BOSTON

THE MINI ROUGH GUIDE

There are more than one hundred and fifty Rough Guide travel, phrasebook, and music titles, covering destinations from Amsterdam to Zimbabwe, languages from Czech to Thai, and music from World to Opera and Jazz

Forthcoming titles include

Argentina • Croatia • Ecuador
Southeast Asia

Rough Guides on the Internet

www.roughguides.com

Rough Guide Credits

Text editor: Don Bapst
Managing editor: Andrew Rosenberg
Series editor: Mark Ellingham
Typesetting: Robert Evers
Cartography: Melissa Baker

Publishing Information

This second edition published July 2000 by
Rough Guides Ltd, 62–70 Shorts Gardens, London WC2H 9AB

Distributed by the Penguin Group:
Penguin Books Ltd, 27 Wrights Lane, London W8 5TZ
Penguin Putnam, Inc. 375 Hudson Street, New York, NY 10014, USA
Penguin Books Australia Ltd, 487 Maroondah Highway,
PO Box 257, Ringwood, Victoria 3134, Australia
Penguin Books Canada Ltd, 10 Alcorn Avenue,
Toronto, Ontario, Canada M4V 1E4
Penguin Books (NZ) Ltd, 182–190 Wairau Road,
Auckland 10, New Zealand

Typeset in Bembo and Helvetica to an original design by Henry Iles.
Printed in Spain by Graphy Cems.

352pp includes index
A catalogue record for this book is available from the British Library.
ISBN 1-85828-521-6

BOSTON

THE MINI ROUGH GUIDE

**by David Fagundes
and Anthony Grant**

**with additional contributions by
Amy K. Brown, Kate Davis
and Rachel Greenblatt**

We set out to do something different when the first Rough Guide was published in 1982. Mark Ellingham, just out of university, was traveling in Greece. He brought along the popular guides of the day, but found they were all lacking in some way. They were either strong on ruins and museums but went on for pages without mentioning a beach or taverna. Or they were so conscious of the need to save money that they lost sight of Greece's cultural and historical significance. Also, none of the books told him anything about Greece's contemporary life – its politics, its culture, its people and how they lived.

So with no job in prospect, Mark decided to write his own guidebook, one which aimed to provide practical information that was second to none, detailing the best beaches and the hottest clubs and restaurants, while also giving hard-hitting accounts of every sight, both famous and obscure, and providing up-to-the-minute information on contemporary culture. It was a guide that encouraged independent travelers to find the best of Greece, and was a great success, getting shortlisted for the Thomas Cook travel guide award, and encouraging Mark, along with three friends, to expand the series.

The Rough Guide list grew rapidly and the letters flooded in, indicating a much broader readership than had been anticipated, but one which uniformly appreciated the Rough Guide mix of practical detail and humor, irreverence and enthusiasm. Things haven't changed. The same four friends who began the series are still the caretakers of the Rough Guide mission today: to provide the most reliable, up-to-date and entertaining information to independent-minded travelers of all ages, on all budgets.

We now publish more than 150 titles and have offices in London and New York. The travel guides are written and researched by a dedicated team of more than 100 authors, based in Britain, Europe, the USA and Australia. We have also created a unique series of phrasebooks to accompany the travel series, along with an acclaimed series of music guides, and a best-selling pocket guide to the Internet and World Wide Web. We also publish comprehensive travel information on our Web site: **www.roughguides.com**

Help Us Update

We've gone to a lot of effort to ensure that this second edition of *The Rough Guide to Boston* is as up-to-date and accurate as possible. However, if you feel there are places we've underrated or over-praised, or find we've missed something good or covered something which has now gone, then please write: suggestions, comments or corrections are much appreciated.

We'll credit all contributions, and send a copy of the next edition (or any other *Rough Guide* if you prefer) for the best letters. Please mark letters: "Rough Guide Boston Update" and send to:

Rough Guides, 62–70 Shorts Gardens, London WC2H 9AB, or
Rough Guides, 345 Hudson St, 4th Floor, New York, NY 10014.

Or send email to: **mail@roughguides.co.uk**
Online updates about this book can be found on
Rough Guides' Web site (see opposite)

The Authors

Born and raised in the Los Angeles area, **David Fagundes** went to college in Cambridge, MA, where he still lives. He has served as an editor for the *Let's Go* series.

Another native Californian, **Anthony Grant** attended Boston University. He has written for *France-Soir*, *The Moscow Times* and *The Malibu Times*.

Acknowledgments

The contributors would like to thank Larry Meehan at the Boston CVB, the Nolan family, Marna Walthall, Danielle Schindler, Nirosha Nimalasurya, Gavin Steckler, Michael Greenblatt and Dave Reeves for their help in updating this edition.

A special thanks to Melissa Baker for her work on maps, to Russell Walton for his attentive proofreading, to Rob Evers and Julia Bovis for their production magic, to Pooja Agarwal for indexing, and Andrew Rosenberg for overseeing this project with his sharp eye.

Thanks also to the many readers who have sent us suggestions for updates via mail and through our Web site. Your ideas are always greatly appreciated.

CONTENTS

Introduction

Boston is as close to the Old World as the New World gets, an American city that proudly trades in on its colonial past, having served a crucial role in the country's development from a few wayward pilgrims right through the Revolutionary War. It occasionally takes its past a bit too seriously – what might pass for a faded relic anywhere else becomes a plaque-covered tourist sight here – but none of that detracts from the city's overriding historic charm nor its present-day energy. Indeed, there are plenty of tall skyscrapers, thriving business concerns and cultural outposts that are part-and-parcel of modern urban America, not to mention excellent mergers of past and present, such as the redeveloped – and bustling – Quincy Market, a paradigm for successful urban renewal. No other city gives a better feel for the events and personas behind the birth of the nation, all played out in Boston's wealth of emblematic and evocative colonial-era sights. But the city's cafés and shops, its attractive public spaces, and the diversity of its neighborhoods – student hives, ethnic enclaves, and stately districts of preserved townhouses – are similarly alluring, going some way to answering the twin accusations of elitism and provincialism to which Boston is perennially subjected.

As the undisputed commercial and cultural center of New England, Boston is the highlight of any trip to the region, truly unmissable as almost every road in the area leads to it (indeed Boston was, until the late-1700s America's most populous and culturally important city). It's also the center of the American university system – more than sixty colleges call the area home, including illustrious Harvard, in the neighboring city of Cambridge. This academic connection has also played a key part in the city's long left-leaning political tradition, which has spawned a line of ethnic mayors, and, most famously, the Kennedy family.

Today, Boston's relatively small size – both physically and in terms of population (it ranks eighteenth among US cities) – and its provincial feel actually serve the city to advantage. Though it has expanded since it was first settled in 1630 through landfills and annexation, it has never lost its core, which remains a tangle of streets clustered around Boston Common that can really only be explored on foot. Steeped in Puritan roots, local residents often display a slightly anachronistic Yankee pride, but it's one which has served to protect the city's identity; indeed, the districts around the Common exude an almost small-town atmosphere, and, until recently at least, were relatively unmarred by chain stores and fast-food joints. Meanwhile, groups of Irish and Italian descent have carved out authentic and often equally unchanged communities in areas like the North End, Charlestown, and South Boston. Even as Boston has evolved from busy port to blighted city to the rejuvenated and prosperous place it is today, it has remained, fundamentally, a city on a human scale.

When to visit

Boston is at its most enjoyable from September through early November, when the weather is cooler and the long lines have somewhat abated (though they are never totally

Boston's climate

	°F Average daily		°C Average daily		Rainfall Average monthly	
	MAX	MIN	MAX	MIN	IN	MM
Jan	36	23	2	-5	3.6	91
Feb	37	25	3	-4	3.6	92
March	45	32	7	0	3.7	94
April	57	41	14	5	3.6	91
May	66	50	19	10	3.2	83
June	77	59	25	15	3.1	78
July	82	65	28	18	2.8	72
Aug	81	64	27	18	3.2	82
Sept	71	57	22	14	3.1	78
Oct	63	46	17	8	3.3	84
Nov	52	39	11	4	4.2	107
Dec	39	27	4	-3	4.0	102

absent), and in late spring – when the magnolia trees on Commonwealth Avenue blossom and the parks spring back to life. The former time also happens to roughly coincide with New England **fall foliage** season – mid-September to mid-October – and Boston is a convenient point of departure to make such specialized trips to the countryside; in the city itself the leaves change colors a bit later, sometimes well into November. Summer is the most popular time to come, both for the warmer weather and frequent festivals, but July and August can be uncomfortably humid, and you'll have to fight with large student-related influxes around graduation time in early June and the beginning of school near Labor Day. Boston **winters** can be harsh affairs:

they tend to run from late November through March, but, thanks to the moderating influence of the Atlantic, mild spells often break the monotony of chilly days and snowfall is lighter than in the interior regions of New England. No matter when you go, be prepared for sudden changes in the weather in the space of a single day: a December morning snow squall could easily be followed by afternoon sunshine and temperatures in the 50s.

THE GUIDE

Introducing the city

Boston is compact for an American city, and its tangle of old streets makes it far easier to get around on foot than by car, especially in the city center. Driving is particularly trying these days due to the "Big Dig," a monumental effort to put Interstate 93 – which cuts through the heart of the city – underground. Boston's **downtown** area is situated on a peninsula that juts into Boston Harbor; most of the other neighborhoods branch out south and west along the thoroughfares of **Washington**, **Tremont** and **Beacon streets**.

Downtown really begins with **Boston Common**, a large public green that holds either on or near its grounds many of the city's most historic sights, including the **State House**, **Old Granary Burying Ground** and **Old South Meeting House**; nothing, however, captures the spirit of the city better than downtown's **Faneuil Hall**, the so-called "Cradle of Liberty," and the always-animated **Quincy Market**, adjacent to the hall. **North End**, Boston's Little Italy, occupies the northeast corner of the peninsula, where it is cut off from the rest of the city by I-93; it, too, is home to a few notable relics, such as **Old North Church** and the **Paul Revere House**. Just across Boston Inner Harbor is **Charlestown**, the quiet berth of the world's oldest commissioned warship, the **USS Constitution**.

The Big Dig

In a city whose roads follow the logic of colonial cow paths, the added confusion wreaked by Boston's highway reconstruction project – the largest and most expensive in US history – does little to help visitors navigate their way around. The primary purpose of this project, known as the **Big Dig**, is to eliminate the unsightly elevated Central Artery – built in the late 1950s without regard for aesthetics, neighborhood dynamics, or traffic growth – by replacing it with a wider, underground version. Unfortunately, the undertaking has ignored another crucial factor this time round: cost. In fact, the initial budget of $2.6 billion has now soared to well over $10 billion, and there's still doubt over whether the Big Dig will be finished by the current estimate of 2004.

Still, the project has pumped millions of construction dollars into the city and will eventually free up 150 acres of land for park and recreational use, while supplying dirt to cap landfills where toxins once seeped into Boston Harbor. This comes as little solace to most Bostonians, especially those who drive; indeed, it's hard to understand what the big deal is unless you're one of them. To get as caught up as the locals, check out *www.bigdig.com*, which has all the history, trivia, artwork, plans, politics, and gossip connected with the project.

North of the Common are the vintage gaslights and red-brick Federalist townhouses that line the streets of **Beacon Hill**, the city's most exclusive residential neighborhood. Charles Street runs south from the Hill and separates Boston Common from the **Public Garden**, which marks the beginning of **Back Bay**. This similarly well-heeled neighborhood holds opulent rowhouses alongside modern landmarks like the **John Hancock Tower**, New England's tallest skyscraper. The gay enclave of the **South End**, known for its hip restaurants, lies south of Back Bay, while the student domains of **Kenmore Square** and **The Fenway** are to its west. The latter spreads out west of Massachusetts Avenue and southwest along Huntington Avenue and is home to local institutions the **Museum of Fine Arts**, the **Isabella Stewart Gardner Museum** and **Fenway Park**. South of these neighborhoods are Boston's vast **southern districts**, which hold little of interest besides the southerly links in Frederick Law Olmsted's series of parks known as the Emerald Necklace, including the dazzling **Arnold Arboretum** and **Franklin Park**, setting for the city zoo. Across the Charles River from Boston is **Cambridge**, synonomous with venerable **Harvard University** but also boasting some of the area's best nightlife and a lively café scene, both of which spill over into neighboring **Somerville**.

The telephone area code for metropolitan Boston is ©617.

Arrival

Boston is the unchallenged travel hub of New England, and if it's not the only place in the region you'll visit, it almost certainly will be the first. Conveniently, all points of entry are located inside the city boundaries, none more than a few miles from downtown.

BY AIR

Busy **Logan International Airport**, servicing both domestic and international flights, sits on Boston's easternmost peninsula, a man-made piece of land sticking far out into Boston Harbor. The airport has five lettered terminals: you'll find **currency exchange** in terminals C and E (daily 2–6pm), plus information centers, car rental, and Automatic Teller Machines (ATMs) in all five. Each is connected by a series of courtesy buses, which also run to the Airport **subway station**. From there, you can take the Blue Line to State or Government Center stations, in the heart of downtown; the ride is about fifteen minutes (85¢). Just as quick, and a lot more fun, is the **water shuttle**, which connects the terminal buses with Rowes Wharf across the harbor (Mon–Thurs every 15min, 6am–8pm; Fri every 30min, 8am–11pm; Sat every 30min, 10am–11pm; Sun every 30min, 10am–8pm; $8). A **taxi** to downtown costs $15–20, plus an extra $4.50 or so in tolls.

BY BUS OR TRAIN

Boston is well served by both **bus** and **rail** travel. It's an especially common stop coming from **New York** or **Washington DC**. Both **Greyhound** buses (©1-800/231-2222) and **Amtrak** trains (©1-800/USA-RAIL) arrive in Boston's **South Station**, at Summer Street and Atlantic Avenue, near the waterfront and just a short walk from downtown. The recently renovated station houses information booths, newsstands, restaurants, and a fantastic old clock, though no currency exchange. The adjacent Red Line subway can quickly whisk you to the center of town or out to Cambridge.

BY CAR

If you're coming by **car**, be aware of the three main highways that lead into town: **I-95** (known as Rte-128) circumscribes the Boston area and is part of the interstate that runs all the way down the east coast; **I-93** (known as the Central Artery) runs through downtown and proceeds up into New Hampshire; and **I-90** (the Massachusetts Turnpike or "Masspike") approaches Boston from due west and is popular with those arriving from New York State.

INFORMATION

Boston's main public tourist office is the **Boston Visitor Information Pavilion** on Boston Common, near the Park Street subway (Mon–Sat 8.30am–5pm, Sun 9am–5pm). You'll find loads of maps and brochures, plus information on historical sights, cultural events, accommodation, restaurants and bus trips. There are also public restrooms, a rarity in Boston. Across the street from the Old State House, at 15 State St, is a **visitors center** maintained by the Boston National Historical Park (daily 9am–5pm); it too has plenty of free brochures, plus a bookstore with lots of material on Boston, New England and Revolutionary history. In Back Bay, there is a visitor **kiosk** in the Prudential Center (Mon–Fri 8.30am–6pm, Sat 10am–6pm, Sun 11.30am–6pm). For information on Boston prior to your arrival, the Greater Boston Convention & Visitors Bureau maintains the free **Boston By Phone** service, which is especially helpful for accommodation bookings (Mon–Fri 9am–5pm; ©1-800/888-5515).

Accommodation listings begin on p.161.

The best sources of up-to-date events' listings are the "Calendar" section in Thursday's *Boston Globe* (50¢) – the premier city newspaper – and the somewhat alternative weekly *Boston Phoenix* (free), published on Thursdays. Both are available at newsstands throughout the city. Free publications with good listings include *The Improper Bostonian* and *Stuff@Night.*

Boston on the Internet

The Boston Globe *www.boston.com*
Daily highlights from the newspaper including valuable up-to-the-minute listings.

Boston Online *www.boston-online.com*
General info on the city, including a dictionary of Bostonian English and a guide to public bathrooms.

Boston Phoenix *www.bostonphoenix.com*
Easily searched site from the alternative weekly with up-to-date arts, music and nightlife listings, restaurant reviews, and lots of cool links.

The Bostonian Society *www.bostonhistory.org*
The official historical society of the city has info on its museum (see p.25) as well as a complete transcript of the Boston Massacre Trial that can be downloaded.

The Greater Boston CVB *www.bostonusa.com*
Everything you'd expect from the city's official site, plus lots of handy links to other sites.

The National Park Service *www.nps.gov*
Helpful for navigating through the many national and state parks around Boston.

Getting Around

Much of the pleasure of visiting Boston comes from being in a city built long before cars were invented. Walking around the narrow, winding streets can be a joy; conversely, driving around them is a nightmare. Be particularly cautious in traffic circles known as "rotaries": when entering, always yield the right of way. If you have a car, better park it for the duration of your trip (see p.292) and get around either by foot or public transit – a system of subway lines and buses run by the Massachusetts Bay Transportation Authority (MBTA, known as the "Ⓣ"; ©1-800/392-6100, *www.mbta.com*).

A good way to save a bit of money while you're in town is to purchase a **Citypass** (*www.citypass.net*; $27.50), a booklet of tickets to six popular attractions – the Isabella Stewart Gardner Museum, the John Hancock Tower, the Kennedy Museum, the Museum of Fine Arts, the New England Aquarium, and the Museum of Science – that can work out to half off total admission – if you visit all six sights within nine days, that is. Citypass is also sold at all six attractions.

SUBWAY

Four **subway** lines transect Boston and continue out into some of its more proximate neighbors. While not the most modern system (the Green Line was America's first underground train, built in the late nineteenth century), it's cheap, efficient, and charmingly antiquated.

See color map 8 for a plan of the subway.

Each line is keyed to a particular color and passes through downtown before continuing on to other districts: the **Red**

Tours

Boston's popular **trolley tours** take you to the city's major sights in around two hours on open-air vehicles painted to look like street cars; most make pick-ups at major hotels and let you hop on and off at various locations.

Narrated trolley tours

Beantown Trolley (©720-6342 or 236-2148). One of the oldest and most popular. $18.

Cityview Luxury Trolley Tours (©363-7899). More comfortable than most. $18.

Discover Boston Multilingual Trolley Tours (©742-1440). Tours in English; audio devices available with French, German, Italian, Japanese, Russian. $24.

Old Town Trolley Tours (©269-7010). Ubiquitous orange-and-green trolleys. $23.

Other tours

Boston by Foot (©367-2345). Informative ninety-minute tours of Beacon Hill, Copley Square, the Waterfront, North End and the Ⓣ, including disused stations. $8.

Boston Duck Tours (©723-DUCK). Restored World War II amphibious landing vehicles make the usual rounds before dipping into the Charles River. Tours depart every half-hour from the Prudential Center, 101 Huntington Ave. $19.

Boston National Historical Park Visitors Center Freedom Trail Tours (©242-5642). Tours led by rangers. Hourly from 10am to 3pm.

Brush Hill Grayline Tours (©720-6342 or 236-2148). Day-long coach tours to surrounding towns such as Lexington, Concord, Plymouth and Salem (late March to Nov).

Line is the safest and most frequent, intersecting South Boston and Dorchester to the south and Cambridge to the north; the **Green Line** hits Back Bay in addition to Kenmore Square, The Fenway and Brookline; the infrequent **Orange Line** traverses the South End and continues down to Roxbury and Jamaica Plain; and the **Blue Line** heads out into East Boston, useful primarily for its stop at Logan Airport. Free transit maps are available at any station. The fare is 85¢, payable with exact change or by tokens purchased at the station; trains run Mon–Sat 5.15am–12.30am, Sun 6am–12.30am.

If you're planning to use public transit a lot, it's a good idea to buy a visitor's "passport," for one ($5), three ($9), or seven days ($18) of unlimited subway and bus use.

BUSES

Buses run less frequently than the subway and are harder to navigate, but they bear two main advantages: they're cheaper (60¢, exact change only) and they provide service to many more points. It's a service used primarily by natives who've grown familiar with the byzantine system of routes; be brave and arm yourself with the *Official Public Transport Map* available at all subway stations. Buses run from 5.30am to 1am.

TAXIS

Given Boston's small scale and the efficiency of its public transit, **taxis** aren't as necessary or prevalent as in cities like New York or London. You can generally hail one along the streets of downtown or Back Bay, though competition gets pretty stiff after 1am when the subway has stopped running and bars and clubs begin to close. If desperate, go to a hotel where cabs cluster or where, at the very least, a bellhop can arrange one. In Cambridge, taxis mostly congregate around Harvard Square.

Boston Cab (✆262-2227) and Bay State Taxi Service (✆566-5000) have 24-hour service and accept major credit cards. Other cab companies include Checker Taxi (✆536-7000) and Town Taxi (✆536-5000). In Cambridge, call the dispatcher (✆495-8294) for Yellow Cabs or Ambassador Cabs.

Downtown Boston

Boston's compact downtown encompasses both the colonial heart and contemporary core of the city. This assemblage of compressed red-brick buildings tucked in the shadow of modern office towers may seem less glamorous than other American big-city centers, but the sheer concentration of historic sights here more than makes up for whatever it lacks in flash. During the day, there's a constant buzz of commuters and tourists; although, come nightfall, the streets thin out considerably. A few notable exceptions are the touristy Quincy Market area, which has a decent, if somewhat downmarket, bar scene; Chinatown, with its popular late night restaurants; and the Theater District, which is particularly animated on weekends.

Skyscrapers aside, downtown is flat territory: hills that once existed here have been smoothed over, though the name of a particularly pronounced peak – Trimountain – lives on in **Tremont Street**, long one of Boston's busiest byways. Today, **King's Chapel**, on Tremont, and the nearby **Old State House** mark the periphery of Boston's earliest town center. The colonies' first church, market, newspaper and prison were all clustered here, though much closer to the shoreline than the plaques that mark their former sites are today. **Spring Lane**, a tiny pedestrian passage off Washington Street, recalls the springs that lured the earliest settlers over to the Shawmut Peninsula from Charlestown. The most evocative streets, however, are those whose essential characters have been less diluted over the years – **School Street**, **State Street** and the eighteenth-century enclave known as **Blackstone Block**, near Faneuil Hall.

You can get the flavor of Boston Harbor, once the world's third busiest, along the **waterfront**, now somewhat isolated on account of the unsightly elevated John F. Fitzgerald Expressway, a chunk of I-93 that's eventually to be put underground (see box p.4). The **Freedom Trail**, a self-guided walking tour that connects an assortment of historic sights by a line of red bricks embedded in the pavement, begins in **Boston Common**, a king-sized version of the tidy green space at the core of innumerable New England villages; close by is the ever-crowded meeting place **Faneuil Hall**. South is the **Financial District**, its short streets still following the tangled patterns of colonial village lanes; west of it is the small but vibrant Chinatown and the adjacent Theater District; below those is the **Leather District**, where empty warehouses and low rents have given rise to a series of art galleries.

The area covered in this chapter is shown in detail on color map 3.

BOSTON COMMON

Map 3, D7–F5. Park Street Ⓣ.

Boston's premier piazza is **Boston Common**, a fifty-acre chunk of green, which is neither meticulously manicured nor especially attractive, though it effectively separates downtown from the posher Beacon Hill and Back Bay districts. It's the first thing you'll see emerging from the **Park Street Ⓣ station**, the central transfer point of America's first subway and a magnet for small demonstrations and, unfortunately, panhandlers. Established in 1634 as "a trayning field" and "for the feeding of Cattell" as a slate tablet opposite the station recalls, the Common is still primarily utilitarian, used by both pedestrian commuters on their way to downtown's office towers and tourists seeking the **Boston Visitor Information Pavilion** (see p.7), just down Tremont Street from the Ⓣ, which is the official starting-point of the Freedom Trail. The shabbiness of the southern side of the Common is offset by the lovely **Beacon Street Promenade**, which runs the length of the northern side, from the gold-domed State House to Charles Street, opposite the Public Garden.

For more detail on the Beacon Street Promenade, see Chapter 5, Beacon Hill and the West End, p.61.

Even before John Winthrop and his fellow Puritan colonists earmarked Boston Common for public use, it served as pasture land for the Reverend William Blackstone, Boston's first white settler. Soon after it disintegrated into little more than a gallows for pirates, alleged witches and various religious heretics; a commoner by the name of Rachell Whall was once hanged here for stealing a bonnet worth 75¢. Newly elected president George Washington made a much-celebrated appearance on the Common in 1789, as did his aide-de-camp, the Marquis de Lafayette, several years later. Ornate eighteenth-century iron fencing encircled the entire park until World War II, when it was taken down for use as scrap metal: it is now said to grace the bottom of Boston Harbor.

One of the few actual sights here is the **Central Burying Ground**, which has occupied the southeast corner of the Common, near the intersection of Boylston and Tremont streets, since 1756. Artist Gilbert Stuart, best known for his portraits of George Washington – the most famous of which is replicated on the dollar bill – died penniless and was interred in Tomb 61. Among the other notables are members of the largest family to take part in the Boston Tea Party, various soldiers of the Revolutionary Army and Redcoats killed in the Battle of Bunker Hill. From the Burying Ground it's a short walk to **Flagstaff Hill**, the highest point on the Common, crowned with the pillar of the Civil War **Soldiers and Sailors Monument**. A former repository of colonial gunpowder, the hill overlooks the **Frog Pond**, once home to legions of unusually large amphibians and site of the first water pumped into the city. It's really just a kidney-shaped pool, used for wading in summer and ice-skating in winter. From here, a path leads to the elegant **Brewer Fountain**, an 1868 bronze replica of one from the Paris Exposition of 1855.

PARK STREET CHURCH

Map 3, F5. July–Aug daily 9am–3pm, rest of year by appointment ✆523-3383; free. Park Street Ⓣ.

The **Park Street Church**, an oversized version of a typical New England village church, has stood just across from Boston Common at the northeast corner of Park and Tremont streets since 1809. Though a rather uninteresting mass of bricks and mortar, its ornate 217-foot-tall white telescoping **steeple** is undeniably impressive. To get an idea of the immensity of the building, including the spire, check out the view from tiny Hamilton Place, across Tremont Street. Ultimately, the structure's reputation rests not on its size but on the scope of events that took place inside: the first Sunday School in the country started here in 1818; the next year, the parish sent the first missionaries to Hawaii; a decade later, William Lloyd Garrison delivered his first public address calling for the nationwide abolition of slavery

(Massachusetts had already scrapped it back in 1783); and on July 4, 1831, the classic ditty *America* ("My country 'tis of thee . . .") was first sung to the church's rafters.

Park Street itself slopes upward along the edge of Boston Common toward the State House. It was once known as **Bulfinch Row** for its many brick townhouses designed by the architect Charles Bulfinch, but today only one remains, the imposing **Amory-Ticknor House** at no. 9, not open, unfortunately, to the public.

For more on Bulfinch and his buildings, see p.65.

OLD GRANARY BURYING GROUND

Map 3, F4. Daily 8am–dusk; free. Park Street Ⓣ.

One of the more peaceful stops on the always-busy Freedom Trail is the **Old Granary Burying Ground**, the resting place of numerous leaders of the American Revolution. Its odd name comes from a grain warehouse that once stood on the site of the adjacent Park Street Church. The two-acre tract, set a few feet above the busy Tremont Street sidewalk, was originally part of Boston Common; today it's hemmed in by buildings on three sides. The fourth, with its Egyptian Revival arch entrance, fronts Tremont Street.

From any angle, you can spot the stocky **obelisk** at dead center that marks the grave of Benjamin Franklin's parents, but some of the most famous gravesites can only be properly appreciated from the Tremont sidewalk, at the southern rim of the plot. On the side closest to Park Street Church, a boulder with an attached plaque marks the tomb of revolutionary **James Otis**, known for his articulate tirades against British tyranny. A few tombs down rest the bones of **Samuel Adams**, the charismatic patriot whose sideline in beer brewing has kept him a household name. Next to his

The Freedom Trail

Boston's history is so visible that the city often stands accused of living in its past, and tourist-friendly contrivances like the **Freedom Trail** only serve to perpetuate the notion. Like many American cities, Boston experienced an economic slump in the postwar years as people migrated to the suburbs. In response, resident William Schofield came up with the idea of a trail highlighting historic Boston sights to lure visitors and their money back into town.

Delineated by a 2.5-mile red-brick stripe in the sidewalk, the trail stretches from the downtown area up into Charlestown, linking sixteen points "significant in their contribution to this country's struggle for freedom." It's a somewhat vague qualifier, resulting in the inclusion of sights that have little to do with Boston's place in the American Revolution. Yes, there's Revolutionary-era Old North Church and Faneuil Hall, but also the *USS Constitution*, assembled fully two decades after the Declaration of Independence, and the Park Street Church, built another fifteen years after that. Unfortunately, some of the touches intended to accentuate the attractions' appeal move closer to tarnishing it. The people in period costume stationed outside some of the sights can't help but grate a little, and the artificially enhanced atmosphere is exaggerated by the $1 million spent by the city to replace most of the painted line with bright-red brick and add pseudo-old signage. Still, the Freedom Trail remains the easiest way to orient yourself downtown, and is especially useful if you'll only be in Boston for a short time. For more info and an interactive timeline of Boston's history, visit *www.thefreedomtrail.org*.

tomb is the group grave of the five people killed in the **Boston Massacre** of 1770, an event which fueled anti-Tory feeling in Boston (see p.27).

Somewhat more secure burial vaults and table tombs – semi-submerged sarcophagi – were preferred by wealthier families. **Peter Faneuil**, who gave his money and his name to Boston's most famous hall, is interred in one of the latter in the left rear corner of the grounds. Midway along the back path is the grave of famed messenger and silversmith **Paul Revere**, opposite that of Judge **Samuel Sewall**, the only Salem Witch Trial magistrate to admit later on that he was wrong. Back across from it on the Park Street Church side, a white pillar marks the likely resting spot of Declaration of Independence signer **John Hancock**. Robert Treat Paine, another signatory, lies along the eastern periphery.

BOSTON ATHENÆUM

Map 3, F4. Park Street Ⓣ.

The **Boston Athenæum**, at 10½ Beacon St, established in 1807, stakes its claim as one of the oldest independent research libraries in the country. In naming their library, the Boston Brahmin founders demonstrated not only their high-minded classicism but marketing sensibility too, as its growing stature was a potent enough force to endow Boston with a lofty sobriquet – the "Athens of America" – that has stuck. The library moved to its present quarters, a replica of the Palazzo da Porta Festa in Vicenza, Italy, in 1849. Best known are its special collections, including the original holdings of the library of King's Chapel, books from the private library of George Washington, and an impressive array of paintings by the likes of John Singer Sargent and Gilbert Stuart.

The Athenæum is in the midst of an extensive restoration and is due to reopen in summer of 2001. Call ©227-0270 for more information.

The crowning glory of the Athenæum is the sedate fifth-floor **Reading Room**; though added in 1914, it's a throwback to a century before. Large Palladian windows afford those stunning views of Old Granary Burying Ground and the skyscrapers beyond.

KING'S CHAPEL BURYING GROUND

Map 3, G4. Daily: June–Oct 9.30am–4pm; Nov–May 10am–4pm; free. Park Street Ⓣ.

Boston's oldest cemetery, the atmospheric **King's Chapel Burying Ground**, at 58 Tremont St, often goes unnoticed by busy passersby. Coupled with its accompanying church, however, it's well worth a tour despite the din of nearby traffic. The graves of several prominent Bostonians are here, and one of the chief pleasures of walking amongst them is to examine the many beautifully etched gravestones, with their winged skulls and contemplative seraphim, such as that of one **Joseph Tapping**, near the Tremont Street side. Others include **John Winthrop**, the first governor of Massachusetts, and **Mary Chilton**, the first Pilgrim to set foot on Plymouth Rock. Near the center of the plot is the tomb of **William Dawes**, the unsung patriot who accompanied Paul Revere on his famous "midnight ride" to Lexington. King's Chapel Burying Ground was one of the favorite Boston haunts of author **Nathaniel Hawthorne**, who drew inspiration from the grave of a certain Elizabeth Pain to create the adulterous character of Hester Prynne for his novel *The Scarlet Letter.*

Hawthorne himself is buried in Concord's Sleepy Hollow Cemetery; see p.144.

The most conspicuous thing about the gray, foreboding chapel that stands on the grounds is its absence of a steeple (there were plans for one, just not enough money). But the belfry does boast the biggest bell ever cast by Paul Revere, which you can't help but notice if you happen to pass by at chime time. A wooden chapel was built on this site first, amid some controversy. In 1686, King James II revoked the Massachusetts Bay Colony's charter and installed Sir Edmund Andros as governor, giving him orders to found an Anglican parish, a move that for obvious reasons didn't sit too well with Boston's Puritan population. The present chapel was completed in 1749, with the pillar-fronted portico added in 1789, when it became one of the first Unitarian Churches.

The best time to enter the building is during one of the weekly chamber music concerts (Tues 12.15–12.45pm). While hardly ostentatious, the elegant Georgian interior provides a marked contrast to the minimalist adornments of Boston's other old churches. It also features America's oldest pulpit and many of its original pews.

WASHINGTON STREET SHOPPING DISTRICT

Map 3, G4–H6.

To a Bostonian, downtown proper comes in two packages: the **Washington Street shopping district** (namely the School Street area and Downtown Crossing) and the adjacent Financial District (see p.27). The former has some of the city's most historic sights – the Old Corner Bookstore, Old South Meeting House and Old State House – but it tends to shut down after business hours, becoming eerily quiet at night. All the stops can be seen in half a day, though you'll obviously need to allow more time if shopping is on your agenda.

Narrow and heavily trafficked today, in colonial times **Washington Street** connected the Old State House to the city gates at Boston Neck, an isthmus that joined the

Shawmut Peninsula to the mainland. That ensured its position as the commercial nerve center of Boston. The best way to begin exploring the area is via **School Street**, anchored on its northern edge by the beautiful **Omni Parker House**, the city's most venerable hotel. It was here that Boston Creme Pie – really a layered cake with custard filling and chocolate frosting all around – was concocted in 1855, and the hotel reportedly still bakes 25 of them a day. More mystifyingly, Ho Chi Minh and Malcolm X each used to wait tables at the hotel's restaurant.

For the rest of its modest length, School Street offers up some of the best in Old Boston charm, beginning with the antique gaslights that flank the severe west wall of King's Chapel. Just beyond is a grand French Second Empire building that served as Boston City Hall from 1865 to 1969. It's near the site of the original location of the **Boston Latin School**, founded in 1635 (a mosaic embedded in the sidewalk just outside the iron gates marks the exact spot). Benjamin Franklin, a statue of whom graces the courtyard, and John Hancock were among the more illustrious graduates of this, America's first public school.

Old Corner Bookstore

Map 3, H4. State Street Ⓣ.

A few doors down from the Latin School site, the gambrel-roofed, red-brick **Old Corner Bookstore** stands at the southern end of School Street where it joins Washington. In the nineteenth century, Boston's version of London's Fleet Street occupied the stretch of Washington from here to Old South Meeting House, with a convergence of booksellers, newspaper headquarters and publishers; most famous among them was Ticknor & Fields, the hottest literary salon Boston ever had. This highly esteemed publishing house was once housed in the bookstore itself and handled the likes of Emerson, Longfellow, Hawthorne and even Dickens and Thackeray. One of America's oldest literary magazines, the staid *Atlantic Monthly*, was published upstairs here for many years, as well; later *The Boston Globe* moved in. It too moved on, but it maintained the site as The Globe Corner Bookstore, an atmospheric travel book shop until its demise in 1997, now vaingloriously reincarnated as the Boston Globe Store, where you can buy merchandise stamped with the newspaper's logo.

Old South Meeting House

Map 3, H4. Daily: April–Oct 9.30am–5pm; Nov–March 10am–4pm; $3, children $1. Downtown Crossing Ⓣ.

Washington Street's big architectural landmark is the **Old South Meeting House**, at no. 310, a charming brick church building recognizable by its tower, a separate but attached structure, that tapers into an octagonal spire. Its exterior clock is the same one installed in 1770, and you can still set your watch by it. An earlier cedarwood structure on the spot burned down in 1711, clearing the way for what is now the second oldest church building in Boston, after Old North Church in the North End. Its Congregationalist origins prescribed simplicity inside and out, with no artifice to obstruct closeness to God. This also endowed Old South with a spaciousness that made it a leading venue for anti-imperial rhetoric. The day after the Boston Massacre, outraged Bostonians assembled here to demand the removal of the troops that were ostensibly guarding the town. Five years later, patriot and doctor Joseph Warren delivered an oration to commemorate the incident; the biggest building in town was so packed that he had to crawl through the window behind the pulpit just to get inside.

More momentously, on the morning of December 16, 1773, nearly seven thousand locals met here, awaiting word from Governor Thomas Hutchinson on whether the Crown would actually impose duty on sixty tons of tea aboard ships in Boston Harbor. When a message was received that it would, Samuel Adams rose and announced, "This meeting can do nothing more to save the country!" His simple declaration triggered the **Boston Tea Party**, perhaps the seminal event leading to the War for Independence (see p.37).

The Meeting House served as a stable, a British riding-school and even a bar before becoming the **museum** it is today. One of the things lost in the transition was the famous original high pulpit; the ornate one standing today is a replica from 1808. There's not much to see other than the building itself, but if you take the audio tour – included in the admission price – you will hear campy re-enactments of a Puritan church service and the Boston Tea Party debates, among other more prosaic sound effects.

Downtown Crossing

Map 3, G6. Downtown Crossing Ⓣ.

Downtown Crossing is a busy pedestrian area, centered on the intersection of Washington and Winter streets, whose strip of department stores and smaller shops recalls the time before malls, and it possesses some fine nineteenth-century commercial architecture besides. Brimming with stores that mostly cater to lower-income shoppers and the pushcart vendors and panhandlers that pester them at nearly every street corner, its nucleus is **Filene's Basement** (see p.265), a magnet for bargain hunters of all socioeconomic stripes and the only "attraction" here really worth your time. Otherwise, unless you have the money and inclination to eat at the historic *Locke-Ober* restaurant on Winter Place, you may as well move on.

For a full review of *Locke-Ober*, see p.192.

Old State House

Map 3, H3. Daily 9.30am–5pm; $3, students $2. State Street Ⓣ.

Skyscrapers dwarf the graceful three-tiered window tower of the red-brick **Old State House**, at the corner of Washington and State streets, amplifying rather than diminishing its colonial-era dignity. This is especially noticeable if you're stuck in traffic on I-93 where the elevated expressway passes by State Street, a view that affords a spectacular juxtaposition of the old and new.

For years, this three-story structure, reminiscent of an old Dutch town hall, was the seat of the Massachusetts Bay Colony and consequently the center of British authority in New England. Later it served as Boston's city hall, and in 1880 it was nearly demolished so that State Street traffic might flow more freely. An attempt was also made to move the site to Chicago, but the House remains in Boston, its fate spared by the Bostonian Society, the city's official historical society, founded specifically to preserve the building; today the site houses the small but comprehensive **Boston History Museum**.

Across from the Old State House, the Boston National Historic Park Visitor's Center, 15 State St, offers loads of information on the city (see p.7).

An impassioned speech in the second-floor Council Chamber by **James Otis**, a Crown appointee who resigned to take up the colonial cause, sparked the quest for independence from Britain fifteen years before it was declared. He argued against the Writs of Assistance, which permitted the British to inspect private property at will. Legend has it that on certain nights you can still hear Otis hurling his anti-British barbs along with the cheers of the crowd he so energized, but museum staff has no comment. The **balcony** overlooking State Street is as famous as Otis' speech, for it was from here on July 18, 1776 that the Declaration of Independence was first read publicly in Boston – a copy having just arrived from Philadelphia. That same night the lion and unicorn figures mounted above the balcony were set ablaze – those currently on display are replicas. Just to show there were no hard feelings, Queen Elizabeth II – the first British monarch to set foot in Boston – read the Declaration of Independence from the balcony as part of the American bicentennial activities in 1976.

As for the museum, the permanent ground-level exhibit, "Colony to Commonwealth," chronicles the role of Boston in the Revolutionary War. Dozens of images and artifacts track, to varying degrees of interest, the events that led up to the establishment of the Commonwealth of Massachusetts (though not, curiously, to the events leading up to US independence). Displays include a bit of tea from Boston's most infamous party; the plaque of royal arms that once hung over Province House, official residence of the colonial governors; the flag that the Sons of Liberty draped from the Liberty Tree (see p.40) to announce their meetings; and the most galvanizing image of the Revolutionary period, Paul Revere's propagandistic engraving of the Boston Massacre. Upstairs are rotating exhibits on the history of the city and, incongruously, a display on old Boston hotels and restaurants.

Boston Massacre Site

Map 3, H3. State Street Ⓣ.

Directly in front of the State Street side of the Old State House, a circle of cobblestones embedded in a small traffic island marks the site of the **Boston Massacre**, the tragic outcome of escalating tensions between Bostonians and the British Redcoats who occupied the city. Riots were an increasingly common occurrence in Boston by the time this deadly one broke out on March 5, 1770. It began when a young wigmaker's apprentice heckled an army officer over a barber's bill. The officer sought refuge in the Custom House (then opposite the Old State House), but when a throng of people gathered at the scene, the mob grew violent, hurling snowballs and rocks at arriving soldiers. When someone threw a club that knocked a Redcoat onto the ice, he rose and fired. Five Bostonians were killed in the ensuing fracas, resulting in Governor Hutchinson's order to relocate occupying troops to Castle Island in Boston Harbor. Two other patriots, John Adams and Josiah Quincy, actually defended the offending eight soldiers in court; six were acquitted, and the two who were found guilty had their thumbs branded.

FINANCIAL DISTRICT

Map 3, I3–I6. South Station or State Street Ⓣ stops.

Boston's **Financial District** hardly conjures the same interest as those of New York and London, but it continues to wield influence in key fields (like mutual funds, invented here in 1925). The area is not entirely devoid of historic interest, though it's generally more manifest in plaques rather than actual buildings. Like most of America's business districts, it beats to an office-hours-only schedule, and many of its little eateries and Irish pubs are closed on weekends, though some brash new restaurants have begun to make inroads. The generally immaculate streets follow the same short, winding paths as they did three hundred years ago; only now, thirty- and forty-story skyscrapers have replaced the wooden houses and churches that used to clutter the area. Still, their names are historically evocative. **High Street**, for example, was once known as Cow Lane and led to the summit of the now vanished eighty-foot-tall Fort Hill. **Arch Street** recalls the decorative arch that graced the Tontine Crescent, a block of stately townhouses designed in 1793 by Charles Bulfinch and unfortunately demolished by the Great Fire of 1872, which began in the heart of the district. Tucked among the relatively generic skyscrapers are several well-preserved nineteenth-century mercantile masterpieces, many of them also Bulfinch designs.

Milk Street and Post Office Square

You can start your tour of the Financial District by heading south from Faneuil Hall or the waterfront, but the most dramatic approach is east from Washington Street via **Milk Street**. A bust of **Benjamin Franklin** surveys the scene from a recessed Gothic niche above the doorway at no. 1, across from the Old South Meeting House. The site marks Franklin's birthplace, though the building itself only dates from 1874. A bit farther down Milk Street, where it intersects Devonshire, the somber, 22-story **John W. McCormack Federal Courthouse** building houses one of Boston's better post offices, with a special section for stamp collectors. An earlier building on this site gave the adjacent, triangular public square its name. Though it's not officially open to the public, you might try sneaking up to the glass atrium atop the building at **One Post Office Square** for jaw-dropping views of Boston Harbor and downtown. The city's skyline encompasses the architectural excesses of the 1980s and a few Art Deco treats too. The best example of the former is the **Bank of Boston** tower at 100 Federal St, with its bulging midsection, nicknamed "Pregnant Alice."

The prime Art Deco specimen, meanwhile, is nearby at 185 Franklin St, the head office of **Bell Atlantic**. The step-top building was a 1947 design; more recently the phone booths outside were given a Deco makeover. If you're here during business hours, check out the fusty nook off the right-hand side of the lobby, home to a replica of the Boston attic room where Alexander Graham Bell first transmitted speech sounds over a wire in 1875. The wooden chamber is a meticulously reassembled version of the original that was installed in 1959. With the exception of an evocative diorama of an old Boston cityscape, it looks like it hasn't been dusted since. Likewise for the 360-degree mural in the lobby that glorifies the exciting world of *Telephone Men and Women at Work*.

Exchange Place, at 53 State St, is a mirrored-glass tower rising from the facade of the old Boston Stock Exchange; the *Bunch of Grapes* tavern, watering hole of choice for many of Boston's revolutionary rabble-rousers, once stood here. Behind it is tiny **Liberty Square**, once the heart of Tory Boston and now mostly of note for its improbable sculpture, commemorating the Hungarian anti-Communist uprising of 1956.

THE CUSTOM HOUSE DISTRICT

Map 3, I3–J3.

The not-quite-triangular wedge of downtown between State and Broad streets and the Fitzgerald Expressway is the unfairly overlooked **Custom House District**, dotted with some excellent architectural draws, chief among which is the **Custom House Tower**. Surrounded by 32 huge Doric columns, it was built in 1847, though the thirty-story Greek Revival tower was only added in 1915. Not surprisingly, it is no longer the tallest skyscraper in New England, but it still has plenty of character, even if its observation deck has been closed since the Marriott Corporation purchased the building.

Another landmark is the **Grain and Flour Exchange Building**, a block away at 177 Milk St, a fortress-like construction that recalls the Romanesque Revival style of prominent local architect H.H. Richardson. Its turreted, conical roof, encircled by a series of pointed dormers, is a bold reminder of the financial stature this district once held. **Broad Street**, built on filled-in land in 1807, is still home to several Federal-style mercantile buildings designed by Bulfinch.

On **State Street**, long a focal point of Boston's maritime prosperity, get a look at the elaborate cast-iron facade of the **Richards Building** at no. 114 – a clipper ship company's office in the 1850s – and the **Cunard Building** at no. 126 – its ornamental anchors recalling Boston's status as the North American terminus of the first transatlantic steamship mail service. Trading activity in the nearby harbor brought a thriving banking and insurance industry to the street along with a collection of rather staid office buildings. A modern exception is the opulent **Fleet Bank** headquarters at no. 75, a medium-sized skyscraper crowned with 3600 square feet of gold leaf and containing a six-story lobby decked out in marble, mahogany and bronze.

FANEUIL HALL MARKETPLACE

Located between the Financial District and the North End, the **Faneuil Hall Marketplace** (rhymes with

"Daniel") is the kind of active, bustling public gathering ground that's none too common in Boston, popular with locals and tourists alike. Built as a market during colonial times to house the city's growing mercantile industry, it declined during the nineteenth century and, like the area around it, was pretty much defunct until the 1960s, when it was quite successfully redeveloped as a restaurant and shopping mall.

Faneuil Hall

Map 3, H2. Daily 9am–5pm; free. State Street Ⓣ.

Much-hyped **Faneuil Hall** itself doesn't appear particularly majestic from the outside; it's simply a small, four-story brick building topped with a Georgian spire, hardly the grandiose auditorium one might imagine would have housed the Revolutionary War meetings that earned its "Cradle of Liberty" sobriquet. The structure once housed an open-air market on its first floor and a space for political meetings on its second, a juxtaposition that inspired local poet Francis Hatch to pen the lines, "Here orators in ages past / Have mounted their attacks, / Undaunted by the proximity / Of sausage on the racks." Faneuil Hall was where revolutionary firebrands such as Samuel Adams and James Otis whipped up popular support for independence by protesting British tax legislation. The first floor now houses a panoply of tourist shops that make for a less than dignified memorial; you'll also find an information desk and a post office. The auditorium on the second floor has been preserved to reflect modifications made by Charles Bulfinch in 1805, the focal point being a massive – and rather preposterous – canvas depicting an imagined scene of Daniel Webster speaking in Faneuil Hall as a range of luminaries from Washington to de Tocqueville look on.

During the War of 1812, folks in Beantown who were suspected of being spies were asked what flew atop Faneuil Hall as a weathervane. Those who knew it was a grasshopper were trusted as true Bostonians; those who didn't were regarded with suspicion, and sometimes even decapitated.

Immediately in front of Faneuil Hall is **Dock Square**, so named for its original location directly on Boston's waterfront; carvings in the pavement indicate the location of Boston's shoreline in 1630. The square's center is dominated by a statue of **Samuel Adams**, interesting mostly for its over-the-top caption: "A Statesman, fearless and incorruptible."

Quincy Market

Map 3, I2. Mon–Sat 10am–9pm, Sun noon–6pm; free. State Street Ⓣ.

The markets just behind Faneuil Hall – three parallel oblong structures that house restaurants, shops and office buildings – were built in the early eighteenth century to contain the trade that had quickly outgrown its space in the hall. The center building, known as **Quincy Market**, holds a superextended corridor lined with stands vending a variety of decent if pricey take-out treats – the mother of the city's modern food courts, it was built in 1822 under the direction of Boston's mayor at the time, Josiah Quincy. To either side of the market are the **North and South Markets**, which hold restaurants and popular chain clothing stores, as well as curiosity shops where narrow specialization is the running gimmick (one sells only plaid clothing, another nothing but puppets). You'll also find the usual complement of street musicians, fire-jugglers and mimes, weather permitting. There's not much to distinguish it from any other shopping complex, although there are several good restaurants and a nice concentration of bars, which are scarce elsewhere in the downtown area. Sitting on a bench in the carnivalesque heart of it all on a summer day, eating scrod while the mobs of townies and tourists mill about, is a quintessential, if slightly contrived, Boston experience.

BLACKSTONE BLOCK AND THE HOLOCAUST MEMORIAL

Map 3, H1.

From Faneuil Hall, traverse the dim, narrow corridor known as Scott's Alley up to Creek Square, where you enter **Blackstone Block**, an area so far bypassed by urban renewal and as such a reasonably authentic remnant of central Boston's original architectural character. Its uneven cobblestoned streets and low brick buildings have remained largely untouched since the 1650s.

Nearby on Union Street jut six tall hollow glass pillars erected as a **memorial** to victims of the Holocaust. Built to resemble smokestacks, the columns are etched with quotes and facts about the human tragedy, with an unusual degree of attention to its non-Jewish victims. Steam rises from grates beneath each of the pillars to accentuate their symbolism, an effect that's particularly striking at night.

GOVERNMENT CENTER

Map 3, G2–H3.

Most visitors pass through the travel hub of **Government Center** during their stay in Boston, and passing through this sea of towering gray government buildings on the former site of **Scollay Square** – once Boston's most notorious den of porn halls and tattoo parlors – is about all you'll want to do in this section of town. As part of a citywide face-lift, Scollay was razed in the early 1960s, eliminating all traces of its salacious past and, along with it, most of its lively character. Indeed, the only thing that remains from the Square's steamier days is the Oriental Tea Company's **Steaming Kettle** advertisement, which has been clouding up the sky across from the Government Center Ⓣ stop since 1873. The area is now overlaid with concrete, and two monolithic edifices tower above: **Boston City Hall**, at the east side of the plaza, and the **John F. Kennedy Federal Building**, on the north. Unless the workings of bureaucracy get you going, the only conceivable reason to stop here is to go to the **visitors center** on the fourth floor of City Hall, which has the usual array of travel information, and some aberrantly clean public restrooms.

THE WATERFRONT

Map 3, K1–L7.

Boston's **waterfront** is still a fairly active area, though no longer the city's focal point, as it was as recently as the mid-1800s. The city's decline as a port left the series of wharves stretching along the harborside below Christopher Columbus Park with no real function, and the construction of the elevated central artery in the 1950s physically separated the area from the rest of the city. Today, the waterfront thrives instead on tourism, with stands selling tacky T-shirts, furry lobsters and the like. Nevertheless, strolling around the wharves on a sunny day affords an unbeatable view of Boston Harbor, and a pleasant respite from the masses that can clog Faneuil Hall and the Common.

The Harborwalk

Like the Freedom Trail, the **Harborwalk** was designed to lure tourist dollars with the promise of an historic theme. On this particular trip back in time, blue plaques illustrate the relevance of various points in Boston's role as a major commercial port – a face of the city that seems ever more a thing of the past, especially with the Harbor's recent notoriety for pollution. While the walk's sights don't have the all-star quality of the historic points on the Freedom Trail (some would need spicing up to pass for mundane), they do provide a decent excuse to take a picturesque stroll along the water, with any enhanced historical context serving as a bonus. Visitors center maps can help steer you on the self-guided stroll which starts at the corner of State Street and Merchant's Row, proceeds along the wharves, and ends up on the Congress Street bridge at the Boston Tea Party museum.

Long Wharf

Map 3, L1.

Long Wharf has been the waterfront's main drag since its construction in 1710. Summer is, not surprisingly, its busiest season, when the wharf is dotted with stands vending kitschy souvenirs and surprisingly good ice cream. This is also the main point of departure for Boston Harbor Cruises (©227-4321; *www.bostonharborcruises.com*), which run **whale-watching** excursions (summer; call for times; $28) as well as ferries to the Harbor Islands (daily 10am–5pm; $8).

Walk out to the end of Long Wharf for an excellent vantage point on **Boston Harbor**. Since the city is surrounded by other land masses, you'll only see a series of peninsulas and islands, which are generally smoky and grinding with industry. It's perhaps most enjoyable – and still relatively safe

– at night, when even the freighters appear graceful against the moonlit water.

New England Aquarium

Map 3, L2. July–Aug Mon, Tues & Fri 9am–6pm, Wed & Thurs 9am–8pm, Sat, Sun & holidays 9am–7pm; Sept–Jun Mon–Fri 9am–5pm, Sat & Sun 9am–6pm; weekdays $12, kids $6; weekends $13.50, kids $7; see Citypass for combination tickets (p.9); ©973-5200. Aquarium Ⓣ.

Next door to Long Wharf is the waterfront's major draw, the **New England Aquarium** at Central Wharf, like many other Boston attractions most fun for kids, though engaging enough for anyone whose sights aren't set too high. Currently in the midst of an ambitious, multimillion-dollar expansion, the Aquarium already has plenty of good exhibits, such as the penguins on the bottom floor. Be sure to play with the special device that allows visitors to maneuver a point of light around the bottom of their pool; the guileless waterfowl mistake the light for a fish and follow it around obediently. In the center of the Aquarium's spiral walkway is an impressive collection of marine life: a three-story cylindrical tank with moray eels, sharks, sting rays and a range of other sea exotica that swim by in unsettling proximity. The Aquarium also runs whale-watching trips out into the harbor in summer (©973-5277).

Boston Tea Party Ship and Museum

Map 3, K7. Daily: June–Aug 9am–6pm; Sept–Nov & March–May 9am–5pm; $8. South Station Ⓣ.

Out of the brief but seminal events of the Boston Tea Party, the curators have forged the **Boston Tea Party Ship and Museum** by combining history with a sense of irreverence. Displays range from the expected (Colonial history) to the tangential (shipbuilding, the English culture of tea, knot-tying), and while the exhibits won't challenge your mind, they're fun in a hokey way – the soundtrack to the museum's informational video, for example, is the dubious 1970s anthem "A Fifth of Beethoven." Once aboard the replica of the notorious ship – which floats alongside the museum's main building off the Congress Street Bridge in Fort Point Channel – you'll be invited to don bright feathers and dump some tea overboard yourself.

The Boston Tea Party

The first major act of rebellion preceding the Revolutionary War, the **Boston Tea Party** was far greater in significance – especially as a popular symbol – than it was in duration. On December 20, 1773, a longstanding dispute between the British government and its colonial subjects, involving a tea tax, came to a dramatic head. At nightfall, an angry mob of about a thousand, which had been whipped into an anti-British frenzy by Samuel Adams at Old South Meeting House, converged on Griffin's Wharf. Around a hundred of them, some dressed in Indian garb, boarded three brigs and threw their cargo of tea overboard. The partiers disposed of 342 chests of tea each weighing 360 pounds – enough to make 24 million cups, and worth more than one million dollars by today's standards. While it had the semblance of spontaneity, the event was in fact planned beforehand, and the mob was careful not to damage anything but the offending cargo. In any case, the "party" transformed protest into revolution; even Governor Hutchinson agreed that afterwards, war was the only recourse. The ensuing British sanctions, colloquially referred to as the "Intolerable Acts," along with the colonists' continued resistance, further inflamed the tension between the Crown and its colonies, which eventually exploded at Lexington and Concord several months later.

Spirited re-creations of the Tea Party are held on occasion here, but don't be taken in: this is not the site of the real Boston Tea Party. It actually took place on what is today dry land, near the intersection of Atlantic and Congress streets. Indeed, at the **Harbor Plaza**, 470 Atlantic St, there's a commemorative plaque engraved with a spirited but silly patriotic poem expressing outrage at "King George's trivial but tyrannical tax of 3p. per pound."

Children's Museum

Map 3, L7. Daily 10am–5pm (Fri until 9pm); $7, kids $6, Fri 5–9pm $1; ✆426-8855. South Station Ⓣ.

Across the Congress Street Bridge is the **Children's Museum**, 300 Congress St, comprising five floors of deceptively educational exhibits that are designed to trick kids into learning about a huge array of topics, from kinematics to the history of popular culture. The key here is interactivity: displays are meant to be touched rather than observed. There is, for instance, the climbing maze in the central shaft that no one over fourteen could possibly get into. Other exhibits are amusing even for adults, particularly those on Japanese youth culture and the replica of "Grandma's House," replete with authentic 1950s furniture, vintage commercials on the television and a meatloaf in the oven.

SEAPORT DISTRICT

The **Seaport District** loosely refers to a harborside area across the Northern Avenue bridge from Boston, accessible by a free shuttle from the South Station Ⓣ, where businesses have recently banded together in an attempt to forge a collective identity. The only real draw here, however, is the excellent range of restaurants near Boston's **Fish Pier** (see p.184 for reviews). There is also a number of odoriferous **lobster wholesalers** on the pier and along Northern Avenue. If you happen to be in the area and love crustaceans, you'll avoid paying standard market price by braving the harrowing sights and smells of these seafood warehouses.

CHINATOWN AND AROUND

Map 3, F8–I8.

Boston's colorful and authentic **Chinatown** lies wedged into just a few square blocks between the Financial and Theater districts, but it makes up in activity what it lacks in size. Just lean against a pagoda-topped payphone on the corner of **Beach and Tyler streets** – the neighborhood's two liveliest thoroughfares – and watch the way life here revolves around the food trade at all hours. By day, merchants barter in Mandarin and Cantonese over the going price of produce; by night, Bostonians arrive in droves to nosh in Chinatown's restaurants. Continue walking down either street, and you'll pass most of the restaurants, bakeries and markets in whose windows you'll see the usual complement of roast ducks hanging from hooks and aquariums filled with future seafood dinners.

For our recommendations on the best restaurants in Chinatown, see p.184.

The prosperity of Boston's Chinatown has increased dramatically in recent years, so much so that the district is expanding to the north, taking up some of the land that lies between it and Downtown Crossing. Despite this growth, the heart of Chinatown contains little in the way of sights, and the atmosphere is best enjoyed by wandering around with no particular destination in mind.

There are a few important landmarks, such as the impressive **Chinatown Gate**, a three-story red-and-gilt monolith guarded by four Fu dogs at the intersection of Hudson and Beach streets, a gift from Taiwan in honor of Chinatown's centennial. Adjacent **Tian An Men Park** provides a place to rest, but it's poorly kept, generally littered with trash and inhabited by fearsomely aggressive pigeons.

Chinatown is at its most vibrant during various festivals, none more so than the **Chinese New Year** (late Jan, early Feb), when frequent parades of papier-mâché dragons fill the streets and the acrid smell of firecrackers permeates the air. During the **Festival of the August Moon**, held, as you may have guessed, in August, there's a bustling street fair. Call the Chinese Merchants' Association for more information (©482-3972).

Combat Zone

Around Washington Street, between Essex and Kneeland, you can still see some vestiges of the old red-light district enigmatically called the **Combat Zone** – not nearly as dangerous as it sounds. Designated by the city as an "adult entertainment zone" in the 1960s after Old Scollay Square was demolished to make room for Government Center, it's still home to a few X-rated theaters and bookshops. The slightly seedy atmosphere is heightened by some low-key drug dealing and prostitution, providing an antidote to the city's much-maligned stuffiness for those Bostonians who need such relief. It doesn't look like the red lights will stay on much longer, however, especially with Chinatown's encroachment; indeed, the former *Naked I Adult Theater*, at 417 Washington St, now stands as Chinatown's first *McDonald's*, decked out with green pagodas and golden arches. Back on the stodgier side is the plaque at the corner of Essex and Washington that marks the site where the so-called **Liberty Tree** stood. This oak, planted in

1646, was a favored meeting point of the Sons of Liberty; the British chopped it down in 1775.

Leather District

Just east of Chinatown, the six square blocks bounded by Kneeland, Atlantic, Essex and Lincoln streets form the **Leather District**, which takes its name from the time when the material was shipped through warehouses here to keep the shoe industry – a mainstay of the New England economy – alive. Since then, the Financial District – with which it is frequently lumped – has taken over as economic hub, and the leather industry has pretty much dried up. The distinction between the Financial and Leather districts is actually quite sharp, and most evident where High Street transitions into **South Street**, the Leather District's main drag. Stout brick warehouses replace gleaming modern skyscrapers, and a melange of merchants and gallery owners take over from the suited bankers. Some of the edifices still have their leather warehouse **signs** on them. Check out the Boston Hide & Leather Co at 15 East St, and the Fur and Leather Services Outlet at 717 Atlantic – but don't expect to see too much going on behind the facades.

Otherwise, the Leather District has little to offer of historical interest, but the area is gradually picking itself up; its abundance of cheap warehouse space attracts a number of **art galleries** and the trendies that go with them, making it the capital of Boston's modest contemporary arts scene. For a list of galleries, see p.262.

THEATER DISTRICT

Map 3, D8–E9.

Just south of Boston Common is the slightly seedy **Theater District**, the chief attractions of which are the flamboyant

Banned in Boston

Boston's Puritan founders would be horrified to find that an area called the **Theater District** exists. Their ingrained allergy to fun resulted in theatrical performances actually being outlawed in Boston until 1792, and in 1878, the Watch & Ward Society was formed to organize boycotts against indecent books and plays. Still the shows went on, and in 1894 vaudeville was born at the lavish (now extinct) B.F. Keith Theater. Burlesque soon followed, prompting the city licensing division in 1905 to deny performances that didn't meet their neo-Puritan codes, thus the phrase "Banned in Boston." As recently as 1970, a production of *Hair* was banned for a month due to its desecration of the American flag.

Yet Boston still managed to become the premier theater tryout town that it is today – high production costs on Broadway have dictated that hits be sifted from misses early on, and Boston was a cost-efficient testing ground. During the 1920s – the heyday of theater in the city – there were as many as forty playhouses in the Theater District alone. But the rise of film meant the fall of theater, and after brief stints as movie halls, many of the grand buildings slid into disrepair and eventual abandonment, including the Art Deco **Paramount**, the crumbling **Opera House** – formerly the Savoy – and the **Modern Theater**, all on lower Washington Street. Others have fared better: the old **Metropolitan Theater**, a movie house of palatial proportions, survives as the glittering **Wang Center**, home of the Boston Ballet; and the **Colonial** is still the grande dame of Boston theater. The **Majestic Theater**, with its soaring Rococo ceiling and Neoclassical friezes, was restored after Emerson College bought it in 1983 and it's now the main stage for the Boston Lyric Opera and Dance Umbrella.

buildings that lend the area its title, such as the Wilbur, Colonial and Majestic. Not surprisingly, you'll have to purchase tickets in order to inspect the theaters' grand old interiors (see p.240). The Colonial is just off **Piano Row** – a section of Boylston Street between Charles and Tremont that was the center of American piano manufacturing and music publishing in the nineteenth and early twentieth centuries. There are still a few piano shops around, but the hip restaurants and clubs in the immediate vicinity are of greater interest. Many are tucked into Charles and Stuart streets around the mammoth **Massachusetts Transportation Building** and cater to the theater-going crowd.

The North End

The North End is a small yet densely populated neighborhood whose narrow streets are chock-a-block with Italian bakeries, restaurants, and some of Boston's most storied sights. Bordered by Boston Harbor and separated from downtown by the noisy, elevated Fitzgerald Expressway (I-93), it may seem an inaccessible district at first, and indeed the protracted "Big Dig" construction project will make getting there a challenge for years to come (see p.4). You can avoid the hassle – and get a much better sense of the area's attractiveness – by entering from the waterfront Christopher Columbus Park, then taking Richmond Street past quiet North Square to Hanover Street, the North End's main drag. Once there, you can cover the must-sees fairly quickly – the Old North Church, Paul Revere House and Copp's Hill Burying Ground – but give yourself time to explore the area's vibrant cafés and food shops (see p.222 & p.260).

Haymarket and North Stret Ⓣ stops offer the best access by public transportation to the North End.

The North End's detached quality goes back to colonial times, when it was actually an island, later to be joined by short bridges to the main part of town, known then as the

South End (and not to be confused with today's South End; see p.74). This physical separation bred antagonism culminating every 5 November in Pope's Day, when North and South Enders paraded effigies of the Pope through their neighborhoods to a standoff on Boston Common where the rival neighbors' attempted to capture each other's pontiff. If the North Enders won, they would burn the South Ender's effigy atop Copp's Hill. Though landfill temporarily ended the district's physical isolation, it remained very much a place apart, and when the Central Artery tore through the city in 1954, the North End became permanently insulated.

In its early days, it was the residence of choice for the wealthy merchant class: Massachusetts Bay Colony governors Hutchinson and Phips owned spacious homes here, as did the notoriously Puritanical Mather family. But most of the British Loyalists who lived here fled to Nova Scotia after the Revolution, hastening de-gentrification. Irish immigrants poured in after the potato famine of 1840; John F. Fitzgerald, JFK's grandfather, was born on Ferry Street, and the late president's mother, Rose, on nearby Garden Street.

The Irish were just the first of several immigrant groups to put down roots in the North End, displaced by Eastern European Jews in the 1850s, and Southern Italians in the early twentieth century. The latter have for the most part stayed put, and the North End is still Boston's most authentically Italian neighborhood. This flavor is most pronounced during the eight annual summer *festas*, during which members of private charity clubs parade figurines of their patron saints (usually the same as those of their home towns in Italy) through the narrow streets. The processions, complete with marching bands, stop every few feet to let people pin dollar bills to streamers attached to the statues.

Thanks to the local mafia, which is still alive if not flourishing, crime (of the nonorganized kind) has long been held at bay here. The ensuing sense of safety, along with comparatively low rents, has made the area attractive to yuppies, who have already gentrified the waterfront while making inroads into rehabilitated tenements in the heart of the district. Despite this recent influx of outsiders, life in North End continues much as it has for decades – complete with laundry dangling from upper-story windows, grandmothers chattering in Italian in front of their apartment buildings, and folks whiling away the hours in local cafés and bars.

The area covered by this chapter is shown in detail on color map 4.

HANOVER STREET

Map 4, C6–F3.

Hanover Street has long been the main connection between the North End and the rest of Boston. Along its length – especially where it meets Parmenter and Richmond – are many of the area's trattorias, cafés and bakeries, giving the street a distinctly European flavor – albeit slightly diluted by the presence of a CVS drugstore, the first, and certainly not the last, chain store intruder on the street. Classic Italian spots remain, including *Mike's Pastry*, at no. 300, where President Clinton has been known to give in to the temptation of cannolis when visiting. The quieter side of the North End reasserts itself on the short blocks north of the Paul Revere Mall, but even these are home to an increasing number of restaurants, geared as much to locals as tourists. Though the area offers little in the way of sights, per se, it's easy to lose half a day just lingering at cafés and browsing in shops here.

NORTH SQUARE

Map 4, D6–E6.

The little triangular wedge of cobblestones and gaslights known as **North Square**, one block east of Hanover between Prince and Richmond streets, is one of the most historic and appealing pockets of Boston, although its actual center is cordoned off by a heavy chain. Here the eateries recede in deference to the **Paul Revere House**, the oldest residential address in the city, at 19 North Square (mid-April to Oct daily 9.30am–5.15pm; Nov to mid-April Tues–Sun 9.30am–4.15pm; $2.50). The small two-story post-and-beam structure, which dates from about 1680, stands on the site of the considerably grander home of Puritan heavyweight Increase Mather (father of Cotton), which burned down in the Great Fire of 1676. A North Ender for most of his life, Revere lived here from 1770 to 1800 (except for much of 1775, when he hid out from the British in Watertown); during these thirty years he sired a sixteen member brood. The house was restored in 1908 to reflect its seventeenth-century appearance; prior to that it served in turn as a grocery store, tenement and cigar factory.

Though the building is more impressive for its longevity than its appearance, the second-story overhang and leaded windows provide quite a contrast to the redbrick buildings around it. On the inside, the first-floor "hall," or living room, resembles a hunting lodge with its low ceiling and enormous fireplace. Examples of Revere's self-made silverwares merit a look upstairs, as does a small but evocative exhibit about the mythologizing of Revere's horseback ride to warn patriots that the British were coming. Fragments of gaudy wallpaper, once considered quite fashionable, adorn the walls throughout the house.

Paul Revere–d

It wasn't until decades after his death that **Paul Revere** achieved fame for his fifteen-mile journey to Lexington to warn John Hancock and Sam Adams of the impending British march inland to seize colonial munitions – and that thanks to a fanciful poem by Henry Wadsworth Longfellow, which failed to note that another patriot, **William Dawes**, made the trip as well. Its opening line, "Listen, my children, and you shall hear / Of the midnight ride of Paul Revere," is as familiar to American schoolchildren as the Pledge of Allegiance. But during his lifetime, this jack-of-all-trades was principally known for his abilities as a silversmith – with a side business in false teeth – and a propagandist for the patriot's cause, not so much as a legendary messenger.

Revere's engraving of the Boston Massacre did much to turn public opinion against the Tories, and he went so far as to stage an exhibition of more patriotic engravings at his North End home on the first anniversary of the incident. He also rode on horseback to carry news of the Boston Tea Party to New York and Philadelphia, only hours after participating in the event. In December 1774, four months before the legendary ride to Lexington, Revere rode to Portsmouth, New Hampshire, to notify locals of the British intent to shore up fortifications there, precipitating the first organized American assault on a royal fortress flying the king's flag. After the Revolution he engraved the first American currency; more profitable was his bell and cannon foundry in the present-day town that bears his name, just north of Boston. He died in 1818 at the age of 83, and rests among his Revolutionary peers in Old Granary Burying Ground (see p.17).

North Street itself was first called Anne's Street, somewhat of a red-light district in the early nineteenth century. It is home to an unusual, obscure relic, too: the **oldest sign**

in Boston. If you look at the building on the corner of North and Richmond streets, you'll see a sign with the initials "W, T, S" affixed to the third floor, a reference to the owners of an inn that stood here in 1694.

A small courtyard, the focus of which is a glass-encased 900-pound bell that Revere cast, separates the Paul Revere House from the **Pierce-Hichborn House** (tours by appointment; ©523-2338; $2.50), the oldest brick house in Boston, a simple Georgian-style residence, built in 1710 by glazier Moses Pierce. Later, it belonged to Paul Revere's cousin, Nathaniel Hichborn, who was considerably wealthier than his more famous cousin, though the sparsely furnished interior of the prosperous shipbuilder's modest home, with its unremarkable period tables and chairs, along with a few decorative lamps and pieces of cabinetry, speaks volumes about Yankee thrift.

ST STEPHEN'S CHURCH AND PAUL REVERE MALL

Map 4, E4–F4.

At Hanover's intersection with Clark Street is **St Stephen's Church**; with its striking three-story recessed brick arch entrance, this is the only church built by Charles Bulfinch in Boston that remains standing (see p.65). Originally called New North Church, it received its new name in 1862 to keep up with the increasingly Catholic population of the North End. Though it seems firmly planted today, the whole building was actually moved back sixteen feet when Hanover Street was widened in 1870. Its other claim to fame is that Rose Kennedy's funeral ceremony was held here in 1995.

Just across Hanover, the famous bronze **statue** of Paul Revere on his borrowed horse marks the edge of the **Paul Revere Mall**. Sometimes called the Prado (an Italian term for a park or open space) this much-needed open space was carved out of a chunk of apartment blocks in 1933 and runs back to tiny **Unity Street** – home of the small redbrick **Clough House**, at no. 21, built by the mason who helped lay the brick of the Old North Church.

OLD NORTH CHURCH

Map 4, E3. Daily 9am–5pm; free.

Were it not for **Old North Church**, 93 Salem St, as a sign affixed to a collection box just inside its entrance reads, "You Might be Making Donations in Pound Notes." Few places in Boston have as emblematic a quality as the simple yet noble Christ Church (as Old North is officially called), rising unobstructed above the homogeneous blocks of red-brick apartments around it. Built in 1723, and inspired by St Andrew's-by-the-Wardrobe in Blackfriars, London, it's the oldest church in Boston, easily recognized by its gleaming 191ft **steeple**; the weathervane perched on top is the colonial original, though the steeple itself is actually a replica – hurricanes toppled both the original in 1804 and its first replacement in 1954. It was a pair of lanterns that secured the structure's place in history, however; the church sexton, Robert Newman, is said to have hung them inside on the night of April 18, 1775 to signal the movement of British forces "by sea" from Boston Common, which then bordered the Charles River. Some historians speculate that the lanterns were actually hung from another church, also called Old North, which occupied the North Square spot where the **Sacred Heart Italian Church** now stands, at no. 12; that irate Tories burned it for firewood in 1776 adds fuel to the theory. What is certain is that Paul Revere had already learned of the impending British advance and was riding to Lexington by the time the lanterns were in place – he simply needed Newman's help to alert Charlestown in case his mission was thwarted. As it turned out, both he and fellow patriot William Dawes were detained by British patrols, but each managed to continue his ride.

The eight bells inside the belfry – which is unfortunately not open to the public – were the first cast for the British Empire in North America and, ironically, have since tolled the death of every US President. The interior itself is spotlessly white and well-lit thanks to the Palladian windows behind the pulpit. Twelve bricks from a prison cell in Boston, England, where an early group of Pilgrims was incarcerated are set into the vestibule wall, and the four cherubim near the organ are eighteenth-century relics looted from a French vessel. You can check your watch by the clock at the rear – made in 1726, it's the oldest one still ticking in an American public building. Wander among the high box pews: no. 62 belonged to General Thomas Gage, commander-in-chief of the British army in North America, while descendants of Paul Revere still lay claim to no. 54. The timber on which the pews rest is supported by 37 basement level brick crypts. One of the 1100 bodies encased therein is that of John Pitcairn, the British major killed in the Battle of Bunker Hill. His remains were tagged for Westminster Abbey, but they never quite made it back home to England.

The church's quirky **souvenir shop** is worth a stop if only for a look at some of its not-for-sale items, such as a vial of Boston Tea Party tea and the bellringers' contract that Paul Revere signed as a mere lad in 1750.

Some of Old North's greatest charms are actually outside the church itself, notably the diminutive **Washington Memorial Garden**, the brick walls of which are bedecked with plaques commemorating one thing or another, and even more inviting and secluded, the unnamed **pocket garden** behind it.

SALEM AND PRINCE STREETS

Map 4, B6–C4.

While the Old North Church is **Salem Street**'s star attraction, in the lower blocks between Prince and Cross streets, Salem is arguably the North End's most colorful artery. The change in atmosphere when venturing here from the commercialized Quincy Market and bland Government Center couldn't be more striking – as soon as you traverse Cross Street (which snakes alongside the elevated expressway), the agreeable onslaught of Italian grocers, aromatic *pasticcerias* and cafés begins. Salem Street itself is so narrow that the redbrick buildings seem to lean into one another, and light traffic makes it a common practice to walk right down the middle of the street. The Naplesesque bustle ends rather abruptly at the intersection with Prince; from here on up the street is primarily residential.

Serpentine **Prince Street** cuts through the heart of the North End on an east-west axis, linking Salem and Hanover streets. At no. 76, the 24-hour **Bova's Bakery** makes a nice range of sweet treats and supplies bread to many North End restaurants. Nearer Hanover Street, **St Leonard's Church** was supposedly the first Italian Catholic church in New England. The ornate interior is a marked contrast to Boston's stark Protestant churches, while the so-called "Peace Garden" in front, with its prosaic plantings and tacky statuary, is in a sense vintage North End.

COPP'S HILL BURYING GROUND

Map 4, D2. Daily dawn–dusk.

Up Hull Street from Old North Church, **Copp's Hill Burying Ground**, with its eerily tilting slate tombstones and stunning harbor views, makes up in atmosphere what it lacks in the way of illustrious deceased. The first burial here, on the highest ground in the North End, took place in 1659. Among the ten thousand interred are nearly a thousand blacks who had lived in New Guinea, a long vanished colonial enclave of free blacks at the foot of the hill. The most famous gravesite here is that of the Mather family, just inside the wrought-iron gates on the northern Charter Street side. Increase Mather and his son Cotton – the latter a Salem Witch Trial judge – were big players in Boston's early days of Puritan theocracy, a fact not at all reflected in the rather diminutive, if appropriately plain, brick vault tomb. Robert Newman, who hung Paul Revere's lanterns in the Old North Church, is buried near the western rim of the plot.

You'll notice that many gravestones have significant chunks missing, the consequence of British soldiers using them for target practice during the 1775 Siege of Boston. The grave of one Captain Daniel Malcolm, toward the left end of the third row of gravestones as you enter the grounds, bears particularly strong evidence of the English maneuvers: three musketball marks scar his epitaph, which calls him a "true son of liberty" and an "enemy of oppression."

The granite **Copp's Hill Terrace**, separated from the burial ground by Charter Street, was the place from which British cannon bombarded Charlestown during the Battle of Bunker Hill. On a particularly hot day in 1919, a 2.3-million-gallon steel storage tank of molasses – used in the production of alcoholic beverages – exploded nearby, creating a syrupy tidal wave fifteen feet high that engulfed entire buildings and drowned 21 people along with a score of horses. Old North Enders – the kind you'll see playing bocci in the little park at the bottom of the terrace – claim you can still catch a whiff of the stuff on an exceptionally hot day.

Charlestown

Charlestown, across Boston Harbor via Charlestown Bridge from the North End, is a largely Irish working-class neighborhood that stands quite isolated from the city, despite its annexation more than a century ago. Not only separated from Boston by the water, its historic core of quiet streets and elegant rowhouses is now all but surrounded by elevated highways and construction projects. A short $1 ferry trip from the waterfront's Long Wharf bypasses the most unsightly areas of the district – as do most of the trolley tours – and deposits you right at the Charlestown Navy Yard, where the area's big draw, the *USS Constitution*, is berthed, just a few minutes' walk from the neighborhood's center.

The earliest Puritan settlers had high hopes for developing Charlestown when they arrived in 1629, but an unsuitable water supply pushed them over to the Shawmut Peninsula, which they promptly renamed Boston (see p.297). Charlestown grew slowly after that, and had to be completely rebuilt after the British burned it down in 1775. Almost as many houses were lost in that blaze as had been burnt in the entire Revolution.

The mid-1800s witnessed the arrival of the so-called "lace-curtain Irish," somewhat better off than their North End compatriots, and the district remains an Irish one at heart. The neighborhood was long a haven for criminals – if a bank was robbed in Boston, police would simply wait out on the Charlestown Bridge for their quarry to come home – and a code of silence still keeps locals from turning in known criminals to the authorities. Longtime residents, known as townies, have acquired a reputation for being standoffish, enhanced greatly after their vehement resistance to school desegregation in the 1970s.

More recently – and much to the townies' chagrin – urban professionals have all but overtaken the Federal and Colonial-style townhomes south of the **Bunker Hill Monument** – Charlestown's other notable sight – and are making inroads along the waterfront where the views from the condos can be spectacular. The rest of the district is fairly nondescript and even somewhat dodgy in parts.

The area covered by this chapter is shown in detail on color map 5.

THE USS CONSTITUTION ("OLD IRONSIDES")

Map 5, F4. Daily 9.30am–sunset; free.

The sprawling **Charlestown Navy Yard** was one of the first and busiest US naval shipyards – riveting together an astounding 46 destroyer escorts in 1943 alone – though it owes most of its present-day liveliness to its grandest tenant, the frigate **USS Constitution** at Constitution Wharf. Though its fate has flipped back and forth during various congressional and presidential administrations, the *USS Constitution* had its full naval commission last returned in 1940, with no change since, making it the oldest commissioned warship afloat in the world. When in 1997 she went on her first unassisted sail in 116 years, news coverage was international in scale, a measure of the public's fondness for the symbolic flagship of the US Navy. Launched two centuries ago to safeguard American merchant vessels from Barbary pirates and secondarily from the French and British navies, she earned her nickname during the War of 1812, when cannonballs fired from the British *HMS Guerrière* bounced off the hull (the iron sides were actually hewn from live oak, a particularly sturdy wood from the southeastern US), leading to the first and most dramatic naval conquest of that war. The ship went on to clinch victory in more than forty battles before she was retired from active battle in the 1830s.

As tall as a twenty-story building and three hundred feet long from bowsprit to back end, she is an impressive sight from any angle, if not quite what she seems – while authentic enough in appearance, roughly ninety percent of the ship has been reconstructed. Even after extensive renovations, Old Ironsides is too frail to support sails for any extended period of time, and the only voyages it makes with any regularity are annual Fourth of July turnarounds in Boston Harbor. But its active commission means that the guides are certified US Navy sailors. Though there's often a line, especially in the summer, it's worth the wait to get a close-up view of the elaborate rigging – some three dozen sails totaling almost an acre in area. After ambling about the main deck, you can scuttle down the nearly vertical stairways to another deck below, where you'll find two long rows of cannons.

The rest of Charlestown Navy Yard

The Yard, part of the Boston National Historical Park, has largely been repurposed as marinas, upscale condos and offices, none of which will really attract your attention, though a few other buildings might. Housed in a substantial granite structure a short walk from Old Ironsides and across from Pier 1, the **USS Constitution Museum** (daily

9am–6pm; free) is worth visiting before you board the ship. Its excellent exhibits help contextualize the vessel and its unparalleled role in American maritime history. One especially evocative display consists of curios which sailors acquired during a two-year round-the-world diplomatic mission begun in 1844, creatively arranged under a forest of faux palm fronds. Among the souvenirs are wooden carved toys from Zanzibar, a chameleon from Madagascar, preserved in a glass jar, and a Malaysian model ship made of cloves. Upstairs you'll find temporary exhibits, as well as replicas of the sailors' hammock-style bunks.

Berthed in between Old Ironsides and the ferry to Long Wharf is the hulking gray mass of the World War II destroyer **USS Cassin Young** (June–Oct 10am–5pm; Nov–May 9.30am–4.30pm; free). You can stride about the expansive main deck and check out some of the cramped chambers below, but it's mostly of interest to World War II buffs. Several similar destroyers were made in Charlestown, but *Cassin Young* was actually built in San Pedro, California and served primarily in the Atlantic and Mediterranean before eventually being transferred to the National Park Service for use as a museum ship in 1978.

At the northern perimeter of the Navy Yard, there's little to see at the narrow, granite **Ropewalk building**, which is closed to the public, but Navy buffs may be interested to know that it's the only surviving structure of its kind in the county. "Ropewalkers" once made all the cordage for US Navy ships. At the opposite end of the Yard, near the point where the Freedom Trail dips under an elevated road to continue toward the Bunker Hill Monument (see p.59), the **Bunker Hill Pavilion** screens a twenty-minute program entitled *Whites of Their Eyes* (April–Nov daily 9.30am–4.30pm; ©241-7576; $3), which attempts to re-create the infamous battle that took place here with blinking lights and voiceovers passing for multimedia.

CITY SQUARE, MAIN STREET AND WINTHROP SQUARE

Map 5: D5, C2, E3.

Toward Charlestown's center, there's a wealth of eighteenth- and nineteenth-century townhouses, many of which you'll pass on your way from the Navy Yard to the Bunker Hill Monument. John Harvard – the young English minister whose library and funds launched the University after his death – lived in Charlestown, as streets bearing his name throughout the district suggest. Directly behind **City Square** – a traffic circle anchored by *Olives* (see p.197 for review), one of Boston's most popular restaurants – Harvard Street curves through the small **Town Hill** district, site of Charlestown's first settled community. You'll also find Harvard Mall and adjacent Harvard Square (not to be confused with the one in Cambridge), both lined with well-preserved homes. The wooden 1795 house of **Deacon John Larkin** – who lent Paul Revere his horse for the ride to Lexington and never got it back – is at 55 Main St, on the eastern edge of Town Hill.

Just up Main Street is the atmospheric **Warren Tavern**, at no. 105, a small three-story wooden structure built soon after the British burned Charlestown in the Battle of Bunker Hill, and named for Dr Joseph Warren, a personal physician to the Adams (presidential) family before he was killed in the Battle of Bunker Hill. From the tavern, crooked Devens Street to the south (called Crooked Lane in 1640) and Cordis Street to the north are packed with historic, private houses. Of these, you'll find the Greek Revival Swallow mansion at **33 Cordis St** the most startling with its white Ionic columns standing tall amidst its quaint New England neighbors. West on Main Street, the monumental **Charlestown Five-Cent Savings Bank Building**, with its steep mansard roof and Victorian Gothic ornamentation, looms above the street-level convenience stores. A good five minutes' walk further west on Main, the **Phipps Street Burying Ground** dates from 1630. While many Revolutionary soldiers are buried here, it's not part of the Freedom Trail – which also means it's less visited than many similar sights, if a bit isolated.

Heading north from Town Hill toward the Bunker Hill Monument, the redbrick townhouses along Monument Avenue are some of the most exclusive residences in Boston. Nearby is **Winthrop Square**, Charlestown's unofficial common, just south of the monument. The prim rowhouses overlooking it form another upscale enclave. Appropriately enough, considering its proximity to Bunker Hill, the common started out as a military training field – a series of bronze tablets at its northeastern edge lists the men killed just up the slope in the Battle of Bunker Hill.

BUNKER HILL MONUMENT

Map 5, E1. Daily 9am–4.30pm; free.

Commemorating the Battle of Bunker Hill – and the final stop on the Freedom Trail – is the **Bunker Hill Monument**, a gray, dagger-like obelisk atop Breed's Hill, where revolutionary troops positioned themselves on the night of June 16, 1775 (see box overleaf). The tower – the first monument built by public subscription and the first to popularize the obelisk style epitomized by the Washington Monument in DC – is centrally positioned in **Monument Square** and fronted by a statue of Colonel William Prescott; at its base is a lodge that houses dioramas of the battle. Inside, 294 steps wind up the 221ft granite shaft to the top; hardy climbers will be rewarded with sweeping views of Boston, the Harbor, surrounding towns and, to the northwest, the stone spire of the **St Francis de Sales Church**, which stands atop the real Bunker Hill.

The Battle of Bunker Hill

The Revolutionary War was at its bloodiest on the hot June day when British and colonial forces clashed in Charlestown. In the wake of the battles at Lexington and Concord two months before, the British had assumed full control of Boston, while the patriots had the upper hand in the surrounding counties. The British, under the command of generals Thomas Gage and "Gentleman Johnny" Burgoyne, intended to sweep the countryside clean of "rebellious rascals." Americans intercepted the plans and fortified **Breed's Hill** – closer to the harbor than **Bunker Hill** for which it was commonly mistaken on Colonial-era maps – with more than a thousand citizen-soldiers, who streamed in on the night of June 16, 1775.

The next morning, spotting a Yankee fort on what they took to be Bunker Hill, the Redcoats, each carrying 125 pounds of food and supplies in preparation for a three-day military foray in the country, rowed across the harbor to take the rebel-held town. On the patriots' side, Colonel William Prescott issued an order to his troops not to fire "'til you see the whites of their eyes," such was their limited store of gunpowder. Though vastly outnumbered, the Americans successfully repelled two full-fledged assaults – the even rows of underprepared and overburdened Redcoats making easy targets. Some British units lost more than ninety percent of their men, and what few officers survived had to push their men forward with their swords to make them fight on. By the third British assault, the Redcoats had shed their gear, but reinforcements were arriving as the Americans' supply of gunpowder dwindled. The rebels continued to fight with stones and musket butts; meanwhile, British cannon fire from Copp's Hill in the North End had turned Charlestown into an inferno. Despite the eventual American loss, the battle did much to persuade the patriots – and the British, who lost nearly half their men who fought in this battle – that continued armed resistance made independence inevitable.

Beacon Hill and the West End

Beacon Hill, a dignified stack of red brick rising over the north side of Boston Common, is Boston at its most provincial. Once home to numerous historical and literary figures – including John Hancock, John Quincy Adams, Louisa May Alcott, and Oliver Wendell Holmes – the area has remained the address of choice for the city's elite, and looking around, it's not hard to fathom why. The narrow, hilly byways are lit with gaslamps and lined with quaint, nineteenth-century townhouses, all part of an enforced preservation that prohibits modern buildings, architectural innovations, or anything else from disturbing the carefully cultivated atmosphere of urban gentility.

In colonial times, Beacon Hill was the most prominent of three peaks, known as the Trimountain, which formed Boston's geological backbone. The sunny south slope was developed into prime real estate and quickly settled by the city's political and economic powers, but the north slope was closer in spirit to the **West End**, a tumbledown port district populated by free blacks and immigrants. The north slope was home to so much salacious activity, in fact, that outraged Brahmins – Beacon Hill's moneyed elite – termed it "Mount Whoredom."

During the twentieth century, this social divide was largely eradicated, though it can still be seen in the somewhat shabbier homes north of **Pinckney Street** and in the tendency of members of polite society to refer to the south slope as "the good side." Still, both sides have much to offer, if of very different character: on the south slope, there's the grandiose **Massachusetts State House**, as well as residences of past and present luminaries, and attractive boulevards like **Charles Street** and the **Beacon Street Promenade**. More down-to-earth, the north slope has its share of atmospheric blocks as well, plus some signature sights of the **Black Freedom Trail**, including the **African Meeting House**.

Most of the area covered by this chapter is shown in detail on color map 3.

BEACON STREET

Map 3, B6–E5.

Running along the south slope of Beacon Hill above the Common, **Beacon Street** was described by Oliver Wendell Holmes in the late nineteenth century as Boston's "sunny street for the sifted few." Its lofty character remains today; a row of stately brick townhouses, fronted by ornate iron grillwork, presides regally over the area. The story behind the **purple panes** in some of their windows – especially nos. 63 and 64 – evinces the street's long association with Boston wealth and privilege. When panes were installed in some of the first Beacon Street mansions, they turned purple upon exposure to the sun, due to an excess of manganese in the glass. At first an irritating accident, they were eventually regarded as the definitive Beacon Hill status symbol due to their prevalence in the windows of Boston's most prestigious homes; some residents have gone so far as to shade their windows purple in imitation.

At 84 Beacon St is the *Bull and Finch Pub*, inspiration for the TV sitcom *Cheers*, a fact the bar never lets you forget; see our listing on p.216.

Across from no. 50, on the **Beacon Street Promenade** that edges Boston Common, is the **Founder's Monument**, commemorating Boston's first European settler, William Blackstone. The Cambridge-educated loner moved from England, with his entire library, to a piece of wilderness he acquired for next to nothing from the Shawmut Indians – the site of present-day Boston. A stone bas-relief depicts the apocryphal moment in 1630 when Blackstone sold most of his acreage to a group of Puritans from Charlestown.

Further up the Promenade, a majestic monument honors **Robert Gould Shaw** and the **54th Massachusetts Regiment**, America's first all-black company to fight in the Civil War. Led by Shaw, scion of a moneyed Boston Brahmin clan, the regiment performed its service bravely, though it was isolated from the rest of the Union army, given the worst of the military's resources, and saddled alternately with menial and dangerous assignments. Most of its members, including Shaw, were killed in a failed attempt to take Fort Wagner from the Confederates. Augustus Saint-Gaudens' 1897 high-relief bronze sculpture depicts the 54th's farewell march down Beacon Street. The names of the soldiers who died in action were belatedly added in 1982 in a list on its reverse side. Robert Lowell won a Pulitzer Prize for his poem on the monument, *For the*

Union Dead, and the regiment's story was depicted in the 1989 film *Glory*.

MASSACHUSETTS STATE HOUSE

Map 3, E4. Mon–Fri 10am–4pm, last tour at 3.15pm; free. Park Street Ⓣ.

Across from the Shaw Memorial, at the confluence of Park and Beacon streets, rises the large gilt dome of the **Massachusetts State House**, the scale and grandeur of which recalls the heady spirit of the newly independent America in which Charles Bulfinch designed it. The original 1795 design actually makes up only a small portion of the existing structure – the huge wings jutting out on either side as well as the extension in the rear were added much later. An all-star team of Revolution-era luminaries contributed to the original construction: built on land donated by John Hancock, its cornerstone was laid by Samuel Adams, and the copper for its dome was rolled in Paul Revere's foundry in 1802 (though it was covered over with gold leaf in the 1870s). Its front lawn is dotted with statuary honoring favorite sons such as Henry Cabot Lodge and JFK. More interesting is the statue of Mary Dyer, which overlooks the spot on Boston Common where she was hanged for adhering to her Quaker faith.

Once inside the labyrinthine interior, make your way up a flight to the second floor, where tours given by nervous, barely post-pubescent volunteers start from **Doric Hall**, though you'd do as well to grab a free map and show yourself around. Littered with statues and murals celebrating even the most obscure Massachusetts historical events and the statesmen who shaped them, the floor's central hallway leads to the impressively sober **Hall of Flags**, a circular room surrounded by tall columns of Siena marble, lit by a vaulted stained-glass window bearing the state seal and hung with the original flags carried by Massachusetts soldiers into battle. On the third floor, a carved wooden fish known as the **Sacred Cod** hangs above the Senate chambers. The senators take this symbol of maritime prosperity so seriously that when Harvard pranksters stole it in the 1930s, they shut down the government until it was recovered.

Behind the State House, on Bowdoin Street, lies pleasant, grassy **Ashburton Park**, centered on a pillar – a replica of a 1789 Bulfinch work – indicating the hill's original summit, which was sixty feet higher. Beacon Hill got its name from the makeshift warning light to ships in the night that once stood in the pillar's place – an iron skillet filled with combustibles and dangled from a 65-ft iron post.

The Architecture of Charles Bulfinch

America's foremost architect of the late eighteenth and early nineteenth centuries, **Charles Bulfinch** developed a distinctive style somewhere between Federal and classical that remains Boston's most recognizable architectural motif. Mixing Neoclassical training with New England practicality, Bulfinch built residences characterized by their rectilinear brick structure and pillared porticoes – examples remain throughout Beacon Hill, most notably at **87 Mt Vernon St** and **45 Beacon St**. While most of his work was residential, Bulfinch, in fact, made his name with the design of various government buildings, such as the 1805 renovation of Faneuil Hall and, more significantly, the Massachusetts State House, whose dome influenced the design of state capitols nationwide.

NICHOLS HOUSE

Map 3, D4. May–Oct Tues–Sat noon–5pm; Nov–Dec & Feb–April Mon & Thurs–Sat noon–4.15pm; $5. Tours start fifteen minutes past the hour. Park Street Ⓣ.

Behind the State House and up the slope of Mount Vernon Street, at no. 55, is the only Beacon Hill residence open regularly to the public, the **Nichols House**; yet another Bulfinch design, the building was most recently the home of eccentric spinster and accomplished landscape gardener Rose Standish Nichols, who counted among her allegiances Fabian Socialism and the International Society of Pen Pals. Miss Rose, as she is known to posterity, lived in the house until her death in the early 1960s – though the faint odor of roses permeating the air here today is supposed to imply that she may still be haunting the hallways. While the detailed tour given by the curator may be gripping only for those with an abiding interest in antique furnishings and decorations – there are some striking Asian tapestries, Federal-period furniture, and an original self-portrait by John Singleton Copley – it does give a brief glimpse on the overstuffed life of leisure led by Beacon Hill's moneyed elite.

LOUISBURG SQUARE AND AROUND

Map 3, C4–C5.

Farther up the slope, between Mount Vernon and Pinckney streets, **Louisburg Square** forms the geographic and gilded heart of Beacon Hill. An oblong green space flanked on either side by rows of stately brick townhouses, it's the city's only private park, owned by the surrounding residents. Encompassed by wrought-iron fencing to keep out the non-resident plebeians and featuring statues of Columbus and Aristides the Just, the square owes its distinction less to its architectural character than to a history of illustrious residents, among them novelist Louisa May Alcott and members of the Vanderbilt family. Today, a sense of elite civic parochialism makes this Boston's most coveted address for a select few: Senator John Kerry and his wife, ketchup heiress Teresa Heinz, own a townhouse here, reportedly purchased for a cool $2 million.

Just below Louisburg Square, between Willow and West Cedar streets, **Acorn Street**, a narrow byway, still has its original early nineteenth-century cobblestones. Barely wide enough for a car to pass through, it was originally built as a minor byway to be lined with servants' residences. Locals have always clung to it as the epitome of Beacon Hill quaint; in the 1960s, residents permitted the city to tear up the street to install sewer pipes only after exacting the promise that every cobblestone would be replaced in its original location. One more block down, **Chestnut Street** features some of the most intricate facades in Boston, particularly Bulfinch's **Swan Houses**, nos. 13, 15 & 17, with their recessed arches and marble columns.

The 's' in Louisburg is not silent, as any Hill resident will tell you should you ask about "Louie-burg Square."

North of Louisburg Square runs **Pinckney Street**, once the sharp division between the opulent south and ramshackle north sections of Beacon Hill. The original developers planned it that way, arranging their stables and estates so that only the back entrances fringed the street. As recently as the 1920s, neighbor Robert Lowell expressed shock at the proximity of his home at 91 Revere St to these shadier environs, claiming that while he lived only fifty yards from Louisburg Square, he was nevertheless "perched on the outer rim of the hub of decency." The distinction is no longer so sharp, and now Pinckney is yet another picturesque Beacon Hill street, all the more worth a stroll thanks to its location at the crest of the hill; on a clear day, from its intersection with Anderson Street, you can see all over the West End and clear across the Charles River to Cambridge.

Charles and Mount Vernon streets

Map 3, A5–B5.

Just west of the square is **Charles Street**, the commercial center of Beacon Hill, lined with scores of restaurants, antique shops and pricey specialty boutiques. A jaunt further down **Mount Vernon Street** along the flat of the hill brings you past some of Beacon Hill's most beautiful buildings. The Federal-style **Charles Street Meeting House** is at the corner of the two streets – a hotbed of political activity in the nineteenth century, it has been repurposed as an office building with a basement café. Farther along, at Mount Vernon's intersection with Brimmer Street, you'll find the vine-covered **Church of the Advent**; with its pointed arches and starkly contrasting building materials – stone and polychrome red bricks – it's a striking example of High Victorian Gothic.

THE ESPLANADE

Map 3, A1–A6.

To the west of Beacon Hill, spanning nine miles along the Charles River, the **Esplanade** is yet another of Boston's well-manicured public spaces, complete with requisite playgrounds, landscaped hills, lakes and bridges. The nicest stretch runs alongside Beacon Hill – and continues into Back Bay – providing a unique, scenic way to appreciate the Hill from a distance as well as a leading hotspot for the city's pretty young things. On summer days the Esplanade is swarming with well-toned joggers and rollerbladers, many of them on the prowl for a partner. Just below the Longfellow Bridge is a **public boathouse**, the point of departure for sailing excursions on the Charles (April–Oct; two-day visitor's pass $50; ©523-1038).

The white half-dome rising from the riverbank along the Esplanade is the **Hatch Shell**, a public performance space best known for its Fourth of July celebration, which features a free concert by the Boston Pops, a pared-down version of the Boston Symphony Orchestra. The popularity of this event has caused it to become terribly overcrowded, but the other summer happenings at the Shell, such as free movies and jazz concerts, occur almost nightly and can be far more accessible. Call ©727-1300 for schedules and upcoming events.

AFRICAN MEETING HOUSE

Map 3, D3. July & Aug daily 10am–4pm; Sept–June Mon–Fri 10am–4pm; donation requested; *www.afroammuseum.org*. Park Street Ⓣ.

Back near the State House, north of Pinckney, **Smith Court** was the center of Boston's substantial pre-Civil War black community, back when the north slope was still a low-rent district; now it's home to a few crucial stops on Boston's **Black Heritage Trail** (see box overleaf). Free blacks who were denied access to participation in Boston's civic and religious life until well into the nineteenth century, worshiped and held political meetings in what became known as the **African Meeting House**, at 8 Smith Court. Informally called the Black Faneuil Hall, the meeting house grew into a center for abolitionist activism: in 1832, William Lloyd Garrison founded the New England Anti-Slavery Society here.

The Black Heritage Trail

Massachusetts was the first state to declare slavery illegal, in 1783, partly as a result of black participation in the Revolutionary War; large communities of free blacks and escaped slaves swiftly sprung up in the North End and Beacon Hill. Very few blacks live in either place nowadays, but the **Black Heritage Trail** traces Beacon Hill's key role in local black history – and is the most important historical site in America devoted to pre-Civil War African-American history and culture. Another in the line of Boston's self-guided walking tours, the trail begins at **Smith Court**, home to the **African Meeting House** and **Abiel Smith School**, and winds around Beacon Hill, passing the memorial for the **54th Massachusetts Regiment** as well as schools, other institutions, and residences ranging from the small, cream clapboard houses of Smith Court to the imposing **Lewis and Harriet Hayden House** at 66 Phillips St, whose master, a former escaped slave himself, regularly opened his door to fugitive abolitionists and slaves alike.

Today, the sober former church is home to the **Museum of Afro-American History**, which, considering the importance of the site it occupies, is rather a disappointment. You won't find much in the way of displays, only a rotating exhibit on the first floor – usually contemporary African-American art – and the meeting house on the second – restored to look like the most basic of churches it once was. Well-informed rangers lead **free tours** and add much to contextualize what little you actually see.

At the end of Smith Court, you can walk along part of the old Underground Railroad used to protect escaped slaves, who once ducked into the doors along narrow **Holmes Alley** left open by sympathizers to the abolitionist cause. The **Abiel Smith School**, at 46 Joy St, built in 1834, was the first public educational institution established for black schoolchildren in Boston. It now showcases exhibits for the Museum of Afro-American History; check out "Separate Schools, Unequal Education," tracing, as the name indicates, the history of racial inequality in the American school system. There's also a gift shop with a wide range of literature related to the African-American experience.

THE WEST END

North of Cambridge Street, the tidy rows of townhouses transition into a more urban spread of office buildings and old brick structures, signaling the start of the **West End**. Once Boston's main port of entry for immigrants, this area was populated by a broad mix of ethnic groups as well as transient sailors who brought a rough-and-tumble sex-and-tattoo industry with them. The eventual drift of Boston's ethnic populations to southern districts, along with 1960s urban renewal, however, has effaced the district's once-lively character with sterile, modern facades.

A vestige of the old West End remains in the small tangle of byways – namely Friend, Portland and Canal streets – behind the high-rise buildings of **Massachusetts General Hospital**, where you'll see urban warehouses interspersed with numerous Irish bars. The *Irish Embassy* and *McGann's* have particularly authentic atmospheres (see "Drinking", p.217), but every bar swells to a fever pitch after Celtics basketball and Bruin hockey games at the nearby **FleetCenter**, 150 Causeway St (tours daily at 11am, 1pm and 3pm; $5), the slick, corporate-named arena on top of North Station.

For ticket information about FleetCenter sports events, see p.274; for music events there, p.229.

Back along Cambridge Street, at no. 141, the brick **Harrison Gray Otis House** (Wed–Sun 11am–5pm, tours hourly; $4), originally built for the wealthy Otis family in 1796, sits incongruously among minimalls and office buildings. In the 1830s, the building served as a Turkish bath before its transformation into a medicine shop and later a boarding house. In the 1920s, the structure was literally rolled back from the present-day median strip to make way for the highway; a painstaking 1970s restoration returned it to the original eye-numbing colors of the Federal style.

Museum of Science

Map 2, G3; Map 3, A1. Daily: July & Aug 9am–7pm (Fri until 9pm), Sept–June 9am–5pm; $10, $7 kids; Citypass accepted (see p.9); ©723-2500. Science Park Ⓣ.

Situated on a bridge over the Charles, right at the northernmost part of the Esplanade (see p.68), Boston's **Museum of Science** consists of several floors of interactive, if patchy and often well-worn, exhibits illustrating basic principles of natural and physical science. There's enough here to entertain kids for most of the day, though that doesn't make it off-limits to fun-loving adults.

The best exhibit is the Theater of Electricity in the Blue Wing, a darkened room full of optical illusions and glowing displays on the presence of electricity in everyday life. The world's largest Van de Graaf generator gives daily electricity shows in which simulated lightning bolts flash and crackle. You can also play virtual volleyball here: the outline of your body appears on a wall-sized screen as you attempt to hit a virtual ball with your virtual shadow. More cerebral is

Mathematica, in which randomly dropped balls fall neatly into a bell curve to demonstrate the notion of probability, and a series of steel spheres orbit around each other in a funnel to replicate the Galilean motion of planets. Check out, too, the Big Dig exhibit on the lower level, where videos and interactive displays provide an engaging chronicle of Boston's Sisyphean attempt to put the unsightly elevated highway I-93 underground (see box, p.4). In what seems a natural expansion, the museum has just added the contents of the former Computer Museum, previously located at Long Wharf, with flashy high-tech exhibits that illustrate the history, and the future, of the machine.

For information on events in the Hayden Planetarium or Omni Theater, call ✆523-6664.

The museum also holds the **Charles Hayden Planetarium** and the **Mugar Omni Theater**, though neither has too much to recommend it. The planetarium hosts talks and presentations throughout the day – free with museum admission – but it's better known for its laser shows, usually set to a soundtrack of classic rock and shown before an audience of precocious children and drug-addled teens. In a similarly showy vein, the Omni Theater's enormous domed IMAX screen and state-of-the-art sound system provide enough sensory impact to make up for the generally vapid content of the films screened there.

Back Bay and the South End

Back Bay, a meticulously planned neighborhood where elegant tree-lined streets form a pedestrian-friendly area that looks much as it did in the nineteenth century, right down to the original gaslights and brick sidewalks, manages a far more cosmopolitan air than similarly affluent Beacon Hill, with which it inevitably draws comparisons. A youthful population helps offset stodginess and keeps the district, which begins at the Public Garden, buzzing with chic eateries, trendy shops and the aura of affluence that goes with both. Its other main draw is a trove of exquisite Gilded Age rowhouses; there really is no end to their fanciful bay windows and ornamental turrets. On its southern border, the sprawl of the South End offers another impressive, if less opulent, collection of Victorian architecture, alongside some of Boston's more inventive restaurants.

For reviews of Back Bay and South End restaurants, see p. 198.

Both neighborhoods were fashioned in response to a shortage of living space in Boston, a problem still somewhat unresolved. In the case of Back Bay, an increasingly cramped Beacon Hill prompted developers to revisit a failed dam project on the Charles River, which had made a swamp of much of the area. With visionary architect and urban planner **Arthur Gilman** at the helm of a huge landfill project, the sludge began to be reclaimed in 1857. Taking his cue from Paris – Haussmann had just designed wide new boulevards for the French capital under Napoléon III – Gilman decided on an orderly street pattern extending east to west from the Public Garden, which had itself been sculpted from swampland only two decades before. By 1890, the cramped peninsula of old Boston was flanked by 450 new acres, on which stood a range of churches, townhouses and schools.

With a few exceptions, the brownstones get fancier the farther from the Garden you go, a result of one-upmanship on the part of architects and those who employed them. It's no surprise that Back Bay quickly became one of Boston's most sought-after addresses, although its popularity subsided somewhat during the Great Depression when single families were unable to afford such opulence. Developers converted many of the spaces into apartments, often gutting the interiors in the process; other properties were purchased by colleges and universities. More recently gentrification has set in, and the demand for whole houses has led to developers actually knocking out many of the apartment walls their predecessors erected.

Whatever may have happened on the inside, the exteriors of most buildings remain unaltered, due largely to landmark preservation laws, and many retain their old wood ornamentation and Victorian embellishments. All this authentic charm contributes to high rents which feed, in turn, the consumer-driven culture on Newbury Street – a far cry from the traditional image of Boston – with its hundreds of upscale shops, designer hair salons and tiny gourmet eateries. The district has its share of urban problems, too, from a shortage of parking space and bad traffic jams to homeless people trawling for designer garbage and an uncomfortably healthy population of rats. But the pervasive grace of the bowfronts and wrought iron terraces provides at least an illusory facade of safety and serenity.

Running parallel to the Charles River in neat rows, Back Bay's east–west thoroughfares – **Beacon**, **Marlborough**, **Newbury** and **Boylston streets** with **Commonwealth Avenue** in their midst – are transsected by eight shorter, streets. These latter have been so fastidiously laid out that not only are their names in alphabetical order, but trisyllables are deliberately intercut by disyllables – Arlington, Berkeley, Clarendon, Dartmouth, Exeter, Fairfield, Gloucester and Herford – until Massachusetts (though Gloucester, purists protest, only looks trisyllabic). Generally, the grandest townhouses are found on Beacon Street and Commonwealth Avenue, though Marlborough is more atmospheric, and Boylston and Newbury are the commercial drags. In the middle of it all is a small green space, **Copley Square**, surrounded by the area's main sights: Trinity Church, the imposing Boston Public Library and the city's classic skyscraper, the John Hancock Tower.

Most of the area covered by this chapter is shown in detail on color map 6.

THE PUBLIC GARDEN

Map 3, B6–C8.

The value of property in Boston goes up the closer its proximity to the lovingly maintained **Public Garden**, a 24-acre park first earmarked for public use in 1859. Of the garden's 125 types of trees, many identified by little brass placards, most impressive are the weeping willows that ring the picturesque man-made **lagoon**. Here you can take a fifteen-minute ride in one of six **Swan Boats** ($1.50), which trace gracious figure-eights in the oversized puddle. The campy pedal-powered conveyances, inspired by a scene in Wagner's opera *Lohengrin*, have been around since 1877 – long enough to become a Boston institution. The boats carry up to twenty passengers at a time, and in the height of summer there is often a line to hop on board – instead of waiting, you can get just as good a perspective on the park from the tiny **suspension bridge** crossing the lagoon.

The park's other big family draw also happens to be fowl-related: a cluster of popular bronze birds collectively called **Mrs Mallard and Her Eight Ducklings**. The sculptures were installed in 1987 to commemorate Robert McClosky's 1941 *Make Way for Ducklings*, a children's tale set in the Public Garden, where parents photograph their toddlers perched atop one of the flock. Of the many other statues and monuments throughout the park, the oldest and oddest is the thirty-foot-tall **Good Samaritan** monument, a granite and red-marble column that is a tribute to, of all things, the anesthetic qualities of ether. Controversy as to which of two Boston men invented the wonder drug led Oliver Wendell Holmes to christen it the "Either Monument." A dignified equestrian statue of **George Washington**, installed in 1869 and the first of its kind, watches over the Garden's Commonwealth Avenue entrance.

COMMONWEALTH AVENUE

Map 6, E3–L3.

Commonwealth Avenue, the 220-foot-wide showcase street of Back Bay, was modeled after the grand boulevards of Paris, and its tree-lined, 100-foot-wide median forms the first link in Frederick Law Olmsted's so-called **Emerald Necklace**, which begins at Boston Common and extends all the way to the Arnold Arboretum in Jamaica Plain. This mall is peppered with several elegantly placed **statues**, though with the exception of a particularly dashing execution of Revolutionary War soldier John Glover – who helped Washington cross the Delaware in 1776 – between Berkeley and Clarendon streets, few of these hold any interest. "Comm Ave," as locals ignobly call it, is at its prettiest in early May, when the magnolia and dogwood trees are in full bloom, showering the brownstone steps with their fragrant pink buds.

The **Baylies Mansion**, at no. 5, now houses the Boston Center for Adult Education, so feel free to slip inside for a look at the opulent ballroom Baylies built expressly for his daughter's coming-out party (in the old-fashioned sense). You'll have to be content to see the **Ames-Webster Mansion**, a few blocks down at 306 Dartmouth St, from the outside. Built in 1872 for US congressman and railroad tycoon Frederick Ames, it features a two-story conservatory, central tower and imposing chimney. Still further down Commonwealth, at no. 314, is the **Burrage House**, a fanciful synthesis of Vanderbilt-style mansion and the French château of Chenonceaux. The exterior of this 1899 urban palace is a riot of gargoyles and sundry carved cherubim; inside it's less boisterous, serving as a retirement home.

First Baptist Church of Boston

Map 6, K3. Mon–Fri 10am–4pm. Arlington Ⓣ.

Rising above the avenue, at no. 110, is the landmark belfry of the **First Baptist Church of Boston**, designed by architect H.H. Richardson in 1872 for a Unitarian congregation, though at bill-paying time only a Baptist group were able to pony up the necessary funds. The puddingstone exterior is topped off by a 176ft **bell tower**, which is covered by four gorgeous friezes by Frédéric-Auguste Bartholdi, of Statue of Liberty fame – a product of his friendship with Richardson that developed at the Ecole des Beaux Arts in Paris. More interesting than what the tableaux depict (baptism, communion, marriage, and death) are some of the illustrious stone-etched visages: those of Emerson, Longfellow, Hawthorne, and Lincoln. Trumpeting angels protrude from each corner, inspiring its inglorious nickname, "Church of the Holy Bean Blowers."

Richardson's lofty plans for the interior never materialized, again for lack of money, but its high ceiling, exposed timbers and Norman-style rose windows are still worth a peek if you happen by when someone's in the church office. Ring the bell on the Commonwealth Avenue side and hope for the best.

NEWBURY AND BOYLSTON STREETS

Map 6, I3–L4.

Newbury Street takes in eight blocks of alternately traditional and eclectic boutiques, art galleries and restaurants, all tucked into Victorian-era brownstones. It's an atmospheric place to browse, though the encroachment of big chain stores like Gap and NikeTown has eroded some of its charm. Wealthy foreign students have colonized cafés like *29 Newbury* and *Emporio Armani Express*, but despite the occasional nod to pretentiousness, the strip's overall mood is surprisingly inviting. And not all is shopping: Newbury and neighboring **Boylston Street** are home to most of the old schools and churches built in the Back Bay area.

In fact, right on the corner of Boylston and Arlington streets is Back Bay's first building, the **Arlington Street Church** (Mon–Fri 10am–5pm), a minor Italianesque masterpiece whose construction in 1861 started a trend that resulted in many downtown congregations relocating to posher quarters in Back Bay. Arthur Gilman, chief planner of Back Bay, designed the clay-colored, squat structure, marked by a host of Tiffany stained-glass windows, added from 1895 to 1930. A history of progressive rhetoric has also earned it some note: abolitionist minister William Ellery Channing intoned against slavery here just a year before the Civil War erupted, and the church was a favored venue of peace activists during the Vietnam War; nowadays there's an active gay congregation. A block down is the prison-like **New England Mutual Life building**, with some national chain stores on the first floor that do little for its character. It's worth nipping inside, nonetheless, for a look at the **murals**, which depict such historic regional events as John Winthrop sailing from Old to New England aboard the *Arbella*, Paul Revere sounding his famous alarm, and the Declaration of Independence being read in Boston for the first time from the balcony of the Old State House (see p.25).

Back on the first block of Newbury Street itself, sandwiched between hair salons and upscale retail stores, is the **Emmanuel Church of Boston**, an unassuming rural Gothic Revival building. Of greater interest is the full-blown Gothic Revival **Church of the Covenant**, further down the street on the same side. Most passersby are too intent on window shopping to notice the soaring steeple, so look up before checking out the interior, famous – like its neighbor, the Arlington Street Church – for its Tiffany stained-glass windows, some of which are thirty feet high. The NAGA Gallery in the chapel is one of Boston's biggest contemporary art spaces, and it's a nice setting for chamber music performances – the Boston Pro Arte Chamber Orchestra was founded here.

Designed as an architect's house, the medieval flight-of-fancy at **109 Newbury St** is arguably more arresting for its two donjon towers than the Cole-Haan footwear inside. A block down at **144 Newbury St** is the Rodier Paris boutique, but again the burnt sienna-colored building with mock battlements hunkered over it steals the show: originally the **Hotel Victoria** in 1886, it looks like a combination Venetian-Moorish castle, not a bad place to have a condo. A block west, on the exposed side of no. 159, is the **Newbury Street Mural**, a fanciful tribute to a hodgepodge of notables from Sam Adams to Sammy Davis, Jr. A key to who's who is affixed to the parking attendant's booth in the lot next to it.

Newbury gets progressively funkier after Exeter Street; the shoppers are more often students and locals than wealthy ladies venturing in from the suburbs. This is where you'll find Boston's most original fashion boutiques and alternative record stores, in addition to several decent restaurants with popular summer sidewalk terraces. On the final block, between Hereford Street and Massachusetts Avenue, a span of nineteenth-century **stables** has been converted to commercial space; check out the cavernous Patagonia clothing shop at no. 346. Looming over Massachusetts Avenue, the colossal Tower Records, at no. 350, is probably the biggest student magnet of all.

For the best stores on Newbury Street, see "Shopping", p.250.

Housed in half of an odd Romanesque-style police and fire station built in 1886 – the other half of which is still home base for Back Bay's firefighters – the **Institute of Contemporary Art**, 955 Boylston St (Map 6, G4; Wed & Fri–Sun noon–5pm, Thurs till 9pm; $6, free Thurs 5–9pm), around the corner from Tower Records, is Boston's main venue for modern art, though it has no permanent collections, only rotating exhibits and installations of mixed success.

BEACON AND MARLBOROUGH STREETS

Map 6, G2–L2.

As a continuation of Beacon Hill's stately main thoroughfare, **Beacon Street** was long the province of blueblood Bostonians. It is the Back Bay street closest to the Charles River, yet its buildings turn their back to it, principally because in the nineteenth century the river was a stinking mess. One such building, the townhouse at no. 137, holds the **Gibson House Museum** (Wed–Sun 1–3pm, tours hourly; $3), which has preserved the home constructed in 1860 for Catherine Hammond Gibson, twenty years after the death of her well-to-do husband. In the somber interior, there's a curious host of Victoriana, including a still-functioning dumbwaiter, antique globes and writing paraphernalia (one of the Gibsons was a noted travel writer), and gilt-framed photos of Catherine's relatives. Notable among the various chinoiserie is a sequined pink velvet cat house, or, if you prefer the Gibsons' term, "pet pagoda." At the far end of Beacon Street, at no. 405, the run-down exterior of **Crossroads Ale House**, a major-league student haunt, might be familiar to a select few thanks to the short-lived TV series *Boston Common*. The turreted **Charlesgate building** at no. 535, a former hotel, has been nicknamed "The Witch's Castle" for obvious reasons by the Emerson College students who now call it home.

Sandwiched between Beacon Street and Commonwealth Avenue is quiet **Marlborough Street**, which with its brick sidewalks and vintage gaslights is one of the most prized residential locales in Boston, after Louisburg Square in Beacon Hill and the first few blocks of Commonwealth Avenue. Even though the townhouses here tend to be smaller than elsewhere in Back Bay, they display a surprising range of stylistic variation, especially on the blocks between Clarendon and Fairfield streets.

COPLEY SQUARE AND AROUND

Map 6, J4.

Bounded by Boylston, Clarendon, Dartmouth and St James streets, **Copley Square** is the busy commercial center of Back Bay. Various design schemes have come and gone since the square was first filled in the 1870s; the present one is a remnant from 1984, a nondescript central grassy expanse and a strange fountain with two stone obelisks on the Boylston Street side. A farmers' market materializes opposite the *Fairmont Copley Plaza Hotel* on Fridays in spring and summer. Fortunately, the periphery holds more interest than the space it surrounds.

Trinity Church

Map 6, K4. Daily 8am–6pm. Copley Ⓣ.

In his meticulous attention to detail – from the polychromatic masonry on the outside to the rather generic stained-glass windows within – Boston architect H.H. Richardson seemed to overlook the big picture of his 1877 **Trinity Church** at 206 Clarendon St – which as one 1923 guidebook averred "is not beautiful." Critics at the time disagreed, dubbing it a masterpiece of Romanesque Revivalism, which Richardson first attempted with his First Baptist Church (see p.78). The hulking exterior is a bit easier on the eye when approached from Clarendon instead of Dartmouth, where you'll get the classic, dead-on view; gazing up at the chunky centered tower from behind affords an unusual, even dizzying perspective. From here, you'll also have an easier time of finding the church's cloister and hidden garden, one of Back Bay's more enchanting quiet spots. Skip the rather spartan interior, which feels more empty than awe-inspiring – unless, of course, you happen to be there on

Friday at 12.15pm in which case there are often free organ recitals. Indeed, the most interesting aspect of Trinity Church is probably its juxtaposition to the John Hancock Tower (see p.86), in whose mirrored panes it's reflected. The church rests rather precariously on 4500 submerged wood pilings – before the advent of modern construction techniques the only way for buildings to stay put in the very moist depths of Back Bay.

Boston Public Library

Map 6, I4. Mon–Thurs 9am–9pm, Fri–Sat 9am–5pm, Sun 1–5pm from Oct–May. Copley Ⓣ.

A decidedly secular building anchoring the end of Copley Square opposite Trinity Church, the **Boston Public Library** is the largest public research library in New England and the first one in America to actually permit the borrowing of books. McKim, Mead & White, the leading architectural firm of its day, built the Italian Renaissance Revival structure in 1852; the visibility of its Dartmouth Street entrance is heightened by the presence of the spiky yet sinuous lanterns overhanging it. The massive inner bronze doors were designed by Daniel Chester French (sculptor of the Lincoln Memorial in Washington DC); beyond them, a musketeer-like statue of Sir Henry Vane stands guard. This early Governor of the Massachusetts Bay Colony believed, or so the inscription relates, that "God, law and parliament" were superior to the king, which apparently didn't do much for his case in 1662, when his freethinking head got the chop.

Beyond the marble grand staircase and beneath the extensively coffered ceilings are a series of **murals**, most impressive of which is a diaphanous depiction of the nine Muses; to its right stands a statue of a smiling naked woman holding a baby in one hand and a bunch of grapes in the other, a replica of an original bacchante which, due to neo-Puritan prudishness, never graced the library's inner courtyard as intended. Just right of that is the gloomy **Abbey Room**, named for Edwin Abbey's murals depicting the Holy Grail legend, and where Bostonians once took delivery of their books. Most of these were kept in the imposing **Bates Reading Room**, which with its 218-foot-long sweep, 50-foot-high barrel-vaulted ceiling, dark oak paneling and incomparable calm, hasn't changed much since its debut more than a century ago. Tranquility also reigns in the library's open-air central **courtyard**, modeled after that of the Palazzo della Chancelleria in Rome.

New Old South Church

Map 6, J4. Mon–Fri 9am–5pm. Copley Ⓣ.

Just opposite the Boston Public Library, on the corner of Boylston and Dartmouth streets, is one of Boston's most attractive buildings – the **New Old South Church**, at 645 Boylston St. There's actually some logic to the name: the congregation in residence at downtown's Old South Meeting House (and church) outgrew it and decamped here in 1875. You need not be a student of architecture to be won over by the Italian Gothic design, most pronounced in the ornate, 220-foot bell tower – a 1937 addition – and copper-roof lantern, replete with metallic gargoyles in the shape of dragons. The dramatic zebra-striped archways on the Dartmouth Street side are unfortunately partially obscured by the entrance to the Copley Ⓣ station. It's not just to be admired from the outside either: its interior is an alluring assemblage of dark woods set against a forest green backdrop, coupled with fifteenth-century English-style stained-glass windows.

John Hancock Tower and Observatory

Map 6, K4. Mon–Sat 9am–11pm, Sun May–Oct 10am–11pm, Nov–April noon–11pm; $4.50, kids free; Citypass accepted (see p.9). Copley Ⓣ.

At 62 stories, the **John Hancock Tower**, at 200 Clarendon St, is the tallest building in America north of New York City, and, in a way, Boston's signature skyscraper – first loathed, now loved, and taking on startlingly different appearances depending on your vantage point. In Back Bay, the characteristically angular edifice is often barely perceptible, due to deft understatement in deference to adjacent Trinity Church and the old brownstones nearby – this modern subtlety in the face of historic landmarks is a signature quality of architect I. M. Pei (of Louvre Pyramid and Bank of China, Hong Kong fame). From Beacon Hill, the tower appears broad-shouldered and stocky; from the South End, taller than it actually is; from across the Charles River, like a crisp metallic wafer. One of the best views is from the **Harvard/Mass Ave Bridge**, with the clouds reflected in the tower's lofty, fully mirrored coat. With such a seamless facade, you'd never guess that soon after its 1976 construction, dozens of windowpanes popped out, showering Copley Square with glass.

The sixtieth floor **observatory** affords the expected stunning views – on a clear day you can see as far as New Hampshire – and a chance to study the city of Boston, splayed out in all directions. A twenty-foot-tall topographical model eases comprehension, as does a miniature sound-and-light exhibit called "Boston 1775." Next door to the tower is the *old* Hancock Tower, which cuts a distinguished profile in the skyline with its truncated step-top pyramid roof. It is locally famous for the neon weather beacon on top which can be decoded with the help of the jingle: "solid blue, clear view; flashing blue, clouds are due; solid red, rain ahead; flashing red, snow instead...," except in summer when red signifies the cancellation of a Red Sox game.

PRUDENTIAL TOWER AND AROUND

Map 6, H5.

Not even the darkest winter night can cloak the ugliness of the **Prudential Tower**, at 800 Boylston St, just west of Copley Square. This 52-story gray intruder to the Back Bay skyline is one of the more unfortunate by-products of the urban renewal craze that gripped Boston and most other American cities in the 1960s – though it did succeed in replacing the Boston & Albany rail yards, a blighted border between Back Bay and the South End. Today its chief attraction is its fiftieth-floor **Skywalk** (Mon–Sat 10am–10pm, Sun noon–10pm; $4), not quite as high as the nearby John Hancock Observatory, but offering the only 360-degree aerial view of Boston. On a clear day you can discern Cape Cod across the waters of Massachusetts Bay and New Hampshire to the north. If you're hungry (or just thirsty) you can avoid the admission charge by ascending two more floors to the *Top of the Hub* restaurant, though your bill will more than finish off the money you saved. The crowded first-floor **Shops at Prudential Center** is about as generic as malls come and adjoins the hulking mass of the equally bland **Hynes Convention Center**.

CHRISTIAN SCIENCE BUILDINGS

Map 6, F5–G6.

People gazing down at Boston from the top of the Prudential Tower are often surprised to see a 224-foot tall Renaissance Revival basilica vying for attention amidst the urban outcroppings lapping at its base. This rather artificial-looking structure is the central feature of the world headquarters of the sprawling **First Church of Christ, Scientist**, at 75 Huntington Ave. With seating for 3000 (and an enormous pipe organ), it dwarfs the earlier, prettier Romanesque **Christian Science Mother Church** just behind it, built in 1894. The nice thing about wandering round the central plaza, a huge concrete block hammered out by I. M. Pei in the early 1970s, is that no one tries to convert you. In fact there may be no better place in Boston to contemplate the excesses of religion than around the center's 670-foot-long red-granite-trimmed **reflecting pool** (which, through some high-tech miracle, manages to cool water for the complex's air conditioning system).

The highlight of a visit here, though, is the unique **Mapparium** (Mon–Sat 10am–4pm; free), tucked into the grand Art Deco lobby of the Christian Science Publishing building, close to Massachusetts Avenue. The curious name refers to an inverted, stained-glass globe, the thirty-foot diameter of which you can cross on a glass bridge. The technicolor hues of the six hundred-plus glass panels, illuminated from behind, reveal the geopolitical reality of the world in the early 1930s when the globe was constructed, as evidenced by names such as Siam, Baluchistan and Transjordan. Intended to symbolize the worldwide reach of the Christian Science movement, the Mapparium has perhaps a more immediate payoff (thanks to the spherical glass surface, which absorbs no sound): whisper "What's Tanganyika called today?" at one end of the bridge and someone on the opposite end will hear it clear as a bell – and perhaps proffer the answer.

BAY VILLAGE

Back near the Public Garden, one of the oldest sections of Boston, **Bay Village**, bounded by Arlington, Church,

Fayette and Stuart streets, functions now as a small atmospheric satellite of Back Bay. This warren of gaslights and tiny brick houses has managed to escape the trolley tours that make other parts of the city feel like a theme park; it's also increasingly popular with Boston's gay population, acting as something of an extension to the nearby South End. The obvious streets to explore – spreading out as they do in the shadow of the area's *Boston Park Plaza Hotel* (see p.165) – are Piedmont, Winchester and Church, but lightly trafficked Melrose and Fayette streets, footsteps beyond them, are also worth inspection. Bay Village wakes up after the sun sets, when men of all ages zero in on spots like the *Luxor*, one of the more popular gay clubs in Boston. Others looking for action head for the district's southern and eastern reaches, where prostitution – catering to various orientations and tastes – has long plagued the neighborhood; campaigns to push the flesh-peddlers out have not amounted to much.

See p.245 for listings of Bay Village's gay clubs.

Bay Village was known alternately as the Church Street District, South Cove and Kerry Village before the current name stuck in the 1960s. The overall resemblance to a miniature Beacon Hill is no accident, as many of the artisans who pieced that district together built their own, smaller houses here throughout the 1820s and 1830s. A few decades later, water displaced from the filling in of Back Bay threatened to turn the district back into a swamp, but Yankee practicality resulted in the lifting of hundreds of houses and shops onto wooden pilings fully eighteen feet above the water level. Backyards were raised only twelve feet, and when the water receded many building owners designed sunken gardens. You can still see some of these in the alleys behind slender Melrose and Fayette streets, but one of the most unusual remnants from the nineteenth century is the **fortress** at the intersection of Arlington and Stuart streets at Columbus Avenue. Complete with drawbridge and fake moat, it was built as an armory for the **First Corps of Cadets**, a private military organization, and has since been relegated to use as an exhibition hall and convention facility for the *Park Plaza Hotel*.

Bay Village's proximity to the theater district made it a prime location for **speakeasies** in the 1920s, not to mention a natural spot for actors and impresarios to take up residence; indeed, the building at **48–50 Melrose Street** originally housed a movie studio. Around the corner from it is the site of the **Cocoanut Grove Fire** of 1942, in which 490 people perished in a nightclub because the exit doors were locked.

THE SOUTH END

Map 6.

Though it lacks obvious tourist attractions, the **South End**, separated from Back Bay by the Copley Place shopping complex, merits a look for its wealth of Victorian architecture and its generally upbeat streetlife, which is in certain respects the most happening in town. There are large black and gay communities here, and the latter has ushered in several trendy cafés and restaurants, most clustered on **Tremont Street** and on gentrified pockets of **Columbus Avenue**.

For listings of South End restaurants, see p.204.

Like Back Bay, the South End was originally a marshland that now sits on landfill. Though the mud-to-mansion process kicked off in 1834 – predating Back Bay – the area really took shape between 1850 and 1875, when the new land was auctioned off. Quaint slivers like **Union Park**

Square were created to attract wealthy buyers, and the neighborhood emerged in piecemeal fashion, unlike the grids of Back Bay. Towards the end of the nineteenth century, the South End went into prolonged decline, as the nouveau riche headed for Back Bay, and immigrants moved in to take their place. In recent years, affluent buyers have snatched up dilapidated brownstones in the South End for renovation, displacing less prosperous Bostonians with skyrocketing real estate prices. Unfortunately, the surrounding areas – some of the poorest in the city – have not benefited from the economic comforts of gentrification, and the tension can be palatable. Random crime, including theft and assaults, are not unheard of in the South End and appropriate caution should be taken, especially at night.

The Golden Triangle and Union Park Square

Map 6, H6–L7.

Not a model of geometric precision, the so-called **Golden Triangle** was named by South End realtors to describe a gentrified zone, loosely bounded by Columbus Avenue and Tremont and Dartmouth streets, that is almost always modified by the term "quaint" – though for once the tag fits. Walk along quiet Chandler and Appleton streets and the appeal is obvious – refurbished bowfronted rowhouses that would be at home in London's Mayfair, with a community feel all but absent in surrounding areas.

Its heart is the intersection of Tremont Street – actually the southernmost edge of the triangle – and **Clarendon Street**, an upmarket crossing home to some of the trendiest restaurants in Boston, such as the acclaimed *Hamersly's Bistro*, at 553 Tremont St. Next door is the domed **Cyclorama Building**, at no. 539, built in 1884 to house an enormous circular painting of the Battle of Gettysburg (since moved to

Gettysburg itself), and now host to the **Boston Center for the Arts** (©426-7700), which features temporary expositions and performances of modern work. If the ornate kiosk in front of it looks a trifle oversized, that's because it was designed as the cupola for a building close by. The world-renowned **Boston Ballet** practices in a postmodern brick building at 19 Clarendon St (call ©695-6950 to schedule a studio tour). Also close by is another attractive space, **Union Park Square**, that you can walk around, although not through. The elegant elliptical park – lined by recently renovated Victorian rowhouses and accented with fountains and formal plantings – is inaccessible, encircled by a wrought-iron fence.

Kenmore Square, The Fenway, and Brookline

At the western edge of Back Bay, the decorous brownstones and smart shops fade into the more casual Kenmore Square and Fenway districts, both a bit removed from the tourist circuit but good fun nonetheless, with a youthful vibe and some of the city's more notable landmarks. The Fenway spreads out beneath Kenmore Square like an elongated kite, taking in a disparate array of sights ranging from Fenway Park, where baseball's star-crossed Red Sox play, to some of Boston's finest high-culture institutions: Symphony Hall, the Museum of Fine Arts and the Isabella Stewart Gardner Museum. Further west and more residential is the suburb of Brookline, which feels like just another sleepy part of the city, though one in which you're unlikely to find yourself spending too much time.

KENMORE SQUARE

Map 6, C2.

Kenmore Square, at the junction of Commonwealth Avenue and Beacon Street, is the unofficial playground for the students of **Boston University**, as most of its buildings can be found here. Back Bay's Commonwealth Avenue Mall leads right into this lively stretch of youth-oriented bars, record stores and casual restaurants that cater to the late-night cravings of local students – as such the Square is considerably more alive when school's in session. Many of the buildings on its north side have been snapped up by BU, such as the bustling six-story Barnes & Noble bookstore, 660 Beacon St, on top of which is perched the monumental **Citgo Sign**, Kenmore's most noticeable landmark. This sixty-square-foot neon advertisement, a pulsing red triangle that is the oil company's logo, has been a popular symbol of Boston since it was placed here in 1965.

You can cross the Brookline Avenue bridge over the Mass Turnpike to the block-long **Lansdowne Street**, a grungy but perennially popular stretch of show-your-ID bars and nightclubs. There's little point in coming here during daylight hours, as it really only wakes up at midnight.

For listings of the area's clubs, see p.233.

BOSTON UNIVERSITY

Map 6, A1; Map 7, J8.

Boston University, one of the country's biggest private schools, has its main campus alongside the Charles River, on the narrow stretch of land between Commonwealth

Avenue and Storrow Drive. Though it boasts a few Nobel-prize winners among its faculty, such as Derek Walcott and Elie Wiesel, the school is more interesting for its inventive reuse of old buildings, such as the dormitory **Myles Standish Hall**, at 610 Beacon St, a scaled-down version of New York's Flatiron Building that once was a hotel where notables like Babe Ruth camped out. One of its rooms also served as the fictional trysting place of Willy Loman in *Death of a Salesman*. Behind it on **Bay State Road**, many of the c.1900 brownstones serve as BU graduate institutes and smaller residence buildings such as **Shelton Hall** where playwright Eugene O'Neill rather undramatically made his own long day's journey into night. The ornate High Georgian Revival mansion at no. 149, meanwhile, holds the office of the current university president. Bay State Road ends at **The Castle**, an ivy-covered Tudor mansion now used for university functions. Just beyond is one of BU's few green spaces, the **Warren Alpert Mall** and its so-called "BU Beach," a sliver of lawn that's been purposefully upswept at the edge to shield busy Storrow Drive from view.

Continuing the repurposing theme back on Commonwealth is the domed **Morse Auditorium**, formerly a synagogue; behind the adjacent College of Communication is the **Sony Nickelodeon**, surprisingly the only art-house movie theater in Boston (though there are others in Cambridge). One long block down is the closest thing the BU campus has to a center, **Marsh Plaza**, with its Gothic Revival chapel and memorial to Martin Luther King, Jr, one of the university's more noted alumni. Further out, Commonwealth Avenue leads into **Allston-Brighton**, home to an edgy mix of students and recent immigrants from several continents, making it a good place to sample various cuisines – especially Asian – at student-friendly prices.

Allston-Brighton restaurants are reviewed on p.207.

FENWAY PARK

Map 6, B3. ©267-8661 Tours April–Oct Mon–Fri 10am, 11am and 1pm; $5. Kenmore or Fenway Ⓣ.

Baseball is treated with reverence in Boston, so it's appropriate that it is played here in what may be the country's most storied stadium, **Fenway Park**, at 24 Yawkey Way, whose giant 37ft-tall left-field wall, aka the "Green Monster," is an enduring symbol of the quirks of early ballparks. Constructed in 1912 in a tiny, asymmetrical wedge just off Brookline Avenue, the parks resulting famously awkward dimensions include an abnormally short right-field line (302 ft) and a fence that doesn't at all approximate the smooth arc of most outfields. That the left-field wall was built so high makes up for some of the short distances in the park and also gives Red Sox' left-fielders somewhat of an advantage over their counterparts – it takes time to get accustomed to the whimsical caroms a ball hit off the wall might take.

Ticket info for games can be found on p.273.

Fenway's fate is somewhat up in the air these days as developers and conservationists quarrel over the cost-effectiveness and feasibility of renovating the existing park versus building a new one. Meanwhile, you can still take tours of the stadium, where greats like Ted Williams, Carl Yazstremski and even Babe Ruth roamed about before becoming a Yankee (see box, opposite), though your best bet is to come see a game – a must for any baseball fan and still a reasonable draw for anyone remotely curious. The season runs from April to October, and tickets are quite affordable, especially if you sit in the bleachers.

The Curse of the Bambino

In 1903, Boston (then nicknamed the "Pilgrims") became the first team to represent the American League in baseball's World Series; their continued financial success allowed them to build a new stadium, **Fenway Park**, in 1912. During their first year there, Boston won the Series again and repeated the feat in 1915, 1916 and 1918, led in the latter years by the young pitcher **George Herman "Babe" Ruth**, who also demonstrated an eye-opening penchant for hitting home runs.

The team seemed poised to become a dynasty, when its owner, Harry Frazee, turned his finances towards a Broadway play starring his ingenue girlfriend and sold off most of the players at bargain prices, including Ruth, who went to the New York Yankees, which went on to become the most successful franchise in professional sports history. On the other hand, Frazee's play, *No, No, Nanette*, flopped. So did his Red Sox team.

Since then, fans have suffered one letdown after another, so much so that they affectionately refer to the Sox fate as "The Curse of the Bambino," in honor of the Babe. One of the more notable instances of the curse rearing its ugly head occurred in 1978, as a late-season collapse was capped off when the Yankees' light-hitting shortstop Bucky Dent slugged a three-run homer to beat the Sox in a one-game playoff; another in 1986, when, just one strike away from clinching the World Series in Game Six against the New York Mets, the Sox began a series of infamous miscues that brought about another crushing loss. As recently as 1999, the team made it to the American League Championship series – only to be dashed by, who else, the Yankees, in Boston's last chance to win another title in the twentieth century.

To read about the Curse of the Bambino being put to the test, pick up Dan Shaughnessy's1991 book of the same name (see "Books", p.314.)

THE BACK BAY FENS AND SYMPHONY HALL

Map 6.

The Fenway's defining element is the **Back Bay Fens**, a snakelike segment of Frederick Law Olmsted's Emerald Necklace that rather uninspiringly takes over where the prim Commonwealth Avenue Mall leaves off. The Fens were fashioned from marsh and mud in 1879, a fact reflected in the name of the waterway that still runs through them today – the **Muddy River**. This narrow channel is crossed in its northernmost part by a medievalesque puddingstone bridge designed by H.H. Richardson. East of Agassiz Road, which roughly splits the Fens in two, local residents maintain small garden plots, one of the better uses of the landscape, though the area also makes an agreeable backdrop for some of Boston's smaller colleges, such as **Simmons** and **Emmanuel**, as well as the **Harvard Medical School**.

The renowned **Berklee College of Music** makes its home on the busy stretch of Massachusetts Avenue south of Boylston Street, an area with several appropriately budget-friendly eateries. Looming a few short blocks south, **Symphony Hall**, where the Boston Symphony Orchestra plays, anchors the corner of Massachusetts and Huntington avenues. The inside of the 1900 McKim, Mead and White design, modeled after the no longer extant Neues Gewandhaus in Leipzig, Germany, resembles an oversized cube, apparently just the right shape to lend it its perfect acoustics. The big English Baroque-style building across the street is **Horticultural Hall**, headquarters of the Massachusetts Horticultural Society, while **Jordan Hall**, venue of the New England Conservatory of Music's chamber music concerts, is a few blocks down on Huntington, at nos. 290–294. The modern campus of **Northeastern University** spreads out on both sides of the avenue about a half-mile further south. There's not much to see here,

The Emerald Necklace

The string of vegetation that stretches through Boston's southern districts, known as the **Emerald Necklace**, grew out of a project conceived in the 1870s, when landscape architect **Frederick Law Olmsted** was commissioned to create for Boston a series of urban parks, as he had done in New York and Chicago. A Romantic naturalist in the tradition of Rousseau and Wordsworth, Olmsted conceived of nature as a way to escape the ills wrought by society, and considered his parks a means for city-dwellers to escape the clamor of their everyday life. He converted much of Boston's remaining open space, which was often disease-ridden marshland, into a sequence of meticulously manicured outdoor spaces beginning with the **Back Bay Fens**, including the **Riverway** along the Boston–Brookline border, and proceeding through **Jamaica Pond** and the **Arnold Arboretum** to Roxbury's **Franklin Park** (see "Southern Districts," p.113). While Olmsted's original skein of parks was limited to these, further development linked the Fens, via the Commonwealth Avenue Mall, to the Public Garden and Boston Common, all of which now function as part of the Necklace, and which make it all the more impressive in scale, although the Necklace's sense of pristine natural wonder has slipped in the century since their creation – the more southerly links in the chain, starting with Fens, have grown shaggy and are unsafe at night.

The **Boston Park Rangers** (daily 9am–5pm; ☎635-7383) organize free walking tours covering each of the Necklace's segments, and hardcore Olmsted fans won't want to miss the **Frederick Law Olmsted National Historic Site** at 99 Warren St (see p.107).

though; it's largely a commuter campus, and as such lacks the collegiate atmosphere of Boston's more happening universities.

MUSEUM OF FINE ARTS

Map 6, B7–C7. Mon & Tues 10am–4.45pm, Wed–Fri 10am–9.45pm (West Wing only after 5pm on Thurs and Fri, $10), Sat & Sun 10am–5.45; $12, free on Wed after 4pm; Citypass accepted (see p.9); ©267-9300; *www.mfa.org*. Museum Ⓣ.

Rather inconveniently located in the south Fenway but well worth the trip, the **Museum of Fine Arts**, at 465 Huntington Ave, is New England's premier art space. Originating in the 1850s as an adjunct of the Boston Athenæum when that organization decided to focus more exclusively on local history rather than art, the collection was given public imprimatur and funding by the Massachusetts Legislature in 1870. After moving around at the end of the nineteenth century, it found its permanent home here in 1906.

Start your tour with the **American painting** on the first floor, a marvelously dense collection featuring important works from the two major figures of the Colonial period: Gilbert Stuart's nationalistic *Washington at Dorchester Heights* is on display along with his portrait of the first US President which graces the one-dollar bill, and John Singleton Copley is represented by his portraits of Revolutionary figures – among them Paul Revere, John Hancock, and Sam Adams – as well as his gruesome narrative *Watson and the Shark*. Romantic naturalist landscapes from the first half of the nineteenth century – such as Albert Bierstadt's quietly majestic *Buffalo Crossing* – dominate several adjoining rooms, mixed in with representations of popular culture, such as William Sidney Mount's *The Bone Player*. From the latter half of the century there are several seascapes by Winslow Homer, Whistler's morose *Nocturne in Blue and Silver: the Lagoon*, and works from the Boston School, notably Childe Hassan's gauzy *Boston Common at Twilight* and John Singer Sargent's provocatively spare *The Daughters of Edward Darley Boit*. A scattering of early-twentieth-century American work rounds out the wing, with Edward Hopper's uncharacteristically hopeful *Room in Brooklyn* and Maurice Prendergast's sentimental renderings of genteel life, *Sunset and Eight Bathers*. Don't miss the **American Decorative Arts**, either: a gloriously nostalgic assemblage of coffee urns, elaborately styled oak furnishings and reconstructed living rooms with period furniture.

The second-floor **European** wing begins with Dutch paintings from the Northern Renaissance, featuring two outstanding Rembrandts, *Artist in his Studio* and *Old Man in Prayer*, and follows with several rooms of grandiose Rococo and Romantic work from the eighteenth and early nineteenth centuries, most interestingly Pannini's self-referential *Picture Gallery with Views of Modern Rome*, Jean-Baptiste Greuze's erotic *Young Woman in White Hat*, and John Martin's epic *The Seventh Plague of Egypt*. The culmination of the wing is the late nineteenth-century collection, which begins with works by the Realist Jean-Francois Millet, whose *Man Turning over the Soil* and *The Sower* exhibit the stark use of color and interest in common subjects that characterized later French artists. Early Impressionists are well-represented by Manet's *Execution of Emperor Maximilian* and Cézanne's *Uncle Dominique*. The Impressionist room also contains Monet's heavily abstracted *Grainstack (Snow Effect)* and *Rouen Cathedral (Morning Effect)*; Degas figures prominently with his madding *Pagans and Degas' Father* and a bronze cast of the famous *Little Dancer*, and there are several land- and cityscapes from Renoir and Pissarro. The room's highlight, however, is its selection of Post-Impressionist art, best of which are Van Gogh's richly hued *Enclosed Field with Ploughman* and *Houses at Auvers* and Gauguin's vibrant narrative of Tahitian life, *Where do we come from? What are we? Where are we going?*

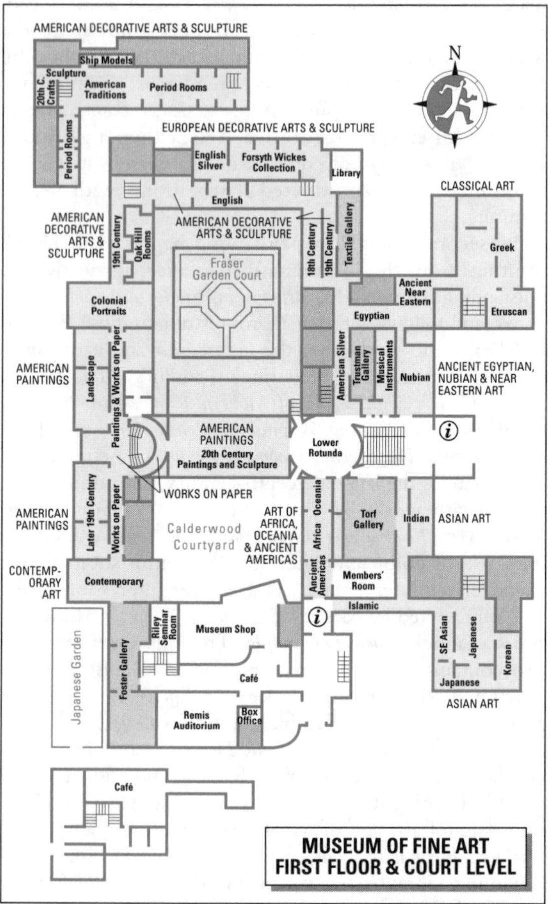
AMERICAN DECORATIVE ARTS & SCULPTURE
Ship Models
Sculpture
20th C. Crafts
American Traditions
Period Rooms
Period Rooms
EUROPEAN DECORATIVE ARTS & SCULPTURE
English Silver
Forsyth Wickes Collection
Library
English
CLASSICAL ART
Greek
Etruscan
Ancient Near Eastern
AMERICAN DECORATIVE ARTS & SCULPTURE
19th Century
Oak Hill Rooms
AMERICAN DECORATIVE ARTS & SCULPTURE
Fraser Garden Court
18th Century
19th Century
Textile Gallery
Colonial Portraits
Egyptian
American Silver
Trustman Gallery
Musical Instruments
Nubian
ANCIENT EGYPTIAN, NUBIAN & NEAR EASTERN ART
AMERICAN PAINTINGS
Landscape
Paintings & Works on Paper
AMERICAN PAINTINGS
20th Century Paintings and Sculpture
Lower Rotunda
WORKS ON PAPER
AMERICAN PAINTINGS
Later 19th Century
Works on Paper
Calderwood Courtyard
ART OF AFRICA, OCEANIA & ANCIENT AMERICAS
Oceania
Africa
Ancient Americas
Torf Gallery
Indian
ASIAN ART
Members' Room
CONTEMPORARY ART
Contemporary
Islamic
Japanese Garden
Foster Gallery
Riley Seminar Room
Museum Shop
Café
Remis Auditorium
Box Office
SE Asian
Japanese
Korean
Japanese
ASIAN ART
Café
MUSEUM OF FINE ART
FIRST FLOOR & COURT LEVEL

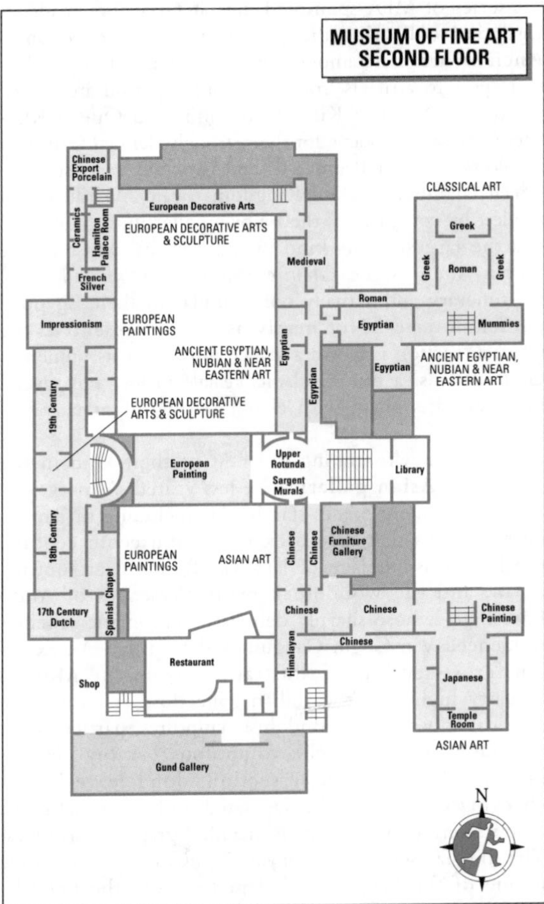

MUSEUM OF FINE ARTS

A series of MFA-sponsored digs at Giza have made its **Egyptian collection** the standout of a fine collection of **Ancient art**. Best among pieces that range from prehistoric pots to artifacts from the Roman period are several imposing statues of King Mercerinus and Queen Kha-Merer-Nebty – notable for their strongly defined features – a colossal head of Ramses II, and two fully reconstructed burial chambers of Old Kingdom royalty. While rather modest by comparison, the Nubian collection is nevertheless the largest of its kind outside Africa. Most of the pieces, such as the *Granite Sphinx of a Nubian King*, are funerary and actually quite similar to their Egyptian contemporaries. Not nearly as well-represented, the Classical section is worth a glance mostly for its numerous Grecian urns, a fine Cycladic *Female Figure*, and several Etruscan sarcophagi with elaborately wrought narrative bas-reliefs.

Though they're among the best of their kind in the world, the **Asian galleries** are less visited. A marvelous array of Japanese pieces stands out, including ornamental munitions that date back to the thirteenth century, the largest assemblage of Japanese Buddhist art outside Japan, and the woodblock print cityscapes of Ando Hiroshige, whose sharply delineated chromatic schemes influenced Van Gogh, Gauguin and Whistler. An excellent cross-section of illustrations from the Mughal Dynasty highlights the Indian collection, and there are also a number of fine Buddhist sculptures, particularly a sinuous *Ganesha* and the voluptuous *Fertility Goddess (Yakshi)*. In the Chinese section, don't leave before checking out the scrolls, decorated with spare naturalist abstractions as well as finely detailed graphic narratives. The life-size statue of *Guanyin, Bodhisattva of Compassion* is one of the best-preserved pieces from the twelfth-century Jin Dynasty.

THE ISABELLA STEWART GARDNER MUSEUM

Map 6, A7. Tues–Sun 11am–5pm; $10 ($11 on weekends); Citypass accepted (see p.9); ©566-1401. Museum Ⓣ.

Less broad in its collection, but more distinctive and idiosyncratic than the MFA, is its neighbor, the **Isabella Stewart Gardner Museum**, at 280 The Fenway. Eccentric Boston socialite Gardner collected and arranged more than 2500 objects in the four-story Fenway Court building she designed herself, making this the only major museum in the country that is entirely the creation of a single individual. It's a hodgepodge of works from around the globe, presented without much attention to period or style; Gardner's goal was to foster the love of art rather than its study, and she wanted the setting of her pieces to "fire the imagination." Your imagination does get quite a workout – there's art everywhere you look, with many of the objects unlabeled, placed in corners or above doorways, for an effect that is occasionally chaotic, but always striking and at times quite effective.

The Gardner Museum hosts a popular weekend chamber and classical music series; see p.237.

The Gardner is best known for its spectacular central **courtyard**, styled after a fifteenth-century Venetian palace, where flowering plants and trees bloom year-round amid statuary and fountains. However, the museum's greatest success is the **Spanish Cloister**, a long, narrow corridor, near the entrace on the first floor, which perfectly frames John Singer Sargent's ecstatic representation of Spanish dance, *El Jaleo*, and also contains fine seventeenth-century Mexican tiles and Roman statuary and sarcophagi.

What was once a first-rate array of seventeenth-century Northern European works was debilitated by a 1990 art heist in which two Rembrandts and a Vermeer were among ten canvases stolen. But the majority of works in the second floor **Dutch Room** remain, most notably an early *Self-Portrait* by Rembrandt and Rubens' austere *Thomas Howard, Earl of Arundel.*

Gardner had an affinity for altars, and her collection contains several, cobbled together from various religious artifacts. A dramatic concentration of these surrounds the third-floor stairwell and includes a medieval stone carving of the beheading of John the Baptist, the particularly agonized *Dead Christ* from twelfth-century Spain, and Giovanni Minelli's maudlin altar painting, the *Lamentation.* Perhaps the most notable sacred art on display, however, is in the **Chapel**, on the third floor, which incorporates sixteenth-century Italian choirstalls and stained glass from Milan and Soissons cathedrals, as well as assorted religious figurines, candlesticks and crucifixes, all surrounding Paul-Cesar Helleu's moody representation of the *Interior of the Abbey Church of Saint-Denis.*

The **Titian, Veronese** and **Raphael Rooms** that complete the third floor comprise a strong showing of Italian Renaissance and Baroque work, including Titian's famous *Europa*, Botticelli's *Tragedy of Lucretia*, and Crivelli's Mannerist *St George and the Dragon.*

BROOKLINE

Map 2.

The leafy, affluent town of **Brookline**, south of Boston University and west of The Fenway, appears as if it's just another well-maintained Boston neighborhood, though in fact it's a distinct municipality. It holds some vaguely diverting attractions, most oriented around bustling **Coolidge Corner**, at the intersection of Beacon and Harvard streets, though it's unlikely any of them will bring you out this way unless you're trying to hit all the Kennedy sights in the greater Boston area.

To reach Brookline, take the Green Line's C branch to Coolidge Corner or D branch to Brookline Village.

Right around this intersection, the **Coolidge Corner Theater**, at 290 Harvard St, is a refurbished art-house cinema (see p.243) sustained by the many students living in the area. A short ways west up Harvard Street, the best among a plethora of Jewish delis and bakeries is *Kupel's*, at no. 421, featuring exceptional bagels. Close by, the **John F. Kennedy National Historic Site**, at 83 Beals St (Wed–Sun 10am–4.30pm; $2) preserves the unremarkable home where JFK happened to be born on May 29, 1917. Inside, a narrated voiceover by the late President's mother, Rose, adds some spice to the rather plain, roped-off rooms.

For a deeper insight into JFK's legacy, visit the Kennedy Library in Dorchester, p.111.

Along Brookline's southern fringe is the **Frederick Law Olmsted National Historic Site**, at 99 Warren St (Fri–Sun 10am–4.30pm; free), the Olmsted family home that provides a retrospective on his life and work and is located, unsurprisingly, in idyllic grounds (see box p.99).

CHAPTER EIGHT

Southern districts

The parts of Boston that most visitors see – Downtown, Beacon Hill, Back Bay, the North End – actually only cover a small proportion of the city's geography. To the south lies a vast spread of residential neighborhoods known collectively as the southern districts, including South Boston, Dorchester, Roxbury and Jamaica Plain, which count just a handful of highlights among them, most notably Dorchester's John F. Kennedy Museum and Library and Jamaica Plain's must-see Arnold Arboretum, with its world renowned Bonsai Collection.

Once rural areas dotted with the swank summer resort homes of Boston's privileged, these districts became populated by middle- and working-class families pushed from the increasingly crowded downtown area in the late nineteenth century. Three-story rowhouses soon replaced mansions, and the moniker "streetcar suburbs" was coined as a catch-all for the newly redefined neighborhoods. In the years immediately following World War II, each was hit to varying degrees by economic decline, and the middle class moved farther afield, leaving the districts to the mostly immigrant and blue-collar communities that remain today.

The areas covered by this chapter can be seen on color map 2.

SOUTH BOSTON

Across Fort Point Channel from downtown and east into Boston Harbor lies **South Boston**, affectionately referred to as "Southie" by its large Irish-American population. Originally a peninsula separated from Boston proper by waterways, it was connected to the city in 1805, and throughout the nineteenth century expanded geographically, via landfill, and in population, thanks to a steady influx of Irish immigrants. South Boston remained solidly blue-collar and Irish until just after World War II, when it was particularly hard hit by recession, and its makeup began to change; despite some subsequent economic revival – especially in the shipbuilding industry – it is better known today for tensions between its old-timers and the newer communities of African-Americans, Hispanics, and gays that have moved into the area. Indeed, the radical AIDS Coalition to Unleash Power met with staunch resistance when the group petitioned in 1994 to march in Southie's annual St Patrick's Day parade; the battle went to the Supreme Court, which upheld the exclusion. South Bostonians showed a different side in a less publicized incident shortly afterward, when the Ku Klux Klan marched in the area and were met with jeers and protests from local residents.

The area's Celtic heritage is quite evident on the main commercial boulevard, **Broadway**, where seemingly every laundromat, convenience store, even Chinese restaurant, has a sign plastered with shamrocks. You'll also find an unsurprising profusion of Irish bars and pubs along West Broadway that make up in enthusiasm for the mother country what they lack in authenticity. *The Blackthorn*, at no. 471, comes closest to the real feel of an Irish pub.

Castle Island and Fort Independence

Map 2, K5. Island open daily dawn–dusk, fort open Sat & Sun noon–3.30pm; free. Broadway Ⓣ, then bus #9 or #11.

South Boston narrows to an end in Boston Harbor on a strip of land called **Castle Island**, off the terminus of William J. Day Boulevard, a favorite leisure spot for Southie residents and, in fact, for many Bostonians. Park and beaches cover the island, though you wouldn't want to swim offshore, since Boston Harbor's waters, while cleaner than in the past, are far from non-toxic – and they're freezing to boot. However, the views of downtown and the harbor are spectacular, best appreciated along the walkway known as the "Sugar Bowl," which follows along a narrow peninsula that curls out into the water.

The island's lone snack bar, *Sullivan's*, is a local institution with tasty seafood and grill fare.

Fort Independence, a stout granite edifice just north of the island, was one of the earliest redoubts in the Americas, originally established in 1634, though it has been rebuilt several times since. Today, what remains is a skeleton of its 1801 version, and its slate-gray walls aren't much to look at from the outside, though the ranger-led weekend tours provide some decent history and folklore about the dank interior corridors. One such story recalls a prisoner held here in the early 1800s for killing another man in a duel. One night, the victim's friends supposedly broke into the prison and chained the assassin into an alcove, then built a brick wall around him and left him to die. A young lawyer in the area by the name of Edgar Allan Poe apparently heard the rumor; he used it as the basis for his story, "The Cask of Amontillado."

DORCHESTER

Occupying the southeast corner of the city, **Dorchester** lies beneath South Boston; originally built on the narrow neck of land that connected Boston to the mainland, it's now a fairly unlovely and uninteresting lower- and middle-class residential neighborhood. North Dorchester was from its earliest days a center of trade and remains a largely industrial area today. South Dorchester has seen more turbulence over the years: once a coveted spot for elite country homes, it followed the "streetcar suburb" pattern of the Southern districts until post World War II, when the middle class left, property values plummeted, and crime and unemployment rose. Today, both parts of Dorchester are home to a broad ethnic mix, notably Irish, Haitians, Vietnamese, Caribbeans and African-Americans. Save for the **John F. Kennedy Museum and Library**, there's not much to see, and parts – especially in South Dorchester – are downright unsafe.

Dorchester Heights Monument

Map 2, I6. Grounds open daily, monument closed. Broadway Ⓣ to #11 bus (G St stop).

At the convergence of South Boston and Dorchester rises the incline of **Dorchester Heights**, a neighborhood of three-story rowhouses whose northernmost point, **Thomas Park**, is crowned by a stone obelisk **monument** commemorating George Washington's bloodless purge of the Brits from Boston. After the Continental Army had held the British under siege in the city for just over a year,

Washington wanted to put an end to the whole thing. On March 4, 1776, he amassed all the artillery he could get his hands on and placed it on the towering peak of Dorchester Heights, so the tired Redcoats could get a good look at the patriots' firepower. Intimidated, they swiftly left Boston – for good.

The park – generally empty and pristinely kept – still commands the same sweeping views of Boston and its southern communities that it did during the Revolutionary War. Unfortunately, the monument is permanently closed to the public, and it's all quite a bit out of the way from any other major points of interest.

John F. Kennedy Museum and Library

Map 2, J7. Daily 9am–5pm; $8; Citypass accepted (see p.9); ✆929-4523. JFK/UMass Ⓣ; free shuttle from the station to the museum every twenty minutes.

As with all presidential museums, the **John F. Kennedy Museum and Library**, at Columbia Point, is faced with the difficult task of extolling a president and icon's virtues while maintaining a veneer of scholarly objectivity, a task it performs with mixed results. But if the museum comes up a bit short in that respect, it still stands out by providing a fascinating glimpse into the culture of a recent era, while being spectacularly sited in an I.M. Pei-designed building (see p.88) overlooking Boston Harbor. The library, meanwhile, is not open to the public, only to researchers with specific requests, and holds JFK's papers from his curtailed term in the Oval Office.

The presentation opens with a well-done eighteen-minute film covering Kennedy's political career through the 1960 Democratic National Covention, narrated by voiceovers by Kennedy himself. The remaining displays cover the presidential campaign of 1960 and highlights of the truncated

Kennedy administration. The campaign exhibits are most interesting for their television and radio ads, which illustrate the squeaky-clean self-image America possessed at that time. Several features on JFK and the media unabashedly play up the contrast between Kennedy's telegenic charisma and Richard Nixon's jowly surliness, citing it as a key factor in JFK's victory over Tricky Dick. The section on the Kennedy administration is more serious, animated by a 22-minute film on the Cuban Missile Crisis that well evokes the tension of the event, if exaggerating Kennedy's heroics. And for Jackie O. fanatics, there's an exhibit that traces her life from early debutante days to her status as First Lady-cum-popular icon.

Oddly enough, the museum is also the repository for Ernest Hemingway's original manuscripts. Call ☎929-4523 for an appointment to see them.

The final section of the museum is perhaps its best: a roomy glass-enclosed space overlooking the harbor, with modest inscriptions bearing some of Kennedy's more memorable quotations – affecting enough to move even the most jaded JFK critic.

ROXBURY

Roxbury has borne the brunt of being one of Boston's most maligned neighborhoods. Occupying most of south-central Boston below the South End and between Dorchester and Jamaica Plain, this once pastoral region was one of the city's most coveted addresses in the seventeenth and eighteenth centuries, when wealthy families built sumptuous country houses here. It wasn't really until the 1950s that the area hit hard times, but the urban blight has left its scars, despite the revitalization of the past decade and an ongoing attempt to restore some of the impressive, if neglected, properties. While it is nowhere as dangerous as the rougher sections of bigger cities like LA or New York, visitors still may feel unwelcome or unsafe in parts, especially at night. The most compelling reason to visit the neighborhood today is the **Franklin Park Zoo**, in yet another of Olmsted's green spaces.

Roxbury's commercial center is **Dudley Square**, the intersection of Dudley and Washington streets, which is little more than the usual mix of shops and convenience stores. If you're in the area, you may want to check out the **Dillaway-Thomas House**, at 183 Roxbury St between Dudley Square and the Roxbury Crossing Ⓣ stop (Wed–Fri 10am–4pm, Sat & Sun noon–5pm; donation requested), a structure built in 1750 and used as a fort in the Revolutionary War. Its first floor is remarkably well-preserved, featuring many details of its original construction, while the upstairs has rotating exhibits of African- and African-American-themed art. Further south, the **Museum of the National Center for Afro-American Artists**, at 300 Walnut Ave (Tues–Sun 1–5pm; $4), housed in the Victorian Gothic "Oak Bend" mansion, has a decent collection of African-American visual art from throughout the twentieth century, highlighted by some richly textured woodcuts by Wilmer Jennings and Hale Woodruff as well as Roy DeCarava's photogravuras of jazz and blues greats.

Franklin Park Zoo

Map 2, F8. April–Oct Mon–Fri 10am–5pm, Sat & Sun 10am–6pm; Nov–March daily 10am–4pm; $6; ✆442-2002. Forest Hills Ⓣ.

The **Franklin Park Zoo**, 1 Franklin Park Rd in Franklin Park – the southernmost link in the Emerald Necklace – has little besides its backdrop to distinguish it from any other zoo, and is perhaps only a must-see if you're traveling with kids. It does boast a decent array of exotic fauna, much of which is contained in the African Tropical Forest, an impressively re-created savanna that's the largest indoor open-space zoo design in North America, and houses gorillas, monkeys and pygmy hippos. The Children's Zoo allows kids to pet and feed rhinos and the like, while Bird's World is a charming relic from the days of Edwardian zoo design: a huge, ornate wrought-iron cage you can walk through while birds fly overhead.

Franklin Park itself was one of Olmsted's proudest accomplishments when it was completed, due to the sheer size of the place, and its scale is indeed astounding – 527 acres of green space, with countless trails for hikers, bikers, and walkers leading through the hills and thickly forested areas. That's about it, as much of the park has unfortunately become overgrown from years of halfhearted upkeep. It's quite easy to get lost among all the greenery and forget that you're in the middle of a city, though this is perhaps not such a hot idea – the park borders some of Boston's more dangerous areas, and can feel quite threatening, especially at night.

JAMAICA PLAIN

Diminutive **Jamaica Plain** – "JP" in local parlance – is one of Boston's more successfully integrated neighborhoods, with a good mix of students, immigrants, and working-class families crowded into its relatively cheap apartments. Located between Roxbury and the section of the Emerald Necklace known as the Muddy River Improvement, the area's activity centers around, appropriately, **Centre Street**, which holds some inventive, and remarkably inexpensive, cafés and restaurants (see p.206 and p.220). Otherwise, head straight for JP's star attraction, the Arnold Arboretum, on its southwestern edge.

Arnold Arboretum

Map 2, D8. Mon–Fri 9am–4pm, Sat & Sun noon–4pm; $1 donation requested. Forest Hills Ⓣ.

The 265-acre Harvard University owned and operated **Arnold Arboretum**, at 125 Arborway, is the most spectacular link in the Emerald Necklace and the southern districts' only must-see sight. Its collection of over 14,000 trees, vines, shrubs and flowers has benefited from more than 100 years of both careful grooming and ample funding, and is now one of the finest in North America. The plants are arranged along a series of paths populated by runners and dog-walkers as well as serious botanists, though it certainly doesn't require any expert knowledge to enjoy the grounds.

The array of Asian species – considered one of the largest and most diverse outside Asia – is highlighted by the **Larz Anderson Bonsai Collection**, brilliantly concentrated along the Chinese Path walkway at the center of the park. Although the staff does an impressive job of keeping the grounds looking fabulous year-round, it's best to visit in spring, when crabapples, lilacs and magnolias complement the greenery with dazzling chromatic schemes. "Lilac Sunday," the third Sunday in May (see "Festivals", p.285), sees the Arboretum at its most vibrant (and busiest), when its collection of lilacs – the second largest in the US – is in full bloom. One of the best ways to appreciate the scope of the place is to make your way to the top of **Bussey Hill** in the Arboretum's center, where you can overlook the grounds in their impressive entirety and, on a clear day, catch a great view of downtown Boston besides.

Cambridge

Past and present stand comfortably opposed in Cambridge – just across the Charles River from Boston, but a world apart in atmosphere and attitude. A city in its own right, Cambridge has the feel of an overgrown college town coupled with the congestion, diversity, and distinctly different neighborhoods that come with being an urban center. A walk down most any street takes you past plaques and monuments honoring literati and revolutionaries who lived and worked in the area as early as the seventeenth century. But along its colonial-period brick sidewalks and narrow, crooked roads, Cambridge vibrates with a vital present: starched businesspeople bustle past a growing homeless population, while clean-cut college students coexist with grungy punks and busloads of tourists look on as vendors purvey goods and street artists perform.

Many residents tend to forget the world beyond the Charles River, and the Puritan parochialism of its founders has turned into a different breed of exclusivity, touched with civic and intellectual elitism. Simultaneously insular and outward-looking, Cambridge's exhilarating mix of colonial past and urban present, its range of residents and activities, and the sense of sheer energy that pervades its classrooms and coffeehouses make it an essential stopover while traveling in the Boston area.

The shape of Cambridge resembles a bow tie with Harvard Square forming the knot. On its southern border is the sinuous Charles River, with Boston on the opposite bank, while the concave northern side is shared with the large, mostly residential town of **Somerville**, popular with locals for its restaurant and café scene.

Cambridge proper is loosely organized around a series of squares – actually confluences of streets that are the focus of each area's commercial activity. By far the most important of these is **Harvard Square**, setting off point for **Harvard University**. Spanning a square mile centered around the Harvard Ⓣ station, the Square and University make up the cultural and academic heart of Cambridge. This is where people converge to check out Ivy League academia, historical monuments, a lively coffeehouse-and-bookstore scene, and a disgruntled counterculture. The area itself is roughly divided into the Square, which radiates out from the Ⓣ stop along Massachusetts Avenue, JFK Street and Brattle Street, and the University, roughly coterminous with Harvard Yard. Its geographic area is small in comparison with the entirety of Cambridge, but the density of attractions here make it one part of town not to be missed. Next to the University District, also easily accessible from Harvard Square, is **Old Cambridge**, the clean, impeccably kept colonial heartland of the city.

Central and **Inman squares**, meanwhile, represent the core of **Central Cambridge**, a neighborhood far more down-to-earth than its university counterpart. Its working-class atmosphere is continued further on in **East Cambridge**, no surprise as both areas grew up around industry rather than academia – though to be sure, East Cambridge gains most of its modern-day interest from the **Massachusetts Institute of Technology** (MIT), one of the world's premier science and research institutions and home to some peculiar architecture as well as an excellent museum. MIT spreads out below **Kendall Square**, which itself is home to a cluster of technology companies.

Above Harvard, **Northwest Cambridge** is an ill-defined corner of Cambridge, a catch-all term for some of the places not identified with the city's more happening districts – and as such it is easily missed. Despite some good shopping and decent restaurants, especially along Huron Avenue and around **Porter Square**, it's more of interest to residents than travelers.

The area covered by this chapter is shown in detail on color map 7.

Some history

Cambridge began inauspiciously in 1630, when a group of English immigrants from Charlestown founded **New Towne** village on the narrow, swampy banks of the Charles River. These Puritans hoped New Towne would become an ideal religious community; to that end, they founded a college in 1636 for the purpose of training clergy. Two years later, the college took its name in honor of a local minister, **John Harvard**, who bequeathed his library and half his estate to the nascent institution. New Towne was eventually renamed Cambridge in honor of the English university where many of its figureheads were educated, and became one of the largest publishing centers in the New World after the importation of the printing press in the seventeenth century. Its university and printing industry established Cambridge as an important center of intellectual activity and political thought, a status that became entrenched in the city over the course of the United States' turbulent early history – particularly during the late eighteenth century when the population was sharply divided between the many artisan and farmer sympathizers of the Revolution and the moneyed Tory minority. When fighting began, the Tories were driven from their mansions on modern-day Brattle Street (then called "Tory Row"), and their place was taken by Cambridge intelligentsia and prominent Revolutionaries.

The area remained unincorporated until 1846, when the Massachusetts Legislature granted a city charter linking Old Cambridge (the Harvard Square area) and industrial East Cambridge as a single municipality. Initially, there was friction between these two very different parts of Cambridge; in 1855, citizens from each area unsuccessfully petitioned for the two regions to be granted separate civic status. The failure of these efforts was followed by a thaw in relations which has resulted in a more cohesive community, though each area retains a distinctive character. The late nineteenth and early twentieth centuries brought substantial growth to the town. A large immigrant population was drawn to opportunity in the industrial and commercial sectors of East Cambridge, while academics increasingly sought out Harvard, whose reputation continued to swell, and the Massachusetts Institute of Technology, which moved here from Boston in 1916. By the 1960s, Cambridge had earned the name "Moscow on the Charles" due to its unabashedly Red character, but as rents have climbed in recent years, it's lost something of its leftist tendencies. Still, with half of its 93,000 residents university affiliates, it remains one of America's intellectual strongholds, regardless of the direction of its political leanings.

HARVARD SQUARE

Map 7, D5.

The Harvard Ⓣ station marks **Harvard Square's** ground zero, where a moody youth brigade stews in the shadow of Yard buildings. When you exit the station, take a pass through the adjacent sunken area known as **The Pit**, a triage center for fashion victims of alternative culture. Disgruntled teens spend entire days sitting here admiring each other's green hair and body piercings while the homeless (and some of the teens) hustle for change and other handouts. This is also the focal point of the **street music scene**, where folk diva Tracy Chapman (a graduate from nearby Tufts University, in Somerville) got her start. The Square reaches its most frenetic state on Friday and Saturday nights and Sunday afternoons, when all the elements converge – crowds mill about; evangelical demonstrators engage in shouting matches with angry youths; and magicians, acrobats and bands perform on every corner.

OLD BURYING-GROUND AND DAWES PARK

Map 7, D4.

North of Harvard Square along Massachusetts Avenue is one of Cambridge's first cemeteries, the **Old Burying-Ground**, whose style and grounds have scarcely changed since the seventeenth century. The epitaphs have an archaic ring to them ("Here lyes..."), and the stone grave markers, some of which date to the middle of the seventeenth century, are adorned in a style between Puritan austerity and medieval superstition: inscriptions praise the simple piety of the staunchly Christian deceased, but are surrounded by death's-heads carved to ward off evil spirits. Its most famous occupants include several of Harvard's first presidents as well as two black veterans of the Revolutionary War, Cato Stedman and Neptune Frost. Be sure to check out the **milestone** at the northeast corner of the cemetery, just inside the gate, whose two-and-a-half-centuries-old inscription is still readily visible. Originally set to mark the then-daunting distance of eight miles to Boston, the letters A. I. identify the stone's maker, Abraham Ireland. You're supposed to apply to the sexton of nearby **Christ Church** for entry, but if the gate at the path behind the simple, eighteenth-century church is open (as it frequently is), you can enter so long as you're respectful of the grounds.

A triangular wedge of concrete squeezed into the intersection of Massachusetts Avenue and Garden Street, **Dawes Park** is named for the patriot who rode to alert residents that the British were marching on Lexington and Concord on April 19, 1775 – the *other* patriot that is, William Dawes. While Longfellow opted to commemorate Paul Revere's midnight ride instead, as have most history classes, the citizens of Cambridge must have appreciated poor Dawes' contribution just as much. Bronze hoofmarks in the sidewalk mark the event, and several placards behind the pathway provide information on the history of the Harvard Square/Old Cambridge area.

CAMBRIDGE COMMON

Map 7, C4.

Cambridge Common, a roughly square patch of green located between Massachusetts Avenue and Garden and Waterhouse streets, has been a site for recreation and community events since Cambridge's earliest settlers first used it as a cow pasture. Tourists flock to the Common for its historical interest, but native Cambridgians congregate in its wide green spaces for frisbee and sunbathing – although after dusk it can be a lonelier, and more dicey, place altogether.

Cambridge's street signs give evidence of the city's early layout, with each road's original name and its year of inception printed below the current tag. For example, Garden Street was created as the Watertown Path in 1630.

Early Harvard commencements took place here, as did public debates and training exercises for the local militia. You can retrace a portion of the old **Charlestown–Watertown path**, along which Redcoats beat a sheepish retreat to Watertown during the Revolutionary War, and which still transects the park from east to west. A broad range of **statuary** dots the southeast corner of the park, and you can't miss the towering monument to Lincoln and other Civil War dead, which all but overshadows the recently added tableau of two emaciated figures nearby, wrought as an unsettling memorial to the Irish Potato Famine.

The most prominent feature on the Common is, however, the revered **Washington Elm**, under which it's claimed George Washington took command of the Continental Army. The elm is at the southern side of the park, near the intersection of Garden Street and Appian Way, and is accompanied by a predictable wealth of commemorative objects: a cannon captured from the British when they evacuated Boston, a statue of Washington standing in the shade of the beloved tree, and monuments to two Polish army captains hired to lead Revolutionary forces – excessive rewards, really, for mercenaries. What the memorials don't tell you is that the city of Cambridge cut down the original Washington Elm in 1946 when it began to obstruct traffic; it stood at the Common's southwest corner, near the intersection of Mason and Garden streets. The present tree is only the offspring of that tree, raised from one of its branches. To further confuse the issue, the Daughters of the American Revolution erected a monument commemorating the southeast corner of the park as the spot where Washington did his historic thing. And recently, American historians have adduced evidence strongly suggesting that Washington never commissioned the troops on the Common at all, but rather in Wadsworth House at Harvard Yard.

RADCLIFFE YARD

Map 7, C5.

Just across Garden Street from Cambridge Common is a less crowded park, **Radcliffe Yard**, originally the center of Radcliffe College, established in 1878 to give women access to (then exclusively male) Harvard. The two colleges merged in the 1970s, and since then Radcliffe has functioned primarily as a resource center for women in higher education. The Yard itself is a picturesque, impeccably preserved quadrangle; enclosed by brick buildings and Ionic columns, it's dotted with fountains and pathways, making it a great place for a summer picnic or stroll.

JFK STREET

Map 7, D5–D6.

The stretch of JFK Street below Harvard Square holds more of the city's many public spaces, certainly the least of which is **Winthrop Square**, site of the original New Towne marketplace and since converted into a bedraggled park. Cross the park and walk down Winthrop Street to the right to get a sense of the sloping topography and narrow street design of early Cambridge. Just to the right of the nightclub *House of Blues* is a **stone wall** that was built along the original shoreline of the Charles River.

John F. Kennedy Park, where JFK Street meets Memorial Drive, was only finished in the late 1980s, making it an infant among Harvard Square's venerable spots. Though certainly not the first pious shrine to the university's favorite modern son, this one is cleaner and more spacious than most other parks in the area. The **memorial** to Kennedy in its center is unusual and worth a look; it's a low granite pyramid surrounded by a moat, covered constantly but imperceptibly by a thin film of flowing water.

HARVARD HOUSES

Harvard's fancy upperclassmen's residences, most of which are nested in the area east of JFK Street and south of Harvard Yard, are a visible – and sometimes ostentatious – reminder of the university's elite past. Nearest the Yard, at 46 Plympton St, **Adams House** once reveled in its role as a haven for the Harvard avant-garde. Such counterculture has now grown feeble, though its subterranean tunnels, decorated with residents' graffiti, give a taste of its once-subversive character. Just south of Adams juts the graceful, blue-topped bell tower of **Lowell House**, at 2 Holyoke Place, which boasts one of Harvard's most beautiful courtyards, surrounded by a compound of sober brick dormitories and fastidiously manicured grounds. Further west on the banks of the Charles rises the purple spire of **Eliot House**, a community that remains a bastion of social privilege despite Harvard's attempts to shed this image. To the east along Memorial Drive lies **Dunster House**, whose red Georgian tower top is a favorite subject of Cambridge's tourist brochures; the clock tower is modeled after Christchurch College's Big Tom in Oxford. Alongside Adams, Dunster has long been considered a center for radical culture – at least by Boston's very proper standards.

HARVARD YARD AND AROUND

Map 7, D8.

The transition from Harvard Square to **Harvard Yard** is brief and dramatic: in a matter of only several feet, the noise and crowds give way to grassy lawns and towering oaks. Its narrow, haphazard footpaths are constantly trafficked by preoccupied students and camera-clicking tour groups. The Yard is where Harvard myth and reality converge – the grandeur of Ivy League aura besieged by the visitor traffic of an amusement park.

The most common entrance is the one directly across from Harvard Square proper, which leads by **Massachusetts Hall** (holding the office of the university president) to the **Old Yard**, a large, rectangular area enclosed by freshman dormitories that has been around since 1636, when it was created as a grazing field for university livestock. In front of stark, symmetrical, slate-gray University Hall is the Yard's trademark icon, the **John Harvard statue**, around which chipper student guides inform tour groups of the oft-told story of the statue's three lies (it misdates the college's founding; erroneously identifies John Harvard as the college's founder; and isn't really a likeness of John Harvard at all). While it's a popular spot for visitors to take pictures, male students at the college prize the statue as a prime spot to urinate in public; anyone managing to pull off the feat is granted a certain honorary status among students on campus – as a result, there are now about twenty surveillance cameras trained on the site, acting as a deterrence.

Along the northwest border of the Yard is stout **Hollis Hall**, the dormitory where Henry David Thoreau lived as an undergraduate. The architectural contrast between modest Hollis, which dates from 1762, and its grandiose southern neighbor, **Matthews Hall**, built around a hundred years later, mirrors Harvard's transition from a quiet training ground for ministers to a wealthy, cosmopolitan university. The **indentations** in Hollis' front steps also hold some historical interest: students used to warm their rooms by heating cannonballs; come time to leave their quarters for the summer, they would dispose of the cannonballs by dropping them from their windows rather than having to carry them down the stairs.

Relentlessly cheerful students lead free tours of the Yard from Holyoke Center, 1350 Massachusetts Ave (June–Aug Mon–Sat 10am, 11.15am, 2pm & 3.15pm, Sun 1.30pm & 3pm; Sept–May Mon–Fri 10am & 2pm, Sat 2pm)

To the east of the Old Yard lie the grander buildings of the **New Yard**, where a vast set of steps leads up to the enormous pillars of **Widener Library**. Named after Harvard grad and *Titanic* victim Harry Elkins Widener, whose mother paid for the project, it's the center of the largest private library collection in the US. Through the entrance and up one flight of stairs is the Widener Memorial Room, flanked by two melodramatic murals by John Singer Sargent. Some of the library's most valuable volumes are displayed here, including a first folio of Shakespeare and a Gutenberg Bible. At the opposite side of the New Yard is **Memorial Church**, whose narrow, white spire strikes a balancing note to the heavy pillared front of Widener; its towering steeple is a classic postcard image of Harvard Yard.

The immense structure just north of the Yard is Harvard's **Science Center**; the big lecture halls on the first floor are the locations of Harvard's most popular classes. Stop by most weekday mornings and you can sit in lectures by popular bigwig professors including Stephen Jay Gould and Milton Friedman. A popular myth has it that the Center was designed to look like a camera, since one of its main benefactors was Polaroid magnate Edwin Land, though any likeness is purely accidental.

North past the Science Center, and just behind the physical science labs, lies the main quad of the famed **Harvard Law School**, focusing on the stern gray pillars of **Langdell Hall**, an imposing edifice on its western border, whose entrance bears the inscription "*Non sub homine, sed sub deo et lege*" ("Not under man, but under God and law"). You can practically smell the stress in the air inside the newly renovated **Harvard Law Library**, officially reserved for Harvard students, though visitor privileges can be applied for at the front desk – not that there's too much worth nosing around for, other than the occasional exhibits on jurisprudence history in the Root and Treasure rooms.

East of the Science Center are the pointed arches and flying buttresses of **Memorial Hall**, built to commemorate the Harvard students who died during the Civil War. Its central vaulted **narthex** is sober and atmospheric; light filtering through the stained-glass windows illuminates inscriptions of the many soldiers' names.

It's hard to miss the conspicuously modern **Carpenter Center** as you walk past Memorial Hall and down Quincy Street, a slab of slate-gray granite amidst Harvard's ever-present brick motif. Completed in 1963 as a center for the study of visual art at Harvard, the Carpenter Center is the only building in America designed by the French architect Le Corbusier, and its jarring difference from its surroundings has drawn a great deal of criticism from staunch Harvard traditionalists. Still, it's a striking and reasonably functional space; be sure to traverse its trademark feature, a **walkway** that leads through the center of the building, meant to reflect the path worn by students on the lot on which the center was constructed. The lower floors of the building frequently house student art exhibits, which are free and open to the public.

HARVARD UNIVERSITY MUSEUMS

Harvard's **museums** have benefited from years of scholarly attention and donors' financial generosity. Largely under-appreciated and underattended by most visitors, not to mention the students themselves, the collections are easily some of the finest in New England.

William Hayes Fogg Art Museum

Map 7, E8. Mon–Sat 10am–5pm, Sun 1–5pm; $5, free Wed 10am–5pm & Sat 10am–noon; ©495-9400.

Housed on two floors and surrounding a lovely mock sixteenth-century Italian courtyard, the collections of the **William Hayes Fogg Art Museum**, at 32 Quincy St, showcase the highlights of Harvard's substantial collection of Western art. Much of the first floor is devoted to Medieval and Renaissance material, mainly religious art with the usual complement of suffering Christs. This part of the collection is best for a series of capitals salvaged from the French cathedral of Moutiers-Saint-Jean, which combine a Romanesque predilection for classical design with Medieval didactic narrative. The rest of the first floor is devoted to portraiture of the seventeenth and eighteenth centuries, featuring two Rubens and a Rembrandt, though it's more notable for a fine display of lesser-known Neapolitan Baroque works, particularly the grotesque *Martyrdom of Saint Sebastian* by Battistello and Francesco Fracazano's robust *Drunken Silenus*. The remainder is rather stale, though the work of local John Singleton Copley figures prominently, and Cavaletto's extraordinarily precise *View of the Piazza San Marco* is not to be missed.

A ticket to the Fogg is also good for entry to the Busch-Reisinger and Sackler museums.

The second floor includes several spaces for rotating exhibits, while its permanent holdings are strongest in Impressionism and modernism, especially the late nineteenth century French contingent of Degas, Monet, Manet, Pissarro and Cézanne.

You'll also see Picasso's *Mother and Child*, famously exemplary of his blue period, a sickly *Self-Portrait, dedicated to Paul Gauguin* by Van Gogh, and Toulouse-Lautrec's queasy *Hangover*. But it's the focus on American counterparts to European late nineteenth- and early twentieth-century artists that truly distinguishes the collection. There's a fine range of John Singer Sargent portraits and a pair of Whistler's moody *Nocturnes*. Sheeler's *Upper Deck*, stands out among the American works: a representation of technology that ingeniously combines realism with abstraction.

Busch-Reisinger Museum

Map 7, E8. Mon–Sat 10am–5pm, Sun 1–5pm; $5, free Wed 10am–5pm & Sat 10am–noon.

Secreted away at the rear of the Fogg's second floor is the entrance to Werner Otto Hall, home of the rich – though somewhat harrowing – **Busch-Reisinger Museum**, concentrating exclusively on the German Expressionists and the work of the Bauhaus. Despite its small size, it's one of the finest collections of its kind in the world, starting off with *fin de siècle* art – including Klimt's *Rue de Rivoli* and *Pear Tree*, a pair of meditations on constructed and natural environments – and moving through Bauhaus standouts like Feininger's angular *Bird Cloud* and Moholy-Nagy's *Light-Space Modulator* – a sculpture-machine set in motion just once a week (Wed 1.45pm) due to its fragility. But the gallery's highlight is its Expressionist portraiture, which includes Kirchner's sardonic *Self-Portrait with a Cat* and Beckmann's nauseated *Self-Portrait in a Tuxedo*.

Arthur M. Sackler Museum

Map 7, E8. Mon–Sat 10am–5pm, Sun 1–5pm; $5, free Wed 10am–5pm & Sat 10am–noon.

Right out of the Fogg and dead ahead is the Arthur M.

Sackler Building, 485 Broadway, three floors of which comprise the **Sackler Museum**, dedicated to the art of classical, Asian and Islamic cultures. The museum's holdings have far outgrown its available space, which is why the first floor is devoted to rotating exhibits. Islamic and Asian art are the themes of the second floor, featuring illustrations from Muslim texts and Chinese landscapes from the past several centuries. The fourth floor is best known for its excellent array of sensuous Buddhist sculptures from ancient China, India and Southeast Asia, and an excellent collection of Japanese woodblock prints. You'll also see a solid display of classical work – standing out from the usual Greek vases and sculpture are intelligent studies on the coins of Alexander the Great and seals from ancient Babylonia.

Harvard Semitic Museum

Map 7, E7. Mon–Fri 10am–4pm, Sun 1–4pm; free.

North past the Sackler is Divinity Avenue, on which another series of museums begins, led by the **Harvard Semitic Museum**, at no. 6, whose informative and impeccably presented displays chronicle Harvard's century-old excavations in the Near East. Pieces range from Egyptian tombs to Babylonian cuneiform, but what makes the collection distinctive is that it focuses nearly as much on the process and methodology of the digs as on their results. For some reason, the Semitic isn't officially part of the consortium known as the Harvard Museums of Cultural and Natural History, so you don't even have to pay admission to see its excellent collection.

Peabody Museum of Archeology and Ethnology

Map 7, E7. Mon–Sat 9am–5pm, Sun 1–5pm; $5.

Officially first in the line-up of Harvard Museums of Cultural and Natural History, and the most prominent among them, the **Peabody Museum of Archeology and Ethnology**, 11 Divinity Ave, displays materials culled from Harvard's anthropological and archeological expeditions. The strength of the museum lies in its collection of pieces from Mesoamerica, ranging from digs in the pueblos of the southwestern United States to artifacts from Incan civilizations. The anthropological material centers mainly on indigenous cultures of America, and includes a detailed presentation on the Ju/wa bushmen of the Kalahari desert. The displays are extensive and informative, covering the history, art, traditions and lifestyles of native peoples from around the world, though the wax dummies in traditional garb and the miniature dioramas can't help but seem hokey and out of place.

One ticket covers entry to the Peabody, Comparative Zoology, Mineralogical and Geological and Botanical museums. All are free between 9am and noon on Saturdays.

Mineralogical and Geological Museum

Map 7, D7. Mon–Sat 9am–5pm, Sun 1–5pm; $5.

Harvard's **Mineralogical and Geological Museum**, another of the University's very specialized museums, is, basically, a bunch of rocks, among them some fairly impressive meteorites. Otherwise, if you don't know much about geology, this probably won't do too much for you. On the other hand, it's reputed to be one of the world's finest mineral collections, and most of the gems are aesthetically as well as academically interesting.

Botanical Museum

Map 7, D7. Mon–Sat 9am–5pm, Sun 1–5pm. $5.

Right next door, and similarly narrow in scope, is the **Botanical Museum**, at 26 Oxford St. You may think this collection is only of interest to botanists, and much of it may well be, but it's still worth a pass to take in the stunning Ware Collection of Glass Models of Plants. This project began in 1887 and terminated almost fifty years later in 1936, leaving the museum with an absolutely unique and visually awesome collection of flower models constructed to the last detail, entirely from glass. It's a spectacle that must be seen to be believed.

Museum of Comparative Zoology

Map 7, D7. Mon–Sat 9am–5pm, Sun 1–5pm. $5.

Housed in the same building as the Botanical Museum, but lacking a knockout centerpiece, the **Museum of Comparative Zoology** is really just the tip of the iceberg of the university's collection of zoological materials, most of which is inaccessible to visitors. Among the rote displays of stuffed dead animals, however, are some fascinating insects preserved in amber and impressive arrays of fossils and ants.

OLD CAMBRIDGE: UPPER BRATTLE STREET

Map 7, A5–D5.

After the outbreak of the American Revolution, Cambridge's bourgeois majority ran the Tories out of town, leaving their sumptuous houses to be used as the quarters of the Continental Army. What was then called Tory Row is modern-day **Brattle Street**, the main drag of the **Old Cambridge** district, a tree-lined neighborhood of stately mansions, behind expansive, impeccably kept lawns.

The **Brattle House**, at 42 Brattle St, just off Harvard Square, fails to reflect the unabashedly extravagant lifestyle of its former resident, William Brattle. It doesn't appear nearly as grand as it once did, dwarfed as it is by surrounding office buildings, nor is it open to the public – no great loss since it now only houses offices. Down the street and to the right, tiny **Farwell Street** features several modest Federal-style houses dating to the early nineteenth century and is the best (and only remaining) example of the square's residential character before it became a teeming center of activity.

The city has labeled every sight of conceivable interest with an explanatory blue oval plaque. Call the Cambridge Historical Commission ✆547-4252 for the exhaustive list.

A sign on the corner of Brattle and Story streets commemorates the site of a tree which once stood near the **Dexter Pratt House**, home of the village blacksmith celebrated by Longfellow in a popular poem that began, "Under a spreading chestnut tree / The village smithy stands, / the smith a mighty man is he, / With large and sinewy hands; / And the muscles of his brawny arms / Are strong as iron bands." In 1876, the chestnut was cut down, despite Longfellow's vigorous opposition, because it was spreading into the path of passing traffic. The city of Cambridge fashioned a chair out of the felled tree, presented it to Longfellow as a birthday present, who then composed a mawkish poem about the whole affair ("From My Easy Chair"), and all was forgiven. These days the house has a more humdrum role, home to the *Blacksmith House* bakery, producers of some of the finest baked treats in greater Boston – which may be the most exciting thing about the place. Beyond the Pratt House, at the intersection of Mason and Brattle streets, the advent of a tree-lined neighborhood of elite mansions signals the edge of Old Cambridge proper.

Longfellow House

Map 7, B5. Wed–Sat 10am–4.30pm, tours every hour; $2. Harvard Ⓣ.

One house you can visit is the **Vassal-Craigie-Longfellow House**, 105 Brattle St, the best-known and most popular of the Brattle Street mansions, where the poet Henry Wadsworth Longfellow lived while serving as a professor at Harvard. It was erected for Royalist John Vassal in 1759, who promptly vacated it on the eve of the Revolutionary War, inhabited by George Washington during the war itself, and used as his headquarters during the siege of Boston. It wasn't until 1843 that it became home to Longfellow, who moved in as a boarder; when he married the wealthy Fanny Appleton, her father purchased the house for them as a wedding gift. Longfellow lived here until his death in 1882, and the house is preserved in an attempt to portray it as it was during his residence. It's a solid, if somewhat strenuously presented, example of Brattle Street's opulence during the nineteenth century. The halls and walls are festooned with Longfellow's furniture and art collection: most surprising is the wealth of nineteenth-century pieces from the Far East, amassed by Longfellow's renegade son Charlie on his world travels. His other son, Ernie, stayed at home, trying – and failing – to make a name for himself as a landscape painter; a number of his unremarkable works also adorn the walls of the house, along with a copy of Gilbert Stuart's famous portrait of George Washington, done by his daughter, Jane Stuart.

Hooper-Lee-Nichols House

Map 7, A5. Tues & Thurs 2–5pm; $2. Harvard Ⓣ.

The second of the Brattle Street mansions open to the public, half a mile west of the Longfellow House and well worth the trip if you've got the stamina, is the **Hooper-Lee-Nichols House**, at no. 159, one of the two oldest residences in Cambridge and the best example of the character of life and style of housing design during Cambridge's Colonial period. The house is particularly unusual for its various architectural incarnations. It began as a stout, post-medieval farmhouse, and underwent various renovations until it became the Georgian mansion it is today. Rooms have been predictably restored with period writing tables, canopy beds and rag dolls, but knowledgeable tour guides spice things up a bit, opening secret panels to reveal centuries-old wallpaper and original foundations.

The Hooper-Lee-Nichols house is officially open Tuesdays and Thursdays 2-5pm, but that doesn't mean someone will be waiting out front for you. Knock vigorously on the front door.

Mount Auburn Cemetery

Map 7, A8–A9. Harvard Ⓣ to Watertown bus #71.

At the intersection of Brattle and Mount Auburn Streets is the **Mount Auburn Cemetery**, whose 170 acres of grounds are more like a beautifully kept municipal park than a necropolis, with as many joggers as there are mourners. The best way to get a sense of the cemetery's scope is to ascend the **tower** that lies smack in its center atop a grassy bluff – from here, you can see not only the entire grounds but, on a clear day, all of downtown Boston and its environs. Of course, like most cemeteries in the Boston area, Mount Auburn also has its share of deceased luminaries, most notably Winslow Homer and Isabella Stewart Gardner; ask the folks in the main office for a map of famous graves if you're interested. You could spend a day walking the grounds; allow at least a few hours.

CENTRAL SQUARE

Map 7, H5.

Central Square, as you might expect, is located roughly in the geographical center of Cambridge, and is appropriately the city's civic center as well, home to its most important government buildings. It's an interesting mix of cultural and industrial Cambridge, a working-class area with an ethnically diverse population and little of the hype that surrounds other parts of town. There's nothing as such to see, but it's a good place to shop and eat, and is home to some of the best nightlife in Cambridge. The Gothic quarters of **City Hall**, 795 Mass Ave (Mon–Fri 8.30am–5pm), house Cambridge's municipal bureaucracy and act as an occasional venue for town meetings or public events, but little else stands out here.

For restaurants and bars in Cambridge, see p.207 & p.220.

INMAN SQUARE

Map 7, G2.

Overshadowed by Cambridge's busier districts, **Inman Square** marks a quiet stretch directly north of Central

Square, centered around the confluence of Cambridge, Beacon and Prospect streets. There's little of interest here either, just a pleasant, mostly residential neighborhood where much of Cambridge's working-class Portuguese-speaking population resides. What does make Inman worth a visit, along with its ethnic markets, is its broad range of excellent restaurants, where you can enjoy some of Cambridge's finest food without breaking the bank. If you're in the area, check out Inman's lone landmark, the charmingly inexpert **Cambridge Firemen's Mural**, at the corner of Cambridge and Antrim streets, a work of public art commissioned to honor local men in red.

EAST CAMBRIDGE AND KENDALL SQUARE

Map 7, L1–L3.

East Cambridge is split into two main areas of activity, though neither has especially much to recommend it unless you're into checking out the corporate headquarters of numerous software companies. In the northernmost region, there's the **CambridgeSide Galleria** (see "Shopping", p.264), a gargantuan shopping multiplex, where mall rats mingle in the neon-lit food court.

Further inland and adjacent to MIT, **Kendall Square** grew from the ashes of the post-industrial desolation of East Cambridge in the Sixties and Seventies to become a glittering testament to the economic revival that sparked Massachusetts in the Eighties. Technology and its profits built the square, and it shows. By day, Kendall bustles with wealthy eggheads lunching in chic eateries; at night, the business crowd goes home and the place becomes largely deserted. The exception to this is the **Kendall Square Cinema**, which draws large crowds to see some of the best art and second-run movies in the area (see "Film", p.244).

MASSACHUSETTS INSTITUTE OF TECHNOLOGY

Map 7, J7–L4.

Occupying 153.8 acres alongside the Charles, the **Massachusetts Institute of Technology** (MIT) provides an intellectual counterweight to the otherwise working-class character of East Cambridge. Originally established in Allston in 1865, MIT moved to this more auspicious campus across the river in 1916 and has since risen to international prominence as a major center for theoretical and practical research in the sciences. Both NASA and the Department of Defense pour funds into MIT in exchange for research and development assistance from the university's best minds.

The campus buildings and geography reflect the quirky, nerdy character of the institute, emphasizing function and peppering it with a peculiar notion of form. Everything is obsessively numbered and coded: you can go to E15 (the Weisner Building) for a lecture in 4.103 (advanced computer-assisted design), which, of course, gets you no closer towards a degree in 17 (political science). Behind the massive pillars that guard the entrance of the **Rogers Building**, at 77 Massachusetts Ave, you'll find a labyrinth of corridors – known to Techies as the **Infinite Corridor** – through which students can traverse the entire east campus without ever going outside. Atop the Rogers Building is MIT's best-known architectural icon, a massive gilt hemisphere called the **Great Dome**. Just inside the entrance to Rogers, you'll find the **MIT Information Center** (Mon–Fri 9am–5pm), which dispenses free campus maps and advice.

MIT has drawn the attention of some of the major architects of the twentieth century, who have used the university's progressiveness as a testing ground for some of their more experimental works. Two of these are located in the courtyard across Massachusetts Avenue from the Rogers Building. The **Kresge Auditorium**, designed by Finnish architect Eero Saarinen, resembles a large tent, though its real claim to fame is that it puzzlingly rests on three, rather than four, corners. In the same courtyard is the **MIT Chapel**, also the work of Saarinen. Shaped like a stocky cylinder and topped with abstract sculpture crafted from paper-thin metals, it's undoubtedly the city's least traditional religious space. The I. M. Pei-designed **Weisner Building** is home to the **List Visual Art Center** (Tues–Sun noon–6pm; free), which displays student works – often and more technologically impressive than visually appealing as they are heavily influenced by science and involve a great deal of computer design.

Of perhaps more interest, down Massachusetts Avenue at no. 265, is the **MIT Museum** (Tues–Fri 10am–5pm, Sat & Sun noon–5pm; $3). The museum has two main permanent displays, the Hologram Museum and the Hall of Hacks, the latter of which provides a retrospective on the various pranks ("hacks") pulled by Techies. Among other things, the madcap funsters have placed a fake cow and a real MIT police car atop the Great Dome, and have wreaked havoc at the annual Harvard–Yale football game by landing a massive weather balloon in the middle of the gridiron. A glimpse at these exploits alone warrants a visit, though there are excellent rotating exhibits as well.

PORTER SQUARE

Map 7, A1.

If Northwest Cambridge has a center, it's **Porter Square**, located a mile north of Harvard Square along Massachusetts Avenue. The walk from Harvard will take you past some of Cambridge's most chic eateries and boutiques, while Porter Square itself is hard to miss – look for the forty-foot red kinetic **sculpture** right outside the subway stop. Just before this gargantuan mobile is the **Porter Exchange**, a mall of mostly unimpressive shops, save for an obscure hallway lined with tiny **Japanese food outlets** – cramped bar-style restaurants where the food is so authentic you'll have to point to the menu to order, unless, of course, you speak Japanese.

DAVIS SQUARE

Just beyond Porter Square, Somerville's **Davis Square** has increasingly become an alternative destination for young area residents looking for the kind of homey cafés and nightspots that used to dot Harvard Square. Coupled with the relatively reasonable rents, this has spurred a gentrification that's worked quickly to erode the square's former working-class atmosphere. In any case, it remains a bit removed from the typical visitor's circuit, though it's as inviting a spot as any to jump on the scenic **Minuteman Bike Trail**, which begins at the Alewife Ⓣ stop and continues through Arlington and Lexington to Bedford (©542-BIKE; *www.massbike.org*).

STRAWBERRY HILL

In the lowest corner of Northwest Cambridge, just to the east of the Fresh Pond reservoir, slopes the gentle grade of **Strawberry Hill**, whose main street, Huron Avenue, runs up and around it. This slice of upper-middle class suburbia is serene and arboreal, one with a charming array of apothecaries and specialty shops. The *Huron Spa*, for example, has a soda fountain where you can sample vanilla cokes and the like, and the bookshelves at Bryn Mawr Book Shop, 373 Huron Ave, still open onto the street.

Day-trips

There's enough of interest in Boston itself to keep you going for several days at the very least. However, the city lies at the center of a dense concentration of historic sights, and there's plenty to see and do within a short distance – not to mention further afield. Perhaps the best inland day-trip you can make within a 25-mile radius of Boston is to the Revolutionary battlegrounds of Lexington and Concord, but the city also makes an excellent base for visiting the numerous quaint and historic towns that line the North Shore of the Massachusetts coast. For many, the notorious witch sights of Salem make that first place of interest, though nearby Marblehead is pretty enough to merit a wander too; after that, you can continue on to somewhat more rustic Gloucester and Rockport, worthwhile if you have the time and are captivated by the faded glories of the New England fishing trade. Route 1 is the quickest way up the coast, though coastal Route 1A is more scenic. Buses run up this direction as well, operated both by the MBTA and by independent tour companies (see p.9) as does the MBTA commuter rail. On the South Shore, Plymouth is the main tourist draw, and in summer a ferry from Boston puts Provincetown, the exuberant old fishing village at the tip of Cape Cod, within easy reach.

LEXINGTON AND CONCORD

The sedate towns of **Lexington** and **Concord**, almost always mentioned in the same breath, trade in on their notoriety as the locations of the first armed confrontation with the British. Lexington is today mostly suburban, while Concord, five miles east, is even sleepier, though it has a bit more character. Most of Concord and Lexington's historical quarters have been incorporated into the **Minute Man National Park**, which takes in the Lexington Battle Green, North Bridge and much of Battle Road, the route the British followed on their retreat from Concord back to Boston. These notorious Battles are evoked in a piecemeal but relentless fashion throughout the park, with scale models, remnant musketry and the odd preserved bullet hole. The **Old Manse** and **The Wayside**, two rambling old Concord houses with bookish pasts, are also situated on the grounds, while some other "literary" sites, such as **Walden Pond** in Concord, are just beyond its boundaries.

Lexington

The main thing to see in **Lexington** is the grassy **Battle Green**, where the American flag flies 24 hours a day. The land serves as Lexington's town common and is fronted by Henry Kitson's famous statue of *The Minute Man*. This musket-bearing figure of Captain John Parker was not dedicated until 1900, but it stands on boulders dislodged from the stone walls behind which the colonial militia fired at the British opponents on April 19, 1775. The **visitors center** (daily: Jan–April 10am–3pm; May–Oct 9am–5pm; Nov & Dec 10am–4pm) on the eastern periphery of the Green has a diorama that shows the detail of the battle, while in the **Buckman Tavern** facing the Green, a British bullet hole has been preserved in an inner door near the restored first-floor tap room. A couple of blocks north, at 36 Hancock St, a plaque affixed to the **Hancock-Clarke House** solemnly reminds that this is where "Samuel Adams and John Hancock were sleeping when aroused by Paul Revere." Exhibits on the free first floor include the drum on which William Diamond beat the signal for the Minute Men to converge and the pistols that British Major John Pitcairn lost on the retreat from Concord. Less interesting is the small wooden **Munroe Tavern**, a bit removed from the town center at 1332 Massachusetts Ave: it served as a field hospital for British soldiers, but for a mere one and one-half hours.

The Buckman Tavern, Hancock-Clarke House and Munroe Tavern are all open mid-March through late Oct Mon–Sat 9am–5pm, Sun 1–5pm; separate 30–45min guided tours of each cost $4.

Concord

One of the few sizeable inland towns of New England at the time of the Revolution, **Concord** retains a pleasant country atmosphere despite its reputation as just another wealthy western suburb. Start your wanderings at the **Colonial Inn**, near the corner of Main and Monument streets, a rambling old hostelry with a traditional dining room and a tavern that served as a makeshift Revolutionary hospital during the war. It's also a good place to stop for a pint or a hearty lunch. From the top of **Hill Burying Ground**, just west of the *Colonial Inn*, you can survey Concord, as did Pitcairn when the Americans amassed on the far side of North Bridge. A few blocks behind it on Route 62 is **Sleepy Hollow Cemetery** – not the one of headless horsemen fame that is located far from here in the

Hudson River Valley. Still, in this Sleepy Hollow, lie Concord literati Emerson, Hawthorne, Thoreau and Louisa May Alcott, atop the graveyard's "Author's Ridge," as signs clearly indicate.

Concord is a forty-minute train ride ($3.25 one way) from Boston's North Station, on the Fitchburg Commuter Rail Line; trains arrive at Concord Station, about half a mile from the city center.

The most hyped spot in Concord is **North Bridge**, site of the first effective armed resistance to British rule in America. If you take the traditional approach from Monument Street, you'll be following the route the British took; just before crossing the bridge, an inscription on the mass grave of some British regulars reads, "They came 3000 miles and died to keep the past upon its throne." The bridge itself, however, looks a bit too well-preserved to provoke much sentiment – no wonder: it's actually a 1954 replica of yet another replica of the original structure.

A stone's throw from North Bridge is the gray-clapboard **Old Manse**, 269 Monument St (April–Oct Mon–Sat 10am–4.30pm, Sun 1–4.30pm; $5), built for Ralph Waldo Emerson's grandfather, the Reverend William Emerson, in 1770. The younger Emerson lived here on and off, though this was where, in 1834, he penned *Nature*, the book that signaled the beginning of the Transcendentalist movement. Of the numerous rooms in the house, all with period furnishings intact, the most interesting is the small upstairs study, where Nathaniel Hawthorne, a resident of the house in the early 1840s, wrote *Mosses from an Old Manse*, a rather obscure book that endowed the place with its name. Hawthorne passed three happy years here shortly after getting married to his wife Sophia, who with her wedding ring etched the words "Man's accidents are God's purposes" into a window pane in the study. Other contemplative etchings can be found on windows downstairs. On the first floor, look for the framed swath of original English-made wallpaper with the British "paper tax" mark stamped on the back.

Right in the middle of town is the *Cheese Shop*, at 29 Walden St, a great place to stop for sandwiches.

Also worth a visit is **The Wayside**, east of the town center at 455 Lexington Rd (April–Oct Tues–Sun 10am–5.30pm; $2), a 300-year-old yellow wooden house that's also a literary landmark, home to both the Alcotts and Hawthornes, though at different times. Louisa May Alcott's girlhood experiences here formed the basis for *Little Women*. Among the antique furnishings, the most unusual is the slanted writing desk at which Hawthorne toiled standing up, in the fourth floor "tower" he added on for that purpose. If you don't feel like taking a guided tour, you can stop in at the small but very well-presented museum at the admissions area for a brief overview. Alcott actually penned *Little Women* next door at the **Orchard House**, where the family lived from 1858 to 1867 and her father, Bronson, founded his School of Philosophy.

Just down the road at no.200, the excellent **Concord Museum** (Mon–Sat 10am–5pm, Sun 1–5pm; $6), on the site of Emerson's apple orchard, has more than a dozen galleries displaying period furnishings from eighteenth- and nineteenth-century Concord, including a sizeable collection of Thoreau's personal effects, such as the bed from his Walden Pond hut. More interesting, however, are the Revolutionary War artifacts throughout, such as one of the signal lanterns hung from the Old North Church in Boston.

WALDEN POND

Though the tranquility that Thoreau sought and savored at **Walden Pond**, just two miles south of Concord proper off Route 126 ($2), is for the most part gone – thanks mainly to the masses of tourists who pour in to retrace his footsteps – the place itself has remained much the same since the author's famed two-year exercise in self-sufficiency begun in 1845. "I did not feel crowded or confined in the least," he wrote of his life in the simple log cabin. Though his semi-fictionalized account of the experience might have you believing otherwise, Thoreau hardly roughed it, taking regular walks into town to stock up on amenities and receiving frequent visitors at his single-room hut. The reconstructed cabin, replete with a journal open on its rustic desk, is situated near the parking lot (you'll have to content yourself with peering through the windows), while the site of the original structure, closer to the shores of the pond, is marked out with stones. The pond itself is quite popular with long-distance swimmers. Spared from development by a band of celebrities led by ex-Eagle Don Henley, the water looks best at dawn, when the pond still "throws off its nightly clothing of mist"; late-risers should plan an off-season visit to maximize their transcendental experience of it all.

SALEM

Salem, an unpretentious city just sixteen miles north of Boston, is the most intriguing destination on the shore, standing out from the other rustic towns that line the coast if only because of its peculiar history. This is where Puritan self-righteousness reached its apogee in the horrific **witch trials** of 1692, and the place has been trying to shake the stigma ever since. Less known were the many years it spent as a flourishing seaport; the remnants from those years only add to the unsettling aura: abandoned wharves, rows of stately sea captains' homes and the astounding display of their riches at the Peabody Essex Museum. Ironically, Salem's dark legacy has proven to be its salvation, leading to a major sprucing-up of its touristy core.

Salem is a twenty- to thirty-minute train ride ($2.50 one way) from North Station in Boston, on the Salem Commuter Rail Line.

Today, the **Salem Heritage Trail** links the town's principal historic sights, the majority of which are tied to the town's gloomy witch-burning days. In an even more ironic twist of history, a sizeable and highly visible contingent of **Wiccans** now lives proudly in modern Salem; these latter-day sorceresses are more than willing to accept modest fees for their fortune-telling services, despite – or perhaps because of – their New Age spirituality. Keep in mind they're as much a part of the tourist industry as everything else in Salem.

The Salem Witch sights

The hokey **Salem Witch Museum**, 19½ Washington Square (daily 10am–5pm; $6), provides some entertaining orientation on the witch hysteria. It's really just a sound-and-light show that makes ample use of wax figures to depict the events of 1692, housed in a suitably spooky one-time Romanesque church. Right in front of it is the imposing statue of a caped **Roger Conant**, founder of Salem's first Puritan settlement. More evocative is the **Witch Dungeon Museum**, at 16 Lynde St (April–Nov daily 10am–5pm; $5), on the west side of town, on the site of the prison where the accused witches were locked up. Inside you're again treated to farcical re-enactments of key events, this time with living players: upstairs, it's the trial of Sarah Good – a pipe-smoking beggar woman falsely accused of witchcraft – based on actual transcripts. Actors then escort visitors to a re-created dungeon with prison cells no bigger than telephone booths. Dank and supremely eerie, it's not hard to believe claims that the place is haunted.

On a less corny note, the **Witch Memorial**, at Charter and Liberty streets, is a simple series of stone blocks etched with the names of the hanged, wedged into a corner of the **Old Burying Point Cemetery**, where one of the witch judges, John Hathorne, is buried.

The Peabody Essex Museum

June–Oct Mon–Sat 10am–5pm, Sun noon–5pm; Nov–May Tues–Sat 10am–5pm, Sun noon–5pm; $8.50; ©978/745-9500 or 1-800/745-4054.

Right up Liberty Street from the Witch Memorial is the **Peabody Essex Museum**, the oldest continuously operating museum in the US, at East India Square on the Essex Street Mall. More than thirty galleries display a staggering mishmash of art and artifacts from around the world, illustrating the importance of Salem as a major point of interaction and trade between the Eastern and Western worlds. Founded by ship captains in 1799 to exhibit their exotic items obtained while overseas, the museum also boasts the biggest collection of nautical paintings in the world. Other galleries hold Chinese and Japanese export art, Asian, Oceanic, and African ethnological artifacts, American decorative arts and, in a preserved house that the museum administers, court documents from the Salem Witch Trials.

The first floor is home to the core museum displays, with creatively curated whaling exhibits that feature not only the requisite scrimshaw but Ambrose Garneray's famous 1835 painting, *Attacking the Right Whale*, and the gaping lower jaw of a sperm whale. Upstairs highlights include a cavernous central gallery with the fanciful figureheads from now demolished Salem ships hung from the walls and the reconstructed salon from America's first yacht, *Cleopatra's Barge*, which took to the seas in 1816. There's also a decent café in case you're hungry.

Salem Maritime National Historic Site

Daily 9am–5pm; ranger-led tours $3.

Little of Salem's original waterfront remains, although the 2000ft-long **Derby Wharf** is still standing, fronted by the imposing Federalist-style **Custom House** at its head. They help comprise the **Salem Maritime National Historic Site**, which maintains a **visitors center** at 174 Derby St. Nathaniel Hawthorne had a three-year stint working at the Custom House that he later described as "slavery." You can only take tours of the office-like interior at irregular hours, but the warehouse in the rear, with displays of tea chests and such, is usually open for casual inspection. Park rangers also give free tours of the adjacent **Derby House** (daily 9am–5pm), whose millionaire owner had it built here, overlooking the harbor, to monitor the shipping empire over which he presided. Next door, the **West India Goods Store** sells the kinds of spices and nautical knick-knacks common to Salem's nineteenth-century shops.

House of the Seven Gables

Tours daily: May–Nov 10am–5pm; Dec–April Mon–Sat 10am–5pm, Sun noon–5pm; $7.

The most famous sight in the waterfront area is undoubtedly the **House of the Seven Gables**, at 54 Turner St, a rambling old mansion by the sea that served as inspiration for

Hawthorne's eponymous novel. Forever the "rusty wooden house with seven acutely peaked gables" that Hawthorne described, this 1688 three-story house has some other notable features, such as the bricked-off "Secret Stairway" that leads to a small room. The house was inhabited in the 1840s by Susan Ingersoll, a cousin of Hawthorne whom he often visited. The author's birthplace, a small undistinguished house built before 1750, has been moved to the grounds; the lovely gardens feature a wishing well.

Eating and drinking

Café Bagel Company, 122 Washington St ©978/740-3180. This is a fairly upbeat spot for a bagel and a coffee.

Lyceum Bar and Grill, 43 Church St ©978/745-7665. Popular spot for Yankee cooking with modern updates.

Nathaniel's, at the *Hawthorne*, 18 Washington Square ©978/744-4080. Upscale comfort food including roasted scrod and grilled pork tenderloin.

Salem Beer Works, 278 Derby St ©978/745-2337. You can try microbrews or nouveau pub food at this glossy brewery.

Salem Diner, 70 Loring Ave ©978/741-7918. Basic diner fare in an original Sterling Streamliner diner car.

MARBLEHEAD

Marblehead is a town of winding streets lined with small but well-preserved private sea captain's homes that lead down to its harbor, which makes for a decent respite from Salem's witch-related sights. Once the domain of Revolutionary War heroes – it was Marblehead boatmen who rowed Washington's assault force across the Delaware River to attack Trenton – it's now mainly home to Boston commuters. One thing that hasn't changed over the years is the town's dramatic setting on a series of rocky ledges overlooking the wide natural harbor, which makes it one of the East Coast's biggest **yachting centers**. The annual Race Week takes place the last week of July.

Settled in 1629, Marblehead has largely escaped commercialism thanks to its occupants' affluence and, oddly, a severe shortage of parking. The latter shouldn't deter you from visiting, however, as this is one of the most picturesque ports in New England. You can get a good look at it from **Fort Sewall**, jutting into the harbor at the end of Front Street, the remnants of fortifications the British originally built in 1644, and later protected the *USS Constitution* in the War of 1812. Closer to the center of town is **Old Burial Hill**, which holds the graves of more than six hundred Revolutionary War soldiers and has similarly sweeping views. **Abbot Hall**, on Washington Street (Mon–Wed & Fri 8am–5pm, Sat 9am–6pm, Sun 11am–6pm), an attractive 1876 town hall which can be seen from far out at sea, houses Archibald Willard's famous patriotic painting *The Spirit of '76*.

If you're looking for a **snack**, try *Flynnie's at the Beach*, on Devereaux Beach (summers only), for inexpensive fish and chips. *The Landing*, 81 Front St, serves fresh seafood in a room overlooking the harbor.

GLOUCESTER

Founded in 1623, **Gloucester** is the oldest fishing and trading port in Massachusetts, though years of overfishing the once cod-rich waters have robbed the town of any aura of affluence it may have had in the past. Just forty miles north of Boston, up Route 1 to 127, the city at least has that past to look back to, because it lacks any serious contemporary goings-on. The ballyhooed **Rocky Neck Art Colony**, for instance, is not much of a colony anymore, though a number of local artists do show their work in area galleries – most are undistinguished; others are downright tacky.

Gloucester's only really compelling attraction is a short drive south along the rocky coast of Route 127: the imposing **Hammond Castle Museum**, at 80 Hesperus Ave (June–Oct daily 10am–5pm; Nov–May weekends only 10am–4pm; $6), whose builder, the eccentric financier and amateur inventor John Hays Hammond, Jr, wanted to bring medieval European relics back to the US. An austere fortress, overlooking the ocean at the spot that served as inspiration for Longfellow's poem *The Wreck of the Hesperus*, brims with the treasures today – from armor and tapestries to an elaborately carved wooden facade of a fifteenth-century French bakery. One of the more interesting artifacts is the partially crushed skull of one of Columbus' shipmates. There's also a murky 30,000-gallon pool whose contents can be changed from fresh to sea water at the switch of a lever.

ROCKPORT

Rockport, about five miles north of Gloucester, is a coastal hamlet that's more self-consciously quaint, though only oppressively so on summer weekends. Its main drag is a thin peninsula called **Bearskin Neck**, lined with old salt-box fishermen's cottages transformed into art galleries and restaurants. The neck rises as it reaches the sea, and there's a nice view of the rocky harbor from the end of it. Otherwise, aside from some decent antique shopping and strolling around **Dock Square**, at the city's center, there isn't much doing here.

Inside the aptly named **Paper House**, a few miles north of here in the small residential neighborhood of Pigeon Cove, everything is made of paper, from chairs and a piano (keys excepted) to a desk made from copies of the *Christian*

Science Monitor. It's the end result of a twenty-year project undertaken in 1922 by a local mechanical engineer who "always resented the daily waste of newspaper." He hasn't really helped the cause.

PLYMOUTH

Though the **South Shore** makes a clean sweep of the coast from suburban Quincy to the former whaling port of New Bedford, the only place really of interest is tiny **Plymouth**, America's so-called "hometown," forty miles south of Boston. It's mostly given over to commemorating, in various degrees of taste and tack, the landing of the 102 Pilgrims here in December 1620.

See p.6 for information on buses from Boston to Plymouth.

The proceedings start off with a solemn pseudo-Greek temple by the sea that encloses the otherwise nondescript **Plymouth Rock**, where the Pilgrims are said to have touched land. As is typical with most sites of this ilk, it is of symbolic importance only – they had already spent several weeks on Cape Cod before landing here. On the hill behind the venerable stone, **The Plymouth National Wax Museum**, at 16 Carver St (daily: March–May & Nov 9am–5pm; June, Sept & Oct 9am–7pm; July–Aug 9am–9pm; closed Dec–Feb; $5), charges admission to its inadvertently kitsch sound-and-light tableaux of the early days of settlement. Down the street is the **Pilgrim Hall Museum**, at 75 Court St (Feb–Dec daily 9.30am–4.30pm; $5.50), where you enter a room filled with furniture, which may or may not have come over on the *Mayflower*, along with numerous pairs of shoes, which the Pilgrims may or may not have worn.

You're better off spending your time at the newly restored replica of the *Mayflower*, called the **Mayflower II** (April–Nov daily 9am–5pm; $6.50), on the State Pier in Plymouth Harbor. Built in Britain by English craftsmen following the detailed and historically accurate plans of an American naval architect at MIT, the *Mayflower II* was ceremoniously docked in Plymouth in 1957 and given to America as a gesture of goodwill. You are free to wander the ship at leisure and there are trained staff members – in contemporary clothing – available to answer any questions.

A combined ticket to the *Mayflower II* and Plimoth Plantation costs $19.

Similar in approach and authenticity is the **Plimoth Plantation**, three miles south of town off Route 3 (April–Nov daily 9am–5pm; $16). Everything you see in the plantation, such as the Pilgrim Village of 1627 and the Wampanoag Indian Settlement, has been created using traditional techniques; even the farm animals were "backbred" to resemble their seventeenth-century counterparts. Again, actors dressed in period garb try to bring you back in time; depending on your level of resistance, it can be quite enjoyable.

A reasonably interesting way to pass time for free is at **Cranberry World**, at 225 Water St, just past the visitors center on the north side of town (May–Nov daily 9.30am–5pm), a slick little museum sponsored by juice giant Ocean Spray. Exhibits show how the tart crimson berries are harvested from local bogs and processed; frequent tours end with free juice samples.

For **food**, the *John Carver Inn*, 25 Summer St (©1-800/274-1620), has a tavern and a restaurant, the *Hearth 'n Kettle*, that are excellent settings for a very American meal or a drink; the *Lobster Hut*, on the waterfront (©508/746-2270), has good, reasonably priced seafood.

PROVINCETOWN

The brash fishing burgh of **Provincetown**, at the very tip of Cape Cod, is a popular summer destination for bohemians, artists and fun-seekers, lured by the excellent beaches, art galleries and welcoming atmosphere. It may be best known for its numerous **gay** visitors, but P-town – as this coastal community of five thousand year-round inhabitants is commonly known – should not be missed by anyone, especially as its just a few hours' ferry ride from Boston.

For history, trivia, listings and plenty more info on Provincetown, visit *www.provincetown.com*

The town and around

Provincetown's center is essentially two three-mile long streets connected by nearly forty tiny lanes of no more than two short blocks each. The first of these two main strips,

Provincetown by ferry

During the busy summer season, it's possible to take a **Bay State Cruise** from Boston to Provincetown. Ferries depart from **Commonwealth Pier** at the World Trade Center (South Station Ⓣ) at 9am and arrive at Provincetown's **Macmillan Wharf** at noon, heading back at 3.30pm for a 6.30pm arrival in Boston. From Memorial Day through June 14, the ferries run on weekends only; from June 20 to Sept 13, they run daily; and weekends thereafter until the end of September. The fare is $30 round-trip, $18 one way. Call ©748-1428 if you need more information.

the aptly named **Commercial Street**, is where the action is, loaded with restaurants, cafés, art galleries, and trendy shops. Jutting right into the middle of Provincetown Harbor, just off Commercial Street, **Macmillan Wharf** is busy as well, though with whale-watching boats, yachts, and colorful old Portuguese fishing vessels. It also houses the new **Whydah Museum**, at no. 16 (July–Columbus Day daily 9am–7pm; $5), which displays some of the bounty from a famous pirate shipwreck off the coast of Wellfleet in 1717. Two blocks north of the wharf, on Town Hill, is the 252-foot granite tower of the **Pilgrim Monument**, named for the Puritans who actually landed near here first before moving on to Plymouth. From the observation deck of the Florentine-style bell tower, accessible by stairs and ramps, the whole Cape (and sometimes Boston) can be seen (July–Aug daily 9am–7pm, May–June & Sept–Oct daily 9am–5pm; $5). At the bottom of the hill on **Bradford Street**, the second of the two strips, is a bas-relief monument to the Pilgrims' **Mayflower Compact**.

In the quiet **West End** of P-Town, many of the weathered clapboard houses are decorated with colored blinds, white picket fences and wildflowers spilling out of every possible crevice. A modest bronze **plaque** on a boulder at the western end of Commercial Street commemorates the Pilgrim's actual landing place. West of town, **Herring Cove Beach** is easily reached by bike and is justly famous for its sunsets, while at the Cape's northern tip, off Route 6, **Race Point Beach**, a wide strip of white sand backed by tall dunes, is the archetypal Cape Cod beach. It abuts the ethereal **Province Lands**, where vast sweeping moors and bushy dunes are buffeted by a deadly sea, site of some 3000 known shipwrecks.

One of the best things to do around Provincetown is to take an organized, but unusual, tour: choose to either ramble about the dunes in a four-wheel-drive vehicle with **Art's Dune Tours**, at Commercial and Standish (April–Oct 10am–dusk; $9; ©508/487-1950); or fly over them in a replica 1938 biplane ($60 for one person, $80 for two; ✆1-888/BIPLANE or 508/428-8732). Twenty-minute flights take off from the Cape Cod Airport, near the intersection of Race Lane and Route 149.

Accommodation

Gifford House Inn & Dance Club, 9–11 Carver St ✆508/487-0688. Popular gay resort with lobby piano bar, restaurant and dance floor. ①–②.

Land's End Inn, 22 Commercial St ✆508/487-0706. Meticulously decorated rooms and suites, many with sweeping ocean views. ②–④.

Sunset Inn, 142 Court St ✆508/487-9810. Clean, quiet rooms in an 1850 captain's house. ①–②.

Provincetown Reservations (✆1-800/648-0364) and Intown Reservations (✆1-800/67P-TOWN) can usually rustle up lodgings at busy times; for accommodation price codes, see box on p.162.

Eating, drinking, and nightlife

Fat Jack's Café, 335 Commercial St ✆508/487-4822. Low-priced, no-nonsense breakfasts; and lunch and dinner specials.

Lobster Pot, 321 Commercial St ✆508/487-0842. Let the landmark neon sign lead you to ultrafresh and affordable crustaceans.

Portuguese Bakery, 299 Commercial St ✆508/487-1803. An excellent stop for baked goods, particularly the fried rabanada, similar to french toast.

Spiritus, 190 Commercial St ✆508/487-2808. One of the cheapest places to fill up on fabulous pizza and gourmet coffee. Open late.

LISTINGS

Accommodation

For such a popular travel destination, Boston has a surprisingly limited range of well-priced accommodation. Though there are still bargains to be found, prices at many formerly moderate hotels have inched into the expense-account range. Your best bet, if you don't mind braving the East Coast winter, is to come off-season, around November through April, when many hotels not only have more vacancies but offer special discounts too. At any other time of year, be sure to make reservations well in advance. September (start of the school year) and June (graduation) are particularly busy months, due to the large student population here.

Increasingly popular in town are **bed and breakfasts**, many of them tucked into renovated brownstones in Beacon Hill, Back Bay and the South End. Short-term **furnished apartments**, spread throughout the city, are another option; most have two-week minimums. There are also a handful of decent **hostels** if you're looking for truly budget accommodation.

HOTELS

If Boston's **hotels** are not suited to every traveler's budget, they do cater to most tastes, and range from the usual

Accommodation price codes

Accommodation prices vary throughout the year, with the highest rates from June to September, and around Christmas and other holidays. Our listings for **hotels** and **B&Bs** feature a code (eg ③) for the least expensive double room available for most of the year:

① under $75	⑤ $165–200
② $75–100	⑥ $200-250
③ $100–130	⑦ $250–300
④ $130–165	⑧ $300–350
⑨ $350+	

The prices do not include **tax**, which is 12.45 percent. Bed and breakfasts are exempt from tax.

assortment of chains to some excellent independently run hotels, the highest concentration of which – including some of the best – are in **Back Bay**. Most of the business hotels are located in or around the **Financial District**, and are not bad if you don't mind being away from the nightlife.

DOWNTOWN

Boston Harbor Hotel

Map 3, L4. 70 Rowes Wharf ©439-7000 or 1-800/752-7077, fax 345-6799. Aquarium Ⓣ.

This hotel provides opulent accommodation in an atmosphere of studied corporate elegance. There's a health club, pool, kowtowing concierge staff, and rooms with harbor and city views, the former substantially pricier. ⑧–⑨

Boston Marriott Long Wharf

Map 3, L2. 296 State St ©227-0800, fax 227-2867. Aquarium Ⓣ.

All the rooms here boast harbor views, but the awesome vaulted lobby is what really makes this *Marriott* stand out. ⑥–⑦

Harborside Inn

Map 3, J2. 185 State St ©723-7500, fax 670-2010. State Ⓣ.

This small new hotel is housed in a renovated 1890s mercantile warehouse across from Quincy Market; the (relatively) reasonably priced rooms – with exposed brick wall, hardwood floors, and cherry furniture – are a welcome surprise for this part of town. ⑤

Le Meridien

Map 3, I5. 250 Franklin St ©451-1900 or 1-800/543-4300, fax 423-2844. State Ⓣ.

Located in the heart of the Financial District, this stern granite building is, appropriately enough, the former Federal Reserve Bank of Boston. The rooms are modern, and the overall atmosphere is a bit stiff. ⑦–⑧

Milner

Map 3, E9. 78 Charles St S ©426-6220 or 1-800/453-1731, fax 350-0360. Boylston Ⓣ.

Recently renovated, this uninspiring but affordable hotel is convenient to the Theater District, Bay Village and the Public Garden. All room rates include a continental breakfast, served in a European-style nook in the lobby. ③

Omni Parker House

Map 3, G4. 60 School St ©227-8600 or 1-800/843-6664, fax 724-4729. Park Ⓣ.

No one can compete with the *Parker House* in the history department: it's the oldest continuously operating hotel in the US. Though the present building only dates from 1927, the lobby, decorated in dark oak with carved gilt moldings, recalls the splendor of the original nineteenth-century building that once housed it. The rooms are small, however, and a bit dowdy. ⑥–⑦

Regal Bostonian Hotel

Map 3, H2. Faneuil Hall Marketplace ✆523-3600 or 1-800/343-0922, fax 523-2454. State Ⓣ.

Splendid quarters in the heart of downtown. The rooms and lobby are festooned with portraits of famous Colonials. ⑥

Swissôtel

Map 3, G6. 1 Avenue de Lafayette ✆451-2600 or 1-800/621-9200, fax 451-2198. Downtown Crossing Ⓣ.

Boston's *Swissôtel* is a plush if peculiarly located option – on the fringes of ragged Downtown Crossing, not the best place to be at night. There's no pedestrian access to the sleek sixteen-story tower; entry is via the parking garage. ⑤–⑥

Tremont House

Map 3, E9. 275 Tremont St ✆426-1400 or 1-800/331-9998, fax 426-0374. NE Medical Center Ⓣ.

The opulent lobby of this 1925 hotel, the former national headquarters of the Elks Lodge, somewhat compensates for its rather small rooms, but if you want to be in the thick of the Theater District you can't do better. ⑤–⑥

BEACON HILL AND THE WEST END

Holiday Inn Select – Government Center

Map 3, C2. 5 Blossom St ✆742-7630 or 1-800/HOLIDAY, fax 742-4192. Bowdoin Ⓣ.

Somewhat misleadingly named – located in the West End and more convenient to Beacon Hill than Government Center – this property has all the modern accoutrements, including a weight room and pool. ⑤–⑥

The John Jeffries House

Map 3, A3. 14 David G. Mugar Way ✆367-1866, fax 742-0313.

Charles Ⓣ.
Mid-scale hotel at the foot of Beacon Hill. There's a cozy lounge for hotel guests, and all rooms include kitchenettes. Though it's wedged in between a busy highway and the local Ⓣ stop, multipaned windows keep most of the sound out. ②–③

The Shawmut Inn

280 Friend St ✆720-5544 or 1-800/350-7784, fax 723-7784. North Station Ⓣ.
Located in the old West End near the FleetCenter, this place has 66 comfortable, modern rooms, all of which come equipped with kitchenettes. ③

BACK BAY AND KENMORE SQUARE

Back Bay Hilton

Map 6, G5. 40 Dalton St ✆236-1100 or 1-800/874-0663, fax 867-6104. Hynes Ⓣ.
Though this chain hotel is fairly charmless, it does have good weekend packages and a guaranteed good American-style breakfast at the hotel's informal restaurant, *Boodle's* (see p.200). It's actually a bit out of Back Bay, closer to the bohemian area of the Berklee College of Music than the shops of Newbury Street – a plus in some folks' eyes. ⑤–⑥

Boston Park Plaza Hotel & Towers

Map 3, C9. 64 Arlington St ✆426-2000 or 1-800/225-2008, fax 426-5545. Arlington Ⓣ.
The *Park Plaza* is practically its own neighborhood, housing the original *Legal Seafoods* restaurant (see p.202) alongside three other eateries, plus offices for American, United and Delta airlines. Its old-school elegance and hospitality, and its central location, however, make it stand out; the high-ceilinged rooms, too, are quite comfortable. ⑤–⑥

Boston Sheraton Hotel & Towers

Map 6, G5. 39 Dalton St ©236-2000 or 1-800/325-3535, fax 236-1702. Hynes Ⓣ.

Accommodations here are a bit nicer than the nondescript exterior might imply, and they mostly play host to convention-goers, who can walk to the nearby Hynes Convention Center and Prudential Center mall without going outside. ④–⑤

The Buckminster

Map 6, C2. 645 Beacon St ©236-7050 or 1-800/727-2825, fax 262-0068. Kenmore Ⓣ.

Though renovated not so long ago, the 1905 *Buckminster* retains the feel of an old Boston hotel with its antique furnishings; its Kenmore Square location also puts it within easy walking distance of Fenway Park and Boston University. Great rates, too. ③

The Chandler Inn

Map 6, K6. 26 Chandler St ©482-3450 or 1-800/842-3450, fax 542-3428. Back Bay Ⓣ.

Small, comfortable hotel that has retained its warm and homey feel despite recent renovations. Free continental breakfast. ②–③

The Colonnade

Map 6, H5. 120 Huntington Ave ©424-7000 or 1-800/962-3030, fax 424-1717. Prudential Ⓣ.

With its beige poured-concrete shell, the *Colonnade* is barely distinguishable from the Church of Christ buildings directly across the street. Still, there are spacious rooms and, in summer, a rooftop pool, the only one in Boston. ⑤

Copley Square Hotel

Map 6, I5. 47 Huntington Ave ©536-9000 or 1-800/225-7062, fax 267-3547. Copley Ⓣ.

Situated on the eastern fringe of Copley Square, this is one of the best bargains in the city; it's also home to the *Café Budapest* (see p.200), one of Boston's most romantic restaurants. Low-key, with a European crowd, and rooms as low as $165 a night. ⑤–⑥

Eliot

Map 6, F3. 370 Commonwealth Ave ✆267-1607 or 1-800/442-5468, fax 536-9114. Hynes Ⓣ.

West Back Bay's answer to the *Ritz*, this calm, plush nine-floor suite hotel has rooms with kitchenettes and luxurious Italian marble baths; they also serve a nice breakfast downstairs. ⑥–⑦

Fairmont Copley Plaza

Map 6, K4. 138 St. James Ave ✆267-5300 or 1-800/795-3906, fax 375-9648. Copley Ⓣ.

Built in 1912 and it shows, from the somewhat severe facade facing Copley Square to the old-fashioned rooms. The hotel has long boasted Boston's most elegant lobby, with its glittering chandeliers, mirrored walls and trompe-l'oeil sky. Even if you don't stay here, have a martini in the fabulous *Oak Bar* (p.219), with its high coffered ceilings and mahogany chairs. ⑧–⑨

Four Seasons

Map 6, D8. 200 Boylston St ✆338-4400 or 1-800/332-3442, fax 423-0154. Arlington Ⓣ.

The tops in city accommodation, with 288 rooms offering quiet, contemporary comfort. The penthouse level health spa has an indoor pool that seems to float over the Public Garden, and the superlative *Aujourd'hui* restaurant (see p.199) is housed here, too. ⑧–⑨

The Lenox

Map 6, I4. 710 Boylston St ✆536-5300 or 1-800/225-7676, fax 236-0351. Copley Ⓣ.

Billed as Boston's version of the *Waldorf-Astoria* when its doors first opened in 1900, the *Lenox* is a far cry from that now, though it's still one of the most comfortably upscale and affordable hotels in the city. Many of the rooms have working fireplaces. ⑦–⑧

Marriott at Copley Place

Map 6, J5. Copley Place ©236-5800 or 1-800/228-9290, fax 236-5885. Copley Ⓣ.

There's not a whole lot of character here, but it's modern, clean, and well-located, with an indoor pool. Ask about lower weekend rates that include full breakfast. ⑤–⑦

Ritz-Carlton

Map 6, L3. 15 Arlington St ©536-5700 or 1-800/241-3333, fax 536-1335. Arlington Ⓣ.

This is the Ritz-Carlton flagship, and even if the rooms can seem a bit cramped, the hotel retains a certain air of refinement. The one thing no one can complain about is the view of the Public Garden, available from the second-floor dining room or street-level *Ritz Bar*. ⑧–⑨

Westin

Map 6, J5. Copley Place ©262-9600 or 1-800/228-3000, fax 424-7483. Copley Ⓣ.

Rooms are modern and spacious at this well-located hotel, always hopping with convention-goers, and a lively place to hole up in winter. Request a room facing the Charles River. ⑥–⑦

CAMBRIDGE

Cambridge Marriott

Map 7, L3. 2 Cambridge Center ©494-6600 or 1-800/228-9290. Kendall Ⓣ.

Stately, well-appointed rooms with a minimum of pretension.

Many overlook the Charles, while the rest have views of industrial Kendall Square. Some weekend packages include sumptuous free brunch. ⑤–⑥

Charles Hotel

Map 7, D5. 1 Bennett St ✆864-1200 or 1-800/882-1818. Harvard Ⓣ.

Clean, bright rooms – some overlooking the Charles – that have a good array of amenities: cable TV, three phones, minibar, Shaker furniture, and access to the adjacent WellBridge Health Spa. There's also an excellent jazz club, *Regattabar* (p.230), and restaurant, *Henrietta's Table* (p.209) on the premises. ⑥

Harvard Square Hotel

Map 7, D5. 110 Mt Auburn St ✆864-5200 or 1-800/458-5886. Harvard Ⓣ.

The rooms here are only adequate, but it has a great location in the midst of Harvard Square, and is fairly affordable. ④

Hyatt Regency Cambridge

Map 7, G7. 575 Memorial Drive ✆492-1234 or 1-800/233-1234, fax 491-6906. Kendall Ⓣ.

Brick ziggurat-like riverside monolith, with luxurious rooms, pool, health club, and a patio with gazebo. Picturesque location on the Charles, but it's a hike from major points of interest. ⑤

Inn at Harvard

Map 7, E5. 1201 Massachusetts Ave ✆491-2222 or 1-800/222-8733, fax 491-6520. Harvard Ⓣ.

This recently built hotel is carefully designed to give the impression of old-school grandeur, and it is so close to Harvard you can smell the ivy. Pleasant but rather small rooms. ⑤–⑥

Royal Sonesta

Cambridge Parkway ✆491-3600 or 1-800/SONESTA, fax 806-4232. Kendall Square Ⓣ.

Luxury quarters with views of the downtown Boston skyline. The fancy rooms have big, sparkling bathrooms; the vast lobby is festooned with strikingly bad art. ⑥–⑦

Sheraton Commander

Map 7, C4. 16 Garden St ©547-4800 or 1-800/535-5007, fax 868-8322. Harvard Ⓣ.

The hotel's name refers to George Washington, who, legend has it, took command of the Continental Army on nearby Cambridge Common (see p.123). Rooms tend to be rather dark and small, though there are some cute frills (eg terrycloth robes). ④–⑥

Susse Chalet Cambridge

211 Concord Turnpike ©661-7800 or 1-800/524-2538, fax 868-8153. Alewife Ⓣ.

Modest rooms in a plain motor lodge located right off a highway and next door to a vintage bowling alley. Free continental breakfast. ②

BED AND BREAKFASTS

The **bed-and-breakfast** industry in Boston is thriving, for the most part because it is so difficult to find accommodation here for under $100 a night – and some B&B's offer just that, at least in the off-season. On the flip side, just as many B&B's cash in on the popularity of their old-world charm, consequently, prices may hover near those of more swank hotels. Some of the best B&B's are outside the city, in either **Cambridge** or **Brookline**, though there are nice in-town options as well. You can make reservations directly with the places we've listed; there are also numerous B&B **agencies** that can do the booking for you (see box, opposite).

B&B and short-term rental agencies

Bed & Breakfast Agency of Boston 47 Commercial Wharf, Boston, MA 02110; ©720-3540 or 1-800/248-9262, 0800/895128 (UK), fax 523-5761; *www.boston-bnbagency.com*. Can book you a room in a brownstone, a waterfront loft or even on a yacht.

Bed & Breakfast Associates Bay Colony Ltd PO Box 57166 Babson Park Branch, Boston, MA 02157; ©449-5302 or 1-800/347-5088, fax 449-5958; *www.bnbboston.com*. Has some real finds in Back Bay and the South End.

Bed & Breakfast – Cambridge & Greater Boston ©720-1492 or 1-800/888-0178, fax 227-0021. Has listings of B&Bs, both hosted and unhosted, and furnished apartments throughout central Cambridge and Boston.

Bed & Breakfast Reservations PO Box 590264 Newtown Center, MA 02459; ©964-1606 or 1-800/832-2632, fax 332-8572; *www.bbreserve.com*. Lists B&Bs in Greater Boston, North Shore and Cape Cod.

Boston Reservations/Boston Bed & Breakfast, Inc ©332-4199, fax 332-5751; *www.bostonreservations.com*. Competitive rates at B&Bs as well as at leading hotels.

Greater Boston Hospitality PO Box 1142 Brookline, MA 02446; ©277-5430, fax 277-7170; *www.bostonbedandbreakfast.com*. Rentals in homes, inns and condominiums.

BEACON HILL

Beacon Hill Bed & Breakfast

Map 3, A5. 27 Brimmer St ©523-7376. Charles Ⓣ.

Only three spacious rooms with fireplaces are available in this well-situated brick townhouse, built in 1869. There are sumptuous full breakfasts; two-night minimum stay, three on holiday weekends. ⑥

BACK BAY AND THE SOUTH END

Copley House

Map 6, H6. 239 W Newton St ✆236-8300 or 1-800/331-1318, fax 424-1815. Prudential Ⓣ.

Furnished apartments on an attractive edge of Back Bay, across from the Copley Plaza shopping center. There's a three-night minimum; ask about the lower weekly rates. ②–③

Copley Inn

Map 6, H6. 19 Garrison St ✆236-0300 or 1-800/232-0306, fax 536-0816. Prudential Ⓣ.

Comfortable rooms with full kitchens, friendly staff and great location make this an ideal place to stay in the Back Bay. Get one night free with a week's stay. ②–③

82 Chandler Street

Map 6, J5. 82 Chandler St ✆482-0408. Back Bay Ⓣ.

Basic rooms with minimal service in a restored, 1863 brownstone that sits on one of the most up-and-coming streets of the South End. Breakfast, when and if it's available, is served on the sunny top floor where you'll also find the best room in the house. ④

463 Beacon Street Guest House

Map 6, G4. 463 Beacon St ✆536-1302. Hynes Ⓣ.

The good-sized rooms in this renovated brownstone, in the heart of Back Bay, come equipped with kitchenettes and other hotel-style amenities. Ask for the top-floor room. ②

Newbury Guest House

Map 6, H3. 261 Newbury St ✆437-7666, fax 262-4243. Copley Ⓣ.

Big 32-room Victorian brownstone that still fills up whenever there's a big convention in town, so call in advance. Continental breakfast included. ③

Oasis Guest House

Map 6, F6. 22 Edgerly Rd ✆267-2262, fax 267-1920. Symphony Ⓣ.
Sixteen comfortable, very affordable rooms, some with shared baths, in a renovated brownstone near Symphony Hall. ①

BROOKLINE

Beacon Inn

1087 and 1750 Beacon St ✆566-0088. Hawes Ⓣ.
Fireplaced lobbies and original woodwork contribute to the relaxed atmosphere in these two nineteenth-century brownstones, part of the same guest house. ②

Brookline Manor Guest House

32 Centre St ✆232-0003 or 1-800/535-5325, fax 734-5815. Coolidge Corner Ⓣ.
This small guest house, on a pleasant stretch off Beacon Street, is just a short subway ride from Kenmore Square. The same management also runs the *Beacon Street Guest House*, at 1047 Beacon St (✆1-800/575-1009). ②

CAMBRIDGE

A Cambridge House

2218 Massachusetts Ave ✆491-6300 or 1-800/232-9989, fax 868-2079. Davis Ⓣ.
A classy B&B, with gorgeous rooms decked out with canopy beds and period pieces. There are full breakfasts plus evening wine-and-cheese in the parlor. It's a bit far out from any points of interest, but worth the trek. ③–④

A Friendly Inn

Map 7, E3. 1673 Cambridge St ✆547-7851. Harvard Ⓣ.

A good deal, just a few minutes' walk from Harvard Square. The rooms are nothing special and the service doesn't exactly live up to the name, but there are private baths, cable TV and laundry service. ③

Irving House

Map 7, E3. 24 Irving St ✆547-4600. Harvard Ⓣ.

A small but quaint option near Harvard Square, with laundry and kitchen facilities. They have both shared and private baths. ②–③

Mary Prentiss Inn

Map 7, C2. 6 Prentiss St ✆661-2929, fax 661-5989. Harvard Ⓣ.

Eighteen clean, comfortable rooms in an impressively refurbished mid-nineteenth-century Greek Revival building. Full breakfast and snacks are served in the living room, or, weather permitting, on a pleasant outdoor deck. Room prices can, however, be as high as $225. ④–⑥

Prospect Place

Map 7, H4. 112 Prospect St ✆864-7500 or 1-800/769-5303. Central Ⓣ.

This Italianate edifice holds a restored parlor inside, along with nineteenth-century period antiques, including two grand pianos, and recently renovated rooms. ②

HOSTELS

There are fairly limited **hostel** accommodations in Boston, and if you want to get in on them, you should definitely book ahead, especially in the summertime.

Berkeley Residence YWCA

Map 6, K5. 40 Berkeley St ✆375-2524, fax 375-2525. Back Bay Ⓣ.

Clean and simple rooms (women only) in a safe location – next door to a police station. All rates include breakfast; dinner is an additional $6.50. Singles are $51, doubles $78, and triples $90; there's a $2 fee for nonmembers.

Greater Boston YMCA

Map 6, F6. 316 Huntington Ave ✆536-7800, fax 267-4653. Symphony Ⓣ.

Good budget rooms, and access to the Y's health facilities (pool, weight room, etc). Singles are $41–56, but you can get a four-person room for $95. Co-ed facilities are available from late June until early September, the rest of the year it is men only. Ten days maximum stay.

HI – Back Bay Summer Hostel

Map 6, C2. 519 Beacon St ✆353-3294; reservation requests to 12 Hemenway St, Boston, MA 02115 ✆536-1027, fax 424-6558. Kenmore Ⓣ.

This converted BU dorm has 63 beds, but is only open June 16–Aug 26. Members $24, nonmembers $27.

HI – Boston

Map 6, G4. 12 Hemenway St ✆536-1027, fax 424-6558. Hynes Ⓣ.

Around the Back Bay–Fenway border, standard dorm accommodation with 3–4 beds per room. Members $20, nonmembers $23.

Irish Embassy Youth Hostel

232 Friend St ✆973-4841, fax 720-3998. North Station Ⓣ.

Boston's only independent youth hostel is above the *Irish Embassy* pub, in the West End and not far from Faneuil Hall. Prices include free admission to pub gigs on most nights, and free barbecues on Tues and Sun. Dorm beds are $15.

Prescott House

36 Church St, Everett ✆389-1990, fax 387-3610. Sullivan Square Ⓣ.

More guest house than hostel, where you can share a dorm room with four to six people for $30 a night, or have a private room with TV and phone for $99. A sporadically operating shuttle may pick you up from Sullivan Square if you call ahead; otherwise it's all a bit far off the path, up in the northern suburb of Everett.

YWCA of Cambridge

Map 7, H5. 7 Temple St ✆491-6050. Central Ⓣ.

Spartan quarters in Cambridge for women only (men aren't allowed on the premises, even for a visit), but space is very limited, so call in advance. Members $30 per night, $90 per week.

Eating

There is no shortage of places to eat in Boston. The city is loaded with bars and pubs that double as restaurants, cafés that serve full and affordable meals, and plenty of higher-end dinner-only options. Historically, weather-beaten Yankees have tended to favor hot and hearty meals made from native ingredients without a lot of fuss. Still, while outsiders may see traditional standbys like broiled scrod, clam chowder and Yankee pot roast as quintessentially New England, to most Bostonians today, such dishes are little more than tourists' cliches. Indeed, the city's vibrant restaurant scene mirrors the growing diversity of Boston's population, with innovative restaurants popping up everywhere; if not always successful, these places have at least scored in weaving elements from more adventurous cuisines into the local food vocabulary.

At **lunchtime** many places offer meals for about half the cost of dinner, a plus if you want to sample some of the food at the pricier and more exclusive restaurants. The city's many sandwich shops, juice bars, burrito joints, and falafel stands cater to the lunch crowd; the areas around the universities are particularly good bets for fast and cheap food. There are also plenty of gourmet shops if you're looking to picnic (see p.260). **Dinner**, usually from 5pm on, is a much more exciting affair, with a wide array of **restaurants** that range from Boston's own local cuisine to ethnic foods of every stripe. You'll probably want to book ahead if you're planning to show up after 6pm; places are generally open until 10 or 11pm, though in Chinatown, there are numerous **late-night** spots. Also, some restaurants close on Sundays and/or Mondays; call ahead on those days to make sure your choice is open.

As for Boston's culinary landscape, there are ever-popular **Italian** restaurants, both traditional Southern and more fancified Northern, that cluster in the **North End**, mainly on Hanover and Salem streets. The city's tiny **Chinatown** packs in not only a fair number of Chinese spots, but **Japanese**, **Vietnamese** and **Malaysian** too. Dim sum, where you choose selections from carts wheeled past your table, is especially big at lunchtime; the best places are always packed on weekends, with lines down the streets. Boston's trendiest restaurants, mostly serving voguish **New American** cuisine, tend to cluster in **Back Bay** and the **South End**.

A complete index of restaurants by cuisine can be found on p.186.

Cambridge's eating options are, for the most part, strung out along Massachusetts Avenue between Central, Harvard, and Porter squares, though funky (and slightly out of the way) Inman Square has a few good spots as well.

BREAKFASTS AND LIGHT MEALS

In most places, save certain areas of downtown, you won't have a problem finding somewhere to **grab a quick bite**, whether it's a diner, deli or café. The establishments we've listed below are all good for light meals, late-night snacks and desserts; see also the bars and cafés listed on p.213, many of which offer food all day.

DOWNTOWN

Brigham's

Map 3, H3. 50 Congress St ©523-9822. State Ⓣ.

The closest thing downtown has to a coffee shop, with an excellent soda fountain. Stick to basic ice cream flavors – chocolate chip, vanilla – and you'll be happiest.

Café Fleuri

Map 3, I4. 250 Franklin St in *Le Meridien* ©451-1900. State, Aquarium or Downtown Crossing Ⓣ.

Though this restaurant does standard upscale meals all day, it's mainly worth checking out on Saturday afternoons (except summers), when its $16.50 all-you-can-eat Chocolate Bar Buffet entitles you to sample everything from Chocolate Grand Marnier Ravioli to Chocolate Croissant Bread Pudding. Truly decadent.

Finagle-a-Bagel

Map 3, H5. 70 Frankin St ©261-1900. Downtown Crossing Ⓣ.

Map 6, I4. 535 Boylston St ©266-2500. Copley Ⓣ.

A small Boston chain with more than fifteen varieties of bagels, from Pumpkin Raisin to Triple Chocolate Chip, that are always served fresh.

Kam Lung Bakery and Restaurant

Map 3, G8. 77 Harrison St ©542-2229. Chinatown Ⓣ.

Tiny take-out joint that vends dim sum as well as bakery treats (sweet rolls, sugary moon pies) and more exotic delicacies (pork buns, meat pies).

Milk Street Café

Map 3, I4. 50 Milk St ©542-3663. State Ⓣ.

Map 3, I5. Post Office Square Park ©350-7273. Downtown Crossing Ⓣ.

Kosher and quick are the keys at these two downtown eateries, popular with suits and vegetarians for the large designer sandwiches and salads.

Sultan's Kitchen

Map 3, J4. 72 Broad St ©338-7819. Aquarium Ⓣ.

The best Turkish food in Boston, this lunch spot is favored by businessmen who queue up for the agreeably spicy Ottoman classics. Take a table in the casual upstairs room and you'll feel a million miles away from nearby tourist-laden Quincy Market.

The Wrap

Map 3, I4. 82 Water St ©357-9013. State Ⓣ.

Sandwiches rolled in tortillas, fruit smoothies, and other lunchtime treats, all quick, easy, and cheap.

NORTH END AND CHARLESTOWN

Ernesto's

Map 4, B6. 69 Salem St ©523-1373. Haymarket Ⓣ.

The cheap, oversized slices of thin-crust pizza served here can't be beat for a quick lunch.

Galleria Umberto

Map 4, C6. 289 Hanover St ©227-5709. Haymarket Ⓣ.

When a place is only open daily from 11am to 2pm, yet there's a line out the door during the limited hours of operation, you know something good is cooking. Here, that something is pizza, cut in greasy, delicious squares.

Rabia's

Map 4, C5. 73 Salem St ©227-6637. Haymarket Ⓣ.

The best thing about this small restaurant is the "Express Lunch" special: a heaped plate of pasta, chicken parmigiana or similar dish is yours to savor for a mere $4 from noon until 2pm, daily.

Sorelle Bakery and Café

Map 5, E2. 1 Monument Ave ©242-2125.

Phenomenal muffins and cookies, plus pasta salads and other lunch fare which you can enjoy on a delightful hidden patio.

BEACON HILL

Buzzy's Fabulous Roast Beef

Map 3, B3. 327 Cambridge St ©242-7722. Charles Ⓣ.

The lunch and after-hours crowds gather here for – what else? – roast beef sandwiches, which really do live up to the hype. Open 24 hours.

Paramount

Map 3, B4. 44 Charles St ©720-1152. Charles Ⓣ.

The Hill's neighborhood diner serves Belgian waffles and frittatas to the brunch crowd regulars by day, decent American standards like hamburgers and meatloaf by night.

Ruby's Diner

Map 3, C2. 280 Cambridge St ©367-3224. Charles Ⓣ.

Very basic breakfast chow, eggs and such, done cheaply and well. Open all night Thurs–Sat.

BACK BAY AND THE SOUTH END

Café de Paris

Map 6, L5. 19 Arlington St ©247-7121. Arlington Ⓣ.

The Parisian pretensions of this spot, where you order your sandwich off a wall menu or select a pre-prepared salad from the counter, are sort of a joke, though people still line up. If you want a pastry, ask for the freshest to avoid disappointment.

Café Jaffa

Map 6, G4. 48 Gloucester St ✆536-0230. Hynes Ⓣ.
Boston's best falafel and other Middle Eastern staples are served in this cool, inviting space with polished wood floors.

Emack & Bolio's

Map 6, H4. 290 Newbury St ✆247-8772. Copley Ⓣ.
Pint-sized ice-cream parlor named for a long-defunct rock band. Try a scoop each of Chocolate Moose and Vanilla Bean Speck in a chocolate-dipped waffle cone to get hooked.

Mike's City Diner

1714 Washington St ✆267-9393. Back Bay Ⓣ.
Classic diner breakfasts and lunches (greasy but good) in an out-of-the way setting in the South End.

Stephanie's on Newbury

Map 6, J3. 190 Newbury St ✆236-0990. Copley Ⓣ.
Though they pride themselves on their smoked salmon potato pancake, what sets *Stephanie's* apart is their sidewalk dining in the prime people-watching territory of Newbury Street, on the site of the former *Harvard Bookstore Café*. Open until midnight.

KENMORE SQUARE

Deli-Haus

Map 6, C2. 476 Commonwealth Ave ✆247-9712. Kenmore Ⓣ.
This student haunt is open 24 hours; try any of the breakfast fare, served all day, or the club sandwich.

CAMBRIDGE

C'est Bon

Map 7, D5. 1432 Massachusetts Ave ✆661-0610. Harvard Ⓣ.
Map 7, D5. 110 Mt Auburn St ✆492-6465. Harvard Ⓣ.

Small, centrally located shop, in two branches, both of which serve up excellent coffee, fresh baked goods, and the best falafel in the area at inexpensive prices. Open late.

Darwin's Ltd

Map 7, C5. 148 Mt Auburn St ©354-5233. Harvard Ⓣ.

The rough-hewn exterior conceals a delightful deli serving the best sandwiches on Harvard Square – wonderfully inventive combinations, such as roast beef, sprouts, and apple slices, served on freshly baked bread.

Herrell's Ice Cream

Map 7, D5. 15 Dunster St ©497-2179. Harvard Ⓣ.

Both the long lines and the profusion of "Best of Boston" awards adorning the walls attest to the well-deserved popularity of this local ice-cream parlor. The chocolate pudding flavor is a particular delight, especially combined with "smoosh-ins," such as Junior Mints or crushed Oreo cookies. Open until midnight.

Porter Square Café and Diner

Map 7, A1. 1933 Massachusetts Ave ©354-3898. Porter Ⓣ.

This place manages to pull off the unlikely combination of coffeehouse and diner culture. It's best for good, cheap American breakfast fare: specials are served all day, and there's a make-your-own omelette option, too.

Toscanini's

Map 7, E5. 1310 Massachusetts Ave ©354-9350. Harvard Ⓣ.

An ever-changing ice-cream list includes original flavors like Khulfee, a concoction of pistachios, almonds, and cardamom.

RESTAURANTS

Boston's restaurants are fairly well spread out, though Back Bay, the South End and Harvard Square have the highest concentrations of worthwhile spots. We've divided our listings up by neighborhood, but you'll also find a complete cross-referenced list by cuisine starting on p.186. Make reservations well ahead of time, especially at the more upscale places.

DOWNTOWN

Bakey's

Map 3, J3. 45 Broad St ✆426-1710. State Ⓣ. Inexpensive

Easily recognized by its decorative sign depicting a man slumped over an ironing board, *Bakey's* was one of the first after-hours Irish pubs to surface in the Financial District. Though it can be pricier if you don't watch what you order ($9 for a turkey sandwich), it's a safe bet if you're caught hungry wandering around this part of town.

The Barking Crab

Map 3, L5. 88 Sleeper St (at the Northern Avenue Bridge) ✆426-CRAB. South Station Ⓣ. Inexpensive.

This endearing seafood shack aims to please with its homey atmosphere, friendly service, and unpretentious menu – centered

Restaurant prices

The restaurant listings are price-coded into five categories: **budget** (under $10), **inexpensive** ($10–15), **moderate** ($15–25), **expensive** ($25–40) and **very expensive** (over $40). This assumes a two-course meal for one person, not including drinks, tax or tip. Much depends of course on what you order, with meat and seafood, as you might expect, on the pricier side. Restaurant tax in Massachusetts is five percent. Most places accept all major credit cards, but eateries in the North End are renowned for accepting only cash.

around anything they can pull from the ocean and fry, sauté, marinate, or grill. Located right on the Boston Harbor with a view of the city skyline.

Bay Tower Room

Map 3, H3. 60 State St ©723-1666. State Ⓣ. Very expensive.
Located on the 33rd floor of a downtown high-rise, the *Bay Tower* is notable mostly for its spectacular views of Boston Harbor. The food is less remarkable – standard fancy American cuisine such as filet mignons and the like.

Ben's Café

Map 3, G4. 45 School St ©227-3370. Government Center or Park Ⓣ. Expensive.
This relaxed French eatery is situated in a French Second Empire building that for a hundred years served as Boston's City Hall. Ask for a table in "The Vault" and go with the prix fixe menu; otherwise head for its airy, hideaway bar, where the price of a drink includes free hors d'oeuvres. Upstairs is the more formal *La Maison Robert*. Closed Sundays.

The Blue Diner

Map 3, I9. 150 Kneeland St ©695-0087. South Station Ⓣ. Inexpensive–moderate.
Campy bar and restaurant with a rare feature among retro diners – good food. A popular spot for a late-night nosh, open until 4am on weekends.

Buddha's Delight

Map 3, G8. 5 Beach St ©451-2395. Chinatown Ⓣ. Inexpensive.
Menu items fall between quotation marks since the "beef" and "chicken" here are actually made from tofu. While the ersatz meats of this vegetarian Vietnamese fare don't exactly taste like the real thing, they're still good. *Buddha's Delight Too* is at 404 Harvard St, Brookline ©739-8830.

Restaurants by cuisine

American

Chinese

French

German

Jacob Wirth p.190

Indian

Bombay Café p.200
Café of India p.208
Kashmir p.201
Rangoli p.207
Tandoor House p.211

Irish

Matt Murphy's p.206

Italian

Artu p.197
Assaggio p.194
Bella Luna p.206
Bertucci's Brick Oven Pizzeria p.204
Café Marliave p.188
Dolce Vita p.195
Gabriele's p.196
Giacomo's p.195
Il Panino p.195
Mama Maria p.195
Marcuccio's p.195
Monica's p.196
Papa Razzi p.202
Pizzeria Regina p.196
Ristorante Toscano p.198
Trattoria Pulcinella p.211

Japanese and Korean

Ginza p.190
Gyuhama p.201
Jae's Café p.190
Kaya p.201
Miyako p.202

Malaysian

Penang p.192

Mediterranean and Middle Eastern

Figs p.196
Lala Rokh p.198
Olives p.197
Steve's Greek-American Cuisine p.203

Mexican and Tex-Mex

Anna's Taqueria p.205
Boca Grande p.207
Border Café p.208
Cactus Club p.200
Zuma's Tex-Mex Café p.194

Continues overleaf

Restaurants by cuisine (continued)

Café Marliave

Map 3, F5. 10 Bosworth St ©423-6340. Park Ⓣ. Moderate.
This Italian-American hideaway is one of Boston's oldest restaurants. Go for the first-rate ravioli and unmistakeably Bostonian ambiance; located behind the *Omni Parker House Hotel* and next to the Province House Steps – the remains of

the seventeenth-century British Government House.

Many of Chinatown's restaurants stay open past 2am, when a fairly lively after-hours scene starts.

The Chart House

Map 3, L2. 60 Long Wharf ©227-1576. Aquarium Ⓣ. Expensive.
Rich food for the rich, though worth the price if you can afford it; the lobster and swordfish are particularly good. For a less highbrow experience, try the downstairs café.

Chau Chow

Map 3, H8. 52 Beach St ©426-6266. Chinatown Ⓣ. Moderate.
One of the first Chinatown restaurants to specialize in seafood, and still one of the best. The setting is stripped-down so there's nothing to distract you from delicious salt-and-pepper shrimp or, if you're in a more adventurous mood, sea cucumber. The *Grand Chau Chow*, just across Beach Street, serves basically the same food at somewhat higher prices and with fancier accoutrements such as tablecloths and linen napkins.

Country Life

Map 3, K4. 200 High St ©951-2685. Aquarium Ⓣ. Inexpensive.
An all-vegetarian buffet near the waterfront, whose cheap and quick meal options vary daily; call the menu hotline (©951-2462) to find out what's cooking.

Dakota's

Map 3, G5. 34 Summer St in the 101 Arch Street Building ©737-1777. Downtown Crossing or Park Ⓣ. Expensive.
Frequented mainly by office workers for lunch and pre-commute dinners, the clubby feel of this expansive American grill restaurant and great food make it the perfect place to dine after visiting nearby Filene's Basement. There are also very

good salads, pasta dishes and Key Lime Pie.

Durgin-Park

Map 3, I2. 340 Faneuil Hall Marketplace ©227-2038. Government Center Ⓣ. Expensive.

A Boston landmark in operation since 1827, *Durgin-Park* has a no-frills Yankee atmosphere and a somewhat surly waitstaff. That doesn't stop folks from coming for the pricey if sizeable pot roast and roast beef dinners in the upstairs dining room. The downstairs raw bar is considerably livelier.

East Ocean City

Map 3, H8. 25–29 Beach St ©542-2504. Chinatown Ⓣ. Moderate.

Another seafood specialist full of aquariums where you can greet your dinner before it appears on your plate. They have especially good soft-shell crabs.

Ginza

Map 3, H8. 16 Hudson St ©338-2261. Chinatown Ⓣ.
1002 Beacon St, Brookline ©566-9688. Moderate.

Open until 4am on weekends, *Ginza* is a popular after-hours spot serving perhaps the best sushi in the city. Any of the vast number of options goes well with a pitcher of warm house sake.

Jacob Wirth

Map 3, E9. 31 Stuart St ©338-8586. Arlington Ⓣ. Moderate.

A German-themed Boston landmark, around since 1868; even if you don't like bratwurst washed down with a hearty lager, something is sure to please. A Boston must.

Jae's Café

Map 3, D9. 212 Stuart St ©451-7788. Arlington Ⓣ.
1281 Cambridge St, Inman Square ©497-8380. #69 bus. Moderate.

The first floor of the Theater District location of this popular chain is a sushi bar and jazz room, while the third is a Korean barbecue where chefs slice and dice at your table. In between lies the main café, with an emphasis on Korean seafood, though you can also create your own noodle dish.

Jimbo's Fish Shanty

Map 2, I4. 245 Northern Ave ©542-5600. South Station Ⓣ. Moderate.

Operated by the proprietor's of *Jimmy's Harborside*, serving basically the same food at lower prices in a more casual atmosphere, without the picturesque views.

Jimmy's Harborside

Map 2, I4. 242 Northern Ave ©423-1000. South Station Ⓣ. Expensive.

Totally tacky, but the harbor views and seafood are beyond reproach. House specialties include the sizeable King Lobsters and the Shore Dinners, a panoply of shellfish harvested along the New England seashore.

King Fung Garden

Map 3, F9. 74 Kneeland St ©357-5262. Chinatown Ⓣ. Inexpensive.

The interior won't impress with its size or style, but the authentic Shangdong province food they serve here will. Inexpensive and delicious, the *King* is best on classics, like pot stickers, scallion pancakes, and (if you let them know in time) Peking duck.

Les Zygomates

Map 3, I8. 129 South St ©542-5108. South Station Ⓣ. Expensive.

The name comes from the French term for the facial muscles that make you smile. An eclectic crowd ranging from bankers to black-clad artistes gather for the inventive Modern French cuisine and the prime selection of wines – more than a hundred international varieties. Enthusiasts can reserve a spot at the "Tuesday Nights" wine-tasting extravaganza ($25).

Locke-Ober Café

Map 3, F5. 3 Winter Place ©542-1340. Park Ⓣ. Very expensive.

Don't be fooled by the name: *Locke-Ober* is very much a restaurant, and one of the most blueblooded in Boston. The fare consists of things like steak tartare and oysters on the half shell, while the setting is dark, ornate, and stuffy. There's an archaic dress code, too – jacket and tie for men.

Mr. Dooley's Boston Tavern

Map 3, J3. 77 Broad St ©338-5656. State Ⓣ. Inexpensive.

Another downtown Irish pub, though with a quieter and more atmospheric interior than the rest. Also known for its live music acts and Traditional Irish Breakfast Sundays – nice, especially since finding anything open around here on Sunday is a challenge.

Penang

Map 3, F8. 685 Washington St ©451-6373. Chinatown Ⓣ. Moderate.

A newcomer to the Chinatown scene, *Penang* takes its name from an island off the northwest coast of Malaysia. The painfully overdone interior is countered by consistently good food: try the *roti canai* appetizer or the copious yam pot dinner.

Pho Pasteur

Map 3, F8 & 9. 682 Washington St and 8 Kneeland St ©482-7467. Chinatown Ⓣ. Cheap.

Two restaurants, both offering a multitude of variations on pho, a Vietnamese noodle dish. The Kneeland location serves only pho, while the one on Washington has other Vietnamese specialties as well – and it's all incredibly cheap.

Pravda 116

Map 3, E8. 116 Boylston St ©482-7799. Arlington Ⓣ. Expensive.

Known more for its faux-hip scene than its Mediterranean-American entrees and reasonably priced tapas, *Pravda 116* also has a small dance club in the rear (see p.232).

Radius

Map 3, J5. 8 High St ✆426-1234. South Station Ⓣ. Expensive.
Housed in a former bank, this ultramodern French restaurant tries to inject a dose of minimalist industrial chic to the cautious Financial District with an über cool decor and innovative menu. New Yorker Michael Schlow's tasty *nouvelle cuisine* is complemented by an extensive wine list.

Salty Dog

Map 3, I2. Faneuil Hall Marketplace ✆742-2094. Government Center Ⓣ. Expensive.
It's worth braving the long waits here for the fresh seafood, such as the particularly good raw oysters and clams and generous lobster dinners, all best enjoyed in the outdoor dining area.

Sam's

Map 3, G3. 100 City Hall Plaza ✆227-0022. Government Center Ⓣ. Inexpensive–Moderate.
Specializing in what they call "modern comfort food," *Sam's* fabulously fresh offerings range from scallops served with mashed potatoes and tropical salsa to pasta tossed with garlic, basil, chicken, green beans, and grapes.

Seasons

Map 3, H2. North and Blackstone sts (in the *Regal Bostonian*) ✆523-4119. Government Center or State Ⓣ. Very expensive.
With inventive, truly excellent Modern American fare, such as stone crab with smoked corn minestrone, *Seasons* has a knack for attracting up-and-coming chefs before sending them on their way to culinary stardom.

Silvertone

Map 3, G5. 69 Bromfield St ✆338-7887. Downtown Crossing Ⓣ. Inexpensive.
Though cocktails are the big draw at this Downtown Crossing

basement bar and eatery, its Caesar salads and roasted salmon with homemade potato chips are excellent and surprisingly inexpensive.

Union Oyster House

Map 3, H2. 41 Union St ©227-2750. Government Center or State Ⓣ. Expensive.

The oldest continuously operating restaurant in America has two big claims to fame: French King Louis-Phillipe lived over the tavern during his youth, and, perhaps apocryphally, the toothpick was first used here. The food is good too: fresh and well-prepared seafood, plus one of Boston's best raw bars.

Zuma's Tex-Mex Café

Map 3, I2. 7 N Market St ©367-9114. State Ⓣ. Inexpensive.

Tex-Mex is a long way from home in Boston, but *Zuma's* comes up with a close approximation, complemented by a garish interior and sassy waitstaff. Especially good are the fajitas, which come to your table billowing with smoke, and the salty, tangy margaritas.

NORTH END

Assaggio

Map 4, D5. 29 Prince St ©227-7380. Haymarket Ⓣ. Moderate.

An extensive wine list allows *Assaggio* to stand on its own as a wine bar, but it's reliable for classic Italian fare with contemporary touches, too. The main dining room, with its ceiling mural of the Zodiac and steady stream of opera music, is calm and relaxing.

The Daily Catch

Map 4, F4. 323 Hanover St ©523-8567. Haymarket Ⓣ. Moderate.
Map 2, I4. 261 Northern Ave ©338-3093. South Station Ⓣ. Moderate.

Ocean-fresh seafood, notably calamari and shellfish, draws big lines to this tiny storefront resto. The cooking is Sicilian-style with megadoses of garlic. The downtown location offers a solid alternative to the touristy Yankee scrod-and-chips thing.

Dolce Vita

Map 4, E5. 237 Hanover St ©720-0422. Haymarket Ⓣ. Inexpensive.
Sit in the quiet upstairs dining room in this longstanding North End spot to savor their famous Ravioli Rose, in a tomato cream sauce. Don't come here if you're in a hurry, though.

Giacomo's

Map 4, F3. 355 Hanover St ©523-9026. Haymarket Ⓣ. Moderate.
This small eatery, with its menu written on a chalkboard attached to a brick wall, serves fresh and flavorful seafood and pasta specialties; try the pumpkin tortellini in sage butter sauce. There's a location in the South End as well, 431 Columbus Ave ©536-5723; dinner only, closed Mondays.

Il Panino

Map 4, C5. 11 Parmenter St ©720-1336. Aquarium Ⓣ. Inexpensive.
A bona fide Boston best, with incredible pasta specials at lunch; a bit more formal by night.

Mama Maria

Map 4, E6. 3 North Square ©523-0077. Haymarket Ⓣ. Expensive.
A favorite special-occasion restaurant, and considered by some to be the best the district has to offer; in any case its location, on historic North Square, is as good a reason as any to come. The Northern Italian fare is of consistently impeccable quality. Dinner only.

Marcuccio's

Map 4, D3. 125 Salem St ©723-1807. Haymarket Ⓣ. Expensive.
Contemporary Italian food in a nice setting, with Pop Art updates of Renaissance masterpieces on the walls. The chef has

a light, piquant touch that works particularly well with seafood dishes, risottos, and salads. No cards; dinner only.

Monica's

Map 4, C4. 67 Prince St ©720-5472. Haymarket Ⓣ. Inexpensive.
Some of the most intensely flavored Italian fare around, prepared and served by Monica's three sons, one of whom drew the cartoons plastered over the walls. They do a brisk takeout (sandwiches and such) at lunch, though the best dishes are reserved for dinner. Monica herself has a gourmet shop around the corner at 130 Salem St (see p.261).

Pizzeria Regina

Map 4, B3. 11½ Thacher St ©227-0765. Haymarket Ⓣ. Inexpensive.
Tasty pizza, served in a neighborhood feed station where the wooden booths haven't budged since the 1940s. Vintage North End.

CHARLESTOWN

Figs

Map 5, D4. 67 Main St ©242-2229. Moderate.
42 Charles St, Beacon Hill ©742-3447.
This noisy, popular offshoot of *Olives* has excellent thin-crust pizzas, topped with such savory items as figs and prosciutto or caramelized onions and arrugula.

Gabriele's

Map 5, H3. 1 First Ave (Charlestown Navy Yard) ©242-4040. Moderate.
This upscale Italian eatery between the USS Constitution Museum and the arrival area for the Long Wharf ferry features the usual suspects – bruschetta, spinach ravioli, chicken parmigiana – but unusually well-executed. Dine on the terrace to catch the breeze on a hot summer's day.

Olives

Map 5, D5. 10 City Square ©242-1999. Very expensive.

Olives is consistently rated Boston's best restaurant, and justifiably so. Chef Todd English turns out New Mediterranean food of unforgettable flavor in sizeable portions, the cause of long lines if you show up after 6pm since there are no reservations save for parties of six or more. Closed Sun and Mon.

BEACON HILL AND THE WEST END

Artu

Map 3, B4. 89 Charles St ©227-9023. Charles Ⓣ.
6 Prince St, North End ©742-4336. Inexpensive.

Though squeezed into a tiny storefront on Charles Street, *Artu* keeps things fresh, flavorful, and affordable. Authentic Italian country cooking focused on soups, risottos, roast meats, and panini. The North End location is larger, but equally charming.

Grand Canal

Map 3, G1. 57 Canal St ©523-1112. North Station Ⓣ. Moderate.

Atmospheric West End Irish pub and restaurant with nineteenth-century accoutrements, such as the linen tablecloths and a great mahogany bar with a mirror behind. Cheap, relatively inexpensive lobster dinners as well as American comfort food.

The Hungry I

Map 3, B4. 71 Charles St ©227-3524. Charles Ⓣ. Very expensive.

A pricey menu and hyped-up romantic surroundings, but the food is delectable – classic American fare with creative twists that change nightly.

The King & I

Map 3, B3. 145 Charles St ©227-3320. Charles Ⓣ.
Inexpensive–moderate.

Excellent, inventive Thai with bold, but not overbearing flavors.

The "Shrimp in Love" is almost worth trying for its name alone.

Lala Rokh

Map 3, C5. 97 Mt Vernon St ©720-5511. Park Ⓣ. Moderate.
Have the waitstaff help you with the inscrutable menu at this exotically plush Azerbaijani restaurant, where you can fill up on the appetizers (such as roasted eggplant *kashk-e-bademjan*) and exotic *torshi* (condiments) alone.

Rebecca's

Map 3, B4. 21 Charles St ©742-9747. Charles Ⓣ. Expensive.
This place brought New American to Beacon Hill when it was still new. The food is still good if it seems a bit more tame these days: grilled salmon, pasta with lemon chicken and pesto, and butternut squash ravioli.

Ristorante Toscano

Map 3, B4. 47 Charles St ©723-4090. Charles Ⓣ. Moderate.
In the midst of the New Italian craze, *Toscano* stayed traditional, and survived. It serves particularly good Southern Italian food, made with classic flair and fresh ingredients.

BACK BAY

Ambrosia

Map 6, I5. 116 Huntington Ave ©247-2400. Prudential or Copley Ⓣ. Expensive–very expensive.
When you get the craving for a Peruvian Purple Potato Springroll or Grilled Pulled Pig Sandwich with Indonesian BBQ Sauce Oil, this is the place. The French Provençal-meets-Asian fusion cuisine is inventively prepared in a high-tech but accessible environment of dazzling floral arrangements, hand-blown crystal and intricate metalwork, though the flavors don't always measure up to the elaborate presentation. At lunch most salads, gourmet sandwiches and other entrees are priced under $12.

Anago

Map 6, I3. 65 Exeter St (in the *Lenox*) ©266-6222. Copley Ⓣ. Expensive.

Comfort food like spit-roasted pork and rotisserie chicken prepared with a thoughtful and not overblown New American accent; desserts include the likes of coconut crème brûlée and ginger poached pear dipped in chocolate.

Aujourd'hui

Map 6, D8. 200 Boylston St (in the *Four Seasons*) ©338-4400 or 1-800/332-3442, fax 423-0154. Arlington Ⓣ. Very expensive.

On the top of everyone's list of Boston's best restaurants, this is a good place to splurge. Nibble roasted Maine lobster – accompanied by crabmeat wontons, pineapple compote and fenugreek broth – from antique china while enjoying the view over the Public Garden.

Back Bay Brewing Company

Map 6, I4. 755 Boylston St ©424-8300. Copley Ⓣ. Moderate.

Of all the brewpubs in Boston, this feels the least like a glorified bar: the breakfast fare is every bit as good as the inventive lunch and dinner offerings. If you just want a brew, though, settle into the comfortable second-floor lounge and take your pick.

Betty's Wok & Noodle Diner

Map 6, F7. 250 Huntington Ave ©424-1950. Symphony Ⓣ. Inexpensive.

Mix and match from a list of rice, noodles, sauces (from Asian Pesto to Cuban Chipotle-Citrus), vegetables, and meats and, minutes later, enjoy a piping hot plateful of tasty Chino-Latino food. Open everyday until 11pm.

Biba

Map 6, L4. 272 Boylston St ©426-7878. Arlington Ⓣ. Very expensive.

Chef Lydia Shire takes culinary eclecticism to absurd heights at this pricey spot, which would be more at home in LA. The food is description-resistant, and there's a category on the menu called "Offal" – draw your own conclusions. *Biba's* over-crowded bar is only slightly safer (see p.218).

The Blue Cat Café

Map 6, F4. 94 Massachusetts Ave ©247-9922. Hynes Ⓣ. Moderate.
Formerly the trendy *575*, this cavernous restaurant/bar has gone back to basics with a rustic decor and all-American staples like pastas and steaks.

Bombay Café

Map 6, F4. 175 Massachusetts Ave ©247-0555. Hynes Ⓣ. Inexpensive.
The chicken tikka and stuffed nan are good bets, as is anything with seafood, at this casual Indian restaurant.

Boodles

Map 6, G5. 40 Dalton St (in the *Back Bay Hilton*) ©236-1100 or 1-800/874-0663, fax 867-6104. Hynes Ⓣ. Moderate.
English-style steakhouse serving the usual grill fare and some eighty microbrews.

Cactus Club

Map 6, F4. 939 Boylston St ©236-0200. Hynes Ⓣ. Inexpensive.
Cavernous Tex-Mex restaurant with funky decor and surprisingly tasty nibbles (including great quesadillas), but equally sought out for its popular bar.

Café Budapest

Map 6, I5. 90 Exeter St (in the *Copley Square Hotel*) ©266-1979. Copley Ⓣ. Expensive.
Some call it the most romantic restaurant in Boston, but really elegance and inadvertent camp (live piano-and-violin renditions of *Hello, Dolly*, for example) are what this gaily hued

basement-level fixture do best. That and iced tart cherry soup followed by chicken paprika.

Cottonwood Restaurant & Café

Map 6, L4. 222 Berkeley St ©247-2225. Arlington Ⓣ.
Map 7, B1. 1815 Massachusetts Ave, Cambridge ©661-7440. Porter Ⓣ. Moderate–expensive.

Creative and tasty Southwestern fare served in a bright setting on the first floor of the 22-story Houghton Mifflin Building. Locally (and justly) famous for its margaritas, this is one of Back Bay's best bets for lunch or Sunday brunch with a twist.

Du Barry Restaurant Français

Map 6, H3. 159 Newbury St ©262-2445. Copley Ⓣ. Expensive.

A bastion of tradition on otherwise trendy Newbury Street, *Du Barry* is one of few classic French restaurants in Boston. Nothing too inventive, just good, hearty staples like *boeuf bourguignon*, and a hidden terrace on which to enjoy them in warmer weather. The quiet bar is popular with locals.

Gyuhama

Map 6, G4. 827 Boylston St ©437-0188. Hynes Ⓣ. Expensive.

A very noisy basement-level sushi bar, favored by many college students for late-night Japanese snacks.

Kashmir

Map 6, G4. 279 Newbury St ©536-1695. Hynes Ⓣ. Moderate.

The food and decor are equally inviting at Newbury Street's only Indian restaurant. Sound bets include shrimp samosas, tandoori rack of lamb and vegetarian curries, all of which go well with the excellent nan bread.

Kaya

Map 6, I4. 581 Boylston St ©236-5858. Copley Ⓣ. Expensive.

This is the place to go when the craving for Japanese–Korean food kicks in; try the teriyaki salmon or steaming shabu shabu.

Legal Seafoods

Map 3, C9. 27 Park Square (in the *Park Plaza Hotel*) ©426-4444. Arlington Ⓣ.

Map 6, J4. 100 Huntington Ave, Level Two Copley Place ©266-7775. Copley Ⓣ.

Map 6, H5. 800 Boylston St, Prudential Center ©266-6800. Prudential Ⓣ.

Map 7, L3. 5 Cambridge Center ©864-3400. Kendall Ⓣ. Expensive.
This local chain is probably the best-known seafood restaurant in America, and for many the best as well. Its trademark is freshness: the clam chowder, Boston scrod and lobster are all top quality. There are some New Asian offerings on the menu, too. Go early to avoid long lines, no matter the location or day of the week.

L'Espalier

Map 6, G3. 30 Gloucester St ©262-3023. Hynes Ⓣ. Very expensive.
A ravishing French restaurant in a Back Bay brownstone. The food is first rate, but the minimalist portions at lofty prices suggest that ambience is factored into your bill.

Miyako

Map 6, G3. 279 Newbury St ©236-0222. Copley Ⓣ. Expensive.
Authenticity comes at a price at this Japanese standby, which has a popular terrace on Newbury Street, a sleek sushi bar inside and a minimalist decor of muted grays and bright floral arrangements.

Papa Razzi

Map 6, J4. 271 Dartmouth St ©536-9200. Copley Ⓣ. Moderate.
Though this urbane, basement-level eatery doesn't look like a chain restaurant, it is – a fact reflected in the menu of standard-

issue bruschetta, salads, and pastas. It's all good, but for more authentic takes head to the North End.

Skipjack's

Map 6, K4. 199 Clarendon St ©536-3500. Arlington Ⓣ. Expensive.
A cool, South Beach-style decor and bold menu distinguish this seafood spot from its rival, the always-busy *Legal Seafoods* – you're as likely to find fresh mahi mahi dipped in lemon and soy as fried scrod with tartar sauce. The Sunday jazz brunch is quite popular.

Sonsie

Map 6, F4. 327 Newbury St ©351-2500. Hynes Ⓣ. Expensive.
The pretension factor is high at this coffeeklatsch, where the ultra-trendy meet over strange marriages of French and Asian food (miso clam soup with spring morels and tofu, grilled salmon with edible blossoms). Consider braving the scene if only for the hot chocolate bread pudding.

Steve's Greek-American Cuisine

Map 6, F4. 316 Newbury St ©267-1817. Hynes Ⓣ. Inexpensive.
Excellent Greek food makes this one of Boston's classic cheap eats. Steve's Greek Salad is a favorite among the Newbury Street lunch crowd, and the Grilled Chicken Sandwich could convert a vegetarian.

Thai Basil

Map 6, J3. 132 Newbury St ©424-8424. Copley Ⓣ. Moderate.
With its excellent seafood, vegetarian, and Pad Thai dishes and a cool, soothing decor in which to enjoy it all, this is the best Thai restaurant in Boston.

Top of the Hub

Map 6, H5. 800 Boylston St ©536-1775. Prudential Ⓣ. Expensive.
There are several benefits of dining atop the 50th floor of the

Prudential Tower, not the least of which is enjoying the excellent city views. There's also surprisingly inventive New England fare and a big, bright space in which to enjoy it.

Turner Fisheries

Map 6, I5. 10 Huntington Ave ✆424-7425. Prudential Ⓣ. Expensive.
The traditional New England seafood at this cheerful spot – scrod, Boston clam chowder, lobster bisque – is as good as any in the city. Most nights feature live jazz performances.

SOUTH END

Bertucci's Brick Oven Pizzeria

Map 6, K5. 43 Stanhope St ✆247-6161. Back Bay Ⓣ. Inexpensive.
Though it may not be the best pizza in Boston, *Bertucci's* more than does the trick; there's also great free garlic bread in this funky South End location.

Claremont Café

Map 6, I7. 535 Columbus Ave ✆247-9001. Back Bay Ⓣ. Moderate.
Diverse appetizers (like cornmeal fried oysters with jicama slaw), imaginatively garnished entrees and particularly flavorful desserts, including a stellar banana creme pie. Closed Mondays.

The Delux Café & Lounge

Map 6, K6. 100 Chandler St ✆338-5258. Back Bay Ⓣ. Moderate.
The South End's cool spot of the moment is this retro hideaway *boîte*; the menu is loosely American fusion, but you basically go for the buzz.

Franklin Café

Map 6, L8. 278 Shawmut Ave ✆350-0010. Back Bay Ⓣ.
Moderate–expensive.
One of the most popular new spots in Boston, this upscale diner has earned local fame for its tasty renditions of Yankee

comfort food like turkey meatloaf with spicy fig sauce.

Geoffrey's

Map 6, K7. 578 Tremont St ©266-1122. Back Bay Ⓣ. Inexpensive.
This cheerful eatery serves a nice range of salads and sandwiches from a menu that also includes more substantial fare like seven-vegetable couscous, asparagus mousse ravioli and huge portions of cake.

Hamersley's Bistro

Map 6, K7. 553 Tremont St ©423-2700. Back Bay Ⓣ. Expensive.
Hamersley's is widely regarded as one of the best restaurants in Boston, and with good cause. Every night star chef-owner Gordon Hamersley dons a baseball cap and takes to the open kitchen, where he dishes out unusual – and unforgettable – French-American fare that changes seasonally.

Mistral

Map 6, K5. 221 Columbus Ave ©867-9300. Back Bay Ⓣ. Expensive.
Still one of *the* places to go in Boston, *Mistral* serves pricey modern Provençal food in a bright, airy space above the Turnpike. How long this star will keep rising is anyone's guess, as the food is mediocre considering the cost. Dinner only.

On the Park

Map 6, K8. One Union Park ©426-0862. Back Bay Ⓣ. Moderate.
The French bistro fare is as much of a draw at this neighborhood restaurant as its secluded setting on the quiet south side of Union Park. The vegetarian cassoulet is a winner. Intimate brunch on weekends.

KENMORE SQUARE, THE FENWAY, AND BROOKLINE

Anna's Taqueria

Map 2, D5. 1412 Beacon St ©739-7300. Coolidge Corner Ⓣ. Cheap.

Exceptional tacos, burritos and quesadillas are the only things on the menu at this bright Mexican eatery, but they're so good a second branch had to be opened around the corner (at 446 Harvard St) to accommodate its legions of devotees.

Audubon Circle

Map 6, C2. 838 Beacon St ©421-1910. Kenmore Ⓣ. Moderate.

The seemingly endless bar grabs your attention first, but it's the food that's worth staying for. Any of the appetizers are good bets, as is anything grilled – from burgers with chipotle ketchup to grilled tuna with banana salsa and fufu (fried plantains mashed with coconut milk). There's a limited selection of homemade desserts.

Matt Murphy's

14 Harvard St, Brookline ©232-0188. Inexpensive.

Authentic Irish comfort food along the lines of warm potato and leek soup with brown bread and rabbit pie with Irish soda bread crust. It's tiny, and you may have to wait, but it's well worth it.

SOUTHERN DISTRICTS

Amrhein's

Map 2, H5. 80 W Broadway, South Boston ©268-6189. Broadway Ⓣ. Moderate.

A Southie landmark and a favorite of local politicians for generations. The good old American comfort food won't dazzle your palate, but it's reasonably priced and you get a lot of it.

Bella Luna

Map 2, E7. 405 Centre St, Jamaica Plain ©524-6060. Green St Ⓣ. Moderate.

Nouvelle pizza with a funky array of fresh toppings (you can order from their list of combinations or design your own) in a festive space. Jazz brunch on Sunday mornings and live entertainment on most weekends.

Bob the Chef

Map 6, G8. 604 Columbus Ave, Roxbury ©536-6204. Mass Ave Ⓣ. Inexpensive–moderate.

The best soul food in New England. Good chitterlings, black-eyed peas and collard greens, and don't miss the "glori-fried chicken," the house specialty. Live jazz on weekends.

ALLSTON-BRIGHTON

Ducky Wok

122–126 Harvard Ave, Allston ©782-8868. Harvard Ave Ⓣ. Inexpensive.

Popular Chinese–Vietnamese restaurant where you select your own fish from a giant tank. The lemongrass chicken, stir-fried peapod stems, and avocado smoothies (for dessert) all stand out.

Rangoli

129 Brighton Ave, Allston ©562-0200. Harvard Ave Ⓣ. Inexpensive.

Southern Indian fare, favoring spicy vegetarian selections. Be sure to try the *dosa*: sourdough pancakes rolled like giant cannoli around a variety of savory fillings.

Wonder Bar

186 Harvard Ave, Allston ©351-2665. Harvard Ave Ⓣ. Moderate.

A bit upscale for the neighborhood, this popular hangout manages to win points for its clay pot concoctions and other innovative snacks; no tennis shoes allowed, though.

CAMBRIDGE

Boca Grande

Map 7, B2. 1728 Massachusetts Ave ©354-7400. Porter Ⓣ. Budget.

Somewhere in between a restaurant and a taco stand, crowded *Boca* vends delectable, if not quite authentic, Mexican fare at incredibly low prices – no entree is above $5. The overstuffed burritos are excellent meals in themselves.

Border Café

Map 7, D5. 32 Church St ©864-6100. Harvard Ⓣ. Moderate.

Cambridge's most popular Tex-Mex place. It's pretty good, though not nearly enough to justify the massive crowds that form on weekend nights. The margaritas are salty and strong, and the food is so pungent that you'll carry its aroma with you for hours afterward.

Café of India

Map 7, C5. 52 Brattle St ©661-0683. Harvard Ⓣ. Inexpensive.

This Indian spot stands out primarily because of its uplifting, woody interior; in summer, the facade is removed for semi-alfresco dining. Its best dishes are tried-and-true Indian standards – chicken tikka, saag paneer, and particularly light and delectable nan bread.

Cambridge Common

Map 7, C4. 1667 Massachusetts Ave ©547-1228. Harvard or Porter Ⓣ. Inexpensive.

Half bar, half restaurant; a popular after-work place for young professionals and graduate students. The "Ultimate Nachos" appetizer could be a meal in itself. A downstairs music venue, the *Lizard Lounge* (p.229), has decent rock and jazz acts almost nightly.

Charlie's Kitchen

Map 7, D5. 10 Eliot St ©492-9646. Harvard Ⓣ. Inexpensive.

Marvelously atmospheric townie hangout in the heart of Harvard Square, with red vinyl booths, sassy waitresses with beehive hairdos, and greasy diner food. The patrons here were smoking cigars before it was hip, and will be doing so long after the craze ends. Try the cheap but filling "Double Cheeseburger Special."

Chez Henri

Map 7, C3. 1 Shepard St ©354-8980. Harvard Ⓣ. Very expensive.

Does paying more at a fancy restaurant actually mean you'll get a vastly superior meal? At *Chez Henri*, the answer is an emphatic yes. If you can get a table (no reservations, and the weekend wait tops one hour even late at night), you'll enjoy what may well be Cambridge's finest cuisine. Chef Paul O'Connell's experiment in fusion brings Modern French together with Cuban influences, best sampled in the light salads and excellent Cuban crab cake appetizers, and the chicken asado that follows.

East Coast Grill

1271 Cambridge St ©491-6568. Harvard or Central Square Ⓣ. Moderate.

A festive and funky atmosphere in which to enjoy fresh seafood (there is a raw bar tucked into one corner) and southern side dishes that take their cue from hearty New England comfort foods.

Henrietta's Table

Map 7, D5. 1 Bennett St (in the *Charles Hotel*) ©661-5005. Harvard Ⓣ. Very expensive.

One of the only restaurants in Cambridge that serves classic New England fare. Rich entrees such as roasted duck or pork chops work well with side dishes of wilted greens or mashed potatoes – although some would say a trip to *Henrietta's* is wasted if it's not for their famous brunch, served every Sunday from noon to 3pm; it costs $32 per person but allows unlimited access to a cornucopia of the farm-fresh treats from around New England.

House of Blues

Map 7, D5. 96 Winthrop St ©491-2583. Harvard Ⓣ. Moderate.

The desultory waitstaff at the original *House of Blues* serves up mediocre Southern food - like jambalaya and ribs – in a decor carefully manufactured to effect a casual roadhouse look. The real reason to come here is for the big name blues performers at the upstairs venue (see p.230).

Iruna

Map 7, D5. 56 JFK St ©868-5633. Harvard Ⓣ. Inexpensive.

Located in a diminutive, unassuming spot in an alley off JFK Street, *Iruna* is a fairly uncrowded spot with authentic Spanish fare. Lunch specials are incredibly cheap, including paella and a rich *arroz con pollo*; dinner is more expensive but equally good.

Mr & Mrs Bartley's Burger Cottage

Map 7, E5. 1246 Massachusetts Ave ©354-6559. Harvard Ⓣ. Inexpensive.

The walls are decorated with references to political humor and popular culture, while the names of the dishes on the menu poke fun at celebrities of the hour. The food itself is loaded with cholesterol. A burger and "frappe" (milkshake) here is a definite experience.

Pho Pasteur

Map 7, D5. 35 Dunster St, in the Garage ©864-4100. Harvard Ⓣ. Inexpensive.

This more upscale Harvard Square incarnation of the successful Chinatown string of Vietnamese joints serves a variety of filling and delicious pho noodle soups beginning at $6. The spring rolls are another treat.

Siam Garden

Map 7, E5. 45½ Mt Auburn St ©354-1718. Harvard Ⓣ. Inexpensive.

Tasty Thai fare in an atmosphere strenuously attempting to invoke images of the exotic East.

Tandoor House

Map 7, H5. 569 Massachusetts Ave ©661-9001. Central Ⓣ. Inexpensive.

Consistently at the top of the list of Cambridge's many fine Indian restaurants, *Tandoor* has excellent chicken saag and a great mushroom bhaji. Definitely the best Indian spot outside Harvard Square, perhaps in the whole city.

Trattoria Pulcinella

Map 7, A3. 147 Huron Ave ©491-6336. Porter Ⓣ. Expensive.

A creative menu blends fresh ingredients with Continental flair. The eggplant-stuffed ravioli with a tomato basil garlic sauce are a must, as is the perfectly decadent tiramisu. Waitstaff is unusually attentive without being intrusive.

Upstairs at the Pudding

Map 7, D5. 10 Holyoke St ©864-1933. Harvard Ⓣ. Very expensive.

The dining room was converted from what was originally the eating area for Harvard's ultra-elite Hasty Pudding Club, and the attitude lingers on. The food is excellent, though, falling somewhere in between New American and Old Colonial, and done with surprising verve – even old standards like a Porterhouse Steak are exciting. Advance reservations are essential.

SOMERVILLE

Dalí

415 Washington St. Harvard Ⓣ. Expensive.

Waitresses dance the flamenco at this upscale tapas restaurant, which features live energetic Spanish music, excellent Sangria and a good wine list.

Redbones

55 Chester St ✆628-2200. Davis Ⓣ. Inexpensive.

All styles of American barbecue are represented in huge portions, accompanied by delectable sides such as collard greens, the sum of which won't likely leave you room for dessert (though the pies are top-notch). Long lines at dinner, so arrive early. No cards.

The Rosebud Diner

381 Summer St ✆666-6015. Davis Ⓣ. Inexpensive.

Authentic diner car with red-vinyl booths, pink neon sign, and chrome detail, that serves the expected burgers, fries, and Boston Creme Pie along with more contemporary favorites like pasta, grilled chicken, and veggie burgers.

Drinking

Despite – or perhaps because of – the lingering Puritan ethic that pervades Boston, people here tend to drink more than they do in the rest of the country, with the consequence that few American cities offer as many different kinds of places to get ploughed per capita. The most prevalent of these is the Irish pub, of which there are high concentrations in the West End and downtown around Quincy Market. Among many unextraordinary such watering holes, several are the real McCoys, drawing as many Irish expatriates as they do Irish-American locals.

More upscale are the bars and lounges of **Back Bay**, along Newbury and Boylston streets, which offer as much attitude as atmosphere. Some of the most popular bars in this area are actually adjuncts of restaurants and hotels. The rest of the city's neighborhood watering holes, pick-up joints and yuppie hotspots are differentiated by their crowds: **Beacon Hill** tends to be older and stuffier; **downtown**, mainly around Quincy Market and the Theater District, draws a healthy mix of tourists and locals; **Kenmore Square** and **Cambridge** are fairly student-oriented.

Predominantly gay bars and cafés can be found beginning on p.246.

The **café** scene is not quite as diverse, but still offers a decent range of places to hang out. The toniest spots are again those that line the Back Bay's **Newbury Street**, where you pay as much for the fancy environs as for the quality of the coffee. Value is much better in the **North End**, whose Italian cafés have somewhat less expensive but generally excellent beverages and desserts. The most lively cafés, however, are across the river in **Cambridge**, unsurprisingly catering to the large student population.

BARS

Bars stop serving at 2am (at the latest), and most strictly enforce the drinking-age minimum of 21. Be prepared to show at least one form of valid identification, either a driver's license or passport. The one potential for after-hours drinking is **Chinatown**, where some restaurants will bring you a pot of beer if you ask for "cold tea."

DOWNTOWN

Bell in Hand Tavern

Map 3, H2. 45 Union St ©227-2098. State or Government Center Ⓣ.
The oldest continuously operating tavern in Boston draws a fairly exuberant mix of tourists and young professionals.

The Black Rose (Roisin Dubh)

Map 3, I3. 160 State St ©742-2286. State Ⓣ.
Down-home Irish pub specializing in imported beers from the Emerald Isle: Harp, Bass Ale, Murphy's, and especially Guinness all flow freely, and things get pretty boisterous on weekends.

Emily's

Map 3, F5. 48 Winter St ©423-3649. Park Ⓣ.
Red-velvet curtains and floor-to-ceiling mirrors give this

downtown spot as much style as any place in Back Bay – without the accompanying attitude. It's mellow on weeknights; on weekends, a DJ spins top-40 mixes to overenthusiastic dancers.

The Good Life

Map 3, G6. 28 Kingston St ©451-2622. Downtown Crossing Ⓣ.
This trendy bar (and restaurant) near Downtown Crossing has generated quite a buzz since its opening a few years ago, due as much to its potent martinis as its 1970s decor.

Governor's Alley

Map 3, G4. 42 Province St ©426-3333. Park Ⓣ.
Although this casual weekday lunch and dinner spot is just off the Freedom Trail, it is happily removed from the Trail's tourist throng. Secure a wooden booth and enjoy big portions of Yankee pub grub, from deli sandwiches to baked stuffed scrod and crab cakes, or repair upstairs to the *Gargoyle Bar* – about as close to a real *Cheers* as you'll find in Boston.

Green Dragon Tavern

Map 3, H2. 11 Marshall St ©367-0055. Government Center Ⓣ.
Another tavern that dates to the Colonial era, this was a popular meeting place for patriots during the Revolution. There's a standard selection of tap beers, a raw bar, and a full menu rife with twee historical humor ("One if by land, two if by seafood").

The Littlest Bar in Boston

Map 3, G4. 47 Province St ©523-9766. Downtown Crossing Ⓣ.
The tiny size of this place is part of the charm, as are the quality pints of Guinness and free music by bands crammed into an alcove – perhaps also the littlest performance space in Boston.

The Purple Shamrock

Map 3, H2. 1 Union St ©227-2060. State or Government Center Ⓣ.
A lively watering hole that draws a broad cross-section of folks,

the *Shamrock* has one of Boston's better straight singles scenes. It gets very crowded on weekends.

The Rack

Map 3, I2. 24 Clinton St ©725-1051. Government Center Ⓣ.
Well-dressed twenty- and thirty-somethings convene at this pool hall to dine, smoke cigars, drink a bewildering variety of cocktails, and, of course, shoot a rack or two. While there are 35 pool tables and a fair share of wannabe hustlers, about half the crowd shows up just to see and be seen.

For more places to shoot pool, see p.278.

CHARLESTOWN

Warren Tavern

Map 5, C2. 2 Pleasant St at Main St ©241-8142. Community College Ⓣ.
An atmospheric place to enjoy a drink, and the oldest standing structure in Charlestown. The *Warren* also has a generous menu of good tavern food.

BEACON HILL AND THE WEST END

The Bull & Finch Pub

Map 3, B6. 84 Beacon St ©227-9605. Arlington Ⓣ.
If you don't already know, and if the conspicuous banners outside don't tip you off, this is the bar that served as the inspiration for the TV show *Cheers*. If you've gotta go, be warned – it's packed with camera-toting tourists; the inside bears little resemblance to the NBC set; the food, though cutely named (eNORMous burgers), is pricey and mediocre; and it's almost certain that nobody will know your name.

Fours

166 Canal St ©720-4455. North Station Ⓣ.

The classiest of the West End's sports bars, with an army of TVs to broadcast games from around the globe and paraphernalia from the Celtics, Bruins, and other local teams. Coach Rick Pitino has been spotted here after Celtic victories.

The Hill

Map 3. D2. 228 Cambridge St ©742-6192. Charles Ⓣ.

The only centrally located bar in Beacon Hill, this classic yuppie bar attracts suits who like to tip back a lot of pricey imported beer; there's often a long line to get in on weekend nights.

Irish Embassy

234 Friend St ©742-6618. North Station Ⓣ.

Up in the West End, this is one of the city's most authentic Irish (rather than Irish-American) pubs, with the crowd to match. Live Irish entertainment most nights, plus broadcasts of Irish soccer games.

McGann's

197 Portland St ©227-4059. North Station Ⓣ.

Similar to the nearby *Irish Embassy*, but with a more upmarket, restauranty feel. There are British eats like shepherd's pie and pan-seared calf's liver if you're in the mood.

Sevens Ale House

Map 3, B3. 77 Charles St ©523-9074. Charles Ⓣ.

While the tourists pack into the *Bull & Finch*, you can drop by this cozy joint to get a taste of what a real Boston neighborhood bar is like. Wide selection of draft beers plus daily specials, substantial food, darts, and a relaxed feel.

21st Amendment

Map 3, F4. 150 Bowdoin St ©227-7100. Bowdoin Ⓣ.

This dimly lit, down-home watering hole is a favorite haunt of legislators from the adjacent State House and students from nearby Suffolk University.

BACK BAY AND THE SOUTH END

Back Bay Brewing Company

Map 6, I4. 755 Boylston St ©424-8300. Copley Ⓣ.

This is actually more a restaurant than bar – despite the name – but the second-floor lounge is one of the city's most inviting spaces to drink a tasty draft. See also p.199.

Biba

Map 6, L4. 272 Boylston St ©426-5684. Arlington Ⓣ.

The first floor is a chic bar packed with Back Bay executives; upstairs is home to *Biba's* trendy restaurant (see p.199).

Bristol Lounge

Map 3, C8. 200 Boylston St ©351-2053. Arlington Ⓣ.

A posh lobby-side lounge in the *Four Seasons* where the desserts are as popular as the drinks.

The Claddagh

Map 6, J6. 113 Dartmouth St ©262-9874. Back Bay Ⓣ.

Big, two-room, Irish-flavored bar and restaurant on the northern cusp of the South End.

Dad's

Map 6, G4. 911 Boylston St ©296-3237. Hynes Ⓣ.

Dim lights and scantily clad barmaids make this a fairly un-Back Bay drinking hole. Down that $6 martini and prepare to cruise.

Daisy Buchanan's

Map 6, H4. 240A Newbury St ©247-8516. Copley Ⓣ.

A real-life beer commercial: young guys wearing baseball caps, professional sports on TV, and a pervasive smell of booze.

Oak Bar

Map 6, J4. 138 St. James Ave (in the *Fairmont Copley Plaza*) ©267-5300. Copley Ⓣ.

Rich wood paneling, high ceilings, swirling cigar smoke and excellent martinis make this one of the more genteel Back Bay spots to drink.

KENMORE SQUARE AND THE FENWAY

Audubon

Map 6, A2. 838 Beacon St ©421-1910. Kenmore Ⓣ.

Sleek, modern bar where a well-dressed crowd gathers for cocktails and fancy bar food before and after games at nearby Fenway Park.

Bill's Bar

Map 6, C3. 5 1/2 Lansdowne St ©421-9678. Kenmore Ⓣ.

A fairly relaxed and homey Lansdowne Street spot, with lots of beer, lots of TV, and occasional live music – in which case expect a cover charge of $5.

Boston Beer Works

Map 6, B3. 61 Brookline Ave ©536-2337. Kenmore Ⓣ.

A brewery located right by Fenway Park – and as such a popular place for the Red Sox faithful to warm up before games and drown their sorrows after. Their signature ale is "Boston Red," but the seasonal brews are also worth a taste. Decent food too.

Copperfield's/Down Under

Map 6, A4. 98 Brookline Ave ©247-8605. Kenmore Ⓣ.

Two adjoining bars, though the difference between them is

minimal: both offer cheap drafts and pool, and are frequented by a raucous collegiate crowd. Cover of $5 on weekends to see loud bands.

SOUTHERN DISTRICTS

Brendan Behan

Map 2, E7. 378 Centre St, Jamaica Plain ©522-5386. Jackson Square Ⓣ.

A dimly lit Irish Pub with a friendly staff. Catch the live music and free buffet available on most weekends.

James's Gate

Map 2, E7. 5-11 McBride St, Jamaica Plain ©983-2000.

Beat Boston's harsh winter by sipping Guinness by the blazing fireplace in this cozy pub, or trying the hearty fare in the restaurant in back. Traditional Irish music on Sundays, open mic on Thursdays.

CAMBRIDGE

The Burren

247 Elm St, Somerville ©776-6896. Davis Ⓣ.

Actually north of Cambridge, in Somerville, but if you're up this far, you can check out the student scene here: lots of baseball caps, baggy jeans, and overflowing crowds.

The Cellar

Map 7, F5. 991 Massachusetts Ave ©876-2580. Harvard Ⓣ.

Two floors, each with a bar, filled with a regular crowd of faculty members, older students, and other locals imbibing fine beers and killer Long Island iced teas.

The Druid

Map 7, G2. 1357 Cambridge St ©497-0965. #69 bus.

Twee Inman Square bar featuring an old Celtic motif, with murals of druid priests and ever-present pints of Guinness; blessedly free of the college scene.

The Field

Map 7, H5. 20 Prospect St ©354-7345. Central Ⓣ.
Although it is located between Harvard and MIT this Irish pub attracts an eclectic non-college crowd. Play pool or darts while you sip one of several varieties of tap beers.

Grafton Street

Map 7, E5. 1280 Massachusetts Ave ©497-0400. Harvard Ⓣ.
Authentic, cozy Irish atmosphere, in which an older, well-dressed set enjoys smooth drafts and equally good food.

Grendel's Den

Map 7, D5. 89 Winthrop St ©491-1160. Harvard Ⓣ.
A favorite spot of locals and grad students for drinking ale; these dark, conspiratorial environs were recently saved by Harvard Law professor Larry Tribe, who lobbied against Puritan blue laws when a nearby church tried to get the place closed. Fantastic happy-hour special offers big plates of appetizers (fried calamari, nachos) for just $1.50 each.

Miracle of Science

Map 7, I5. 321 Massachusetts Ave ©868-2866. Central Ⓣ or #1 bus.
Suprisingly hip despite its status as an MIT hangout. There's a noir decor and a trendy crowd of well-dressed professionals; can get quite crowded on weekend nights.

Rialto

Map 7, D5. 1 Bennett St ©661-5050. Harvard Ⓣ.
The bar adjunct to the chichi restaurant of the same name caters to a wealthy crowd that matches the plush atmosphere.

Dress semi-formally and be prepared to pay big-time for the drinks and cocktails, which are admittedly excellent.

Shay's

Map 7, D5. 58 JFK St ©864-9161. Harvard Ⓣ.

Relaxed contrast to the crowded and sweaty student-oriented sports bars of Harvard Square. Unwind with grad-students over wine and quality beer.

CAFÉS

At many **cafés** in Boston and Cambridge, you can get an excellent full meal just as easily as you can a cup of coffee. Below are the best choices for casual hanging out, day or night; there are also plenty of cafés more suited for meals listed throughout the "Eating" chapter (p.177).

NORTH END

Café Pompeii

Map 4, E5. 280 Hanover St ©227-1562. Haymarket Ⓣ.

Though you may not enjoy the garish murals, mediocre pizza or marginal homemade ice cream, this is the only real late night joint in the North End, open till 4am.

Caffé dello Sport

Map 4, F4. 308 Hanover St ©523-5063. Haymarket Ⓣ.

A continuous stream of Rai Uno soccer matches is broadcast from the ceiling-mounted TV sets, making for an agreeable din amongst a very local crowd. Opens very early.

Caffé Paradiso

Map 4, E5. 255 Hanover St ©742-1768. Haymarket Ⓣ.

Not much on atmosphere, but the pastries are, hands-down, the best in the North End.

Caffé Vittoria

Map 4, E5. 296 Hanover St ©227-7606. Haymarket Ⓣ.

A Boston institution, the *Vittoria*'s atmospheric original section, with its dark wood paneling, pressed tin ceiling, murals of the Old Country, and Sinatra-blaring Wurlitzer, is vintage North End. There's also a cavernous downstairs grotto, and a no-smoking-allowed street-level addition, both equally fine for sipping one of their excellent cappuccinos.

A Different Drummer Café

Map 4, C5. 135 Salem St ©523-6263. Haymarket Ⓣ.

Have a grilled cheese sandwich with your coffee at this small, decidedly un-Italian café right in the middle of the North End.

BEACON HILL

Curious Liquids

Map 3, F4. 22B Beacon St ©720-2836. Park Ⓣ.

What makes this one of Boston's premier cafés is not the specialty coffees (though the "midnight silk mocha" is outstanding), but the stylish setting, with two floors of comfy overstuffed chairs, as well as books and games for your amusement.

Panificio

Map 3, B3. 144 Charles St ©227-4340. Charles Ⓣ.

Fine cups o' Joe, fresh tasty pastries (biscotti is the standout), and some of the best home-baked bread in the city.

BACK BAY AND THE SOUTH END

Caffé Romano

Map 6, L3. 33 Newbury St ©266-0770. Arlington Ⓣ.

Affordable pastries, sandwiches and coffee drinks on the first and toniest block of Newbury Street. Those who require a dose of aesthetics will be gratified by the rotating installations of contemporary paintings.

The Other Side Cosmic Café

Map 6, F4. 407 Newbury St ©536-9477. Hynes Ⓣ.
This ultracasual spot on "the other side" of Massachusetts Avenue, cut off from the trendy part of Newbury Street, offers gourmet sandwiches, "creative green salads," and fresh juices. Local band videos and short art films are shown Monday nights; there's a jazz/ambient brunch on weekends.

Trident Booksellers & Café

Map 6, G4. 338 Newbury St ©267-8688. Copley Ⓣ.
A window seat at this bookstore café (see p.253), perennially popular with the cool student set, is the ideal vantage point from which to observe the flood of young passersby outside.

Twelve Church

Map 6, L6. 12 Church St ©348-0012. Arlington Ⓣ.
Tiny neighborhood coffeehouse in Bay Village with a nice range of fresh baked goods.

29 Newbury

Map 6, L3. 29 Newbury St ©536-0290. Arlington Ⓣ.
A small upscale café/bar and eatery with good, if pricey, salads and the like. In warmer weather, the self-consciously hip crowd migrates to the sidewalk terrace. Wear black, dangle sunglasses, enjoy the crème brûlée. Open until 1.30am.

SOUTHERN DISTRICTS

Black Crow Caffe

Map 2, E7. 2 Perkins St, Jamaica Plain ©983-9231. Jackson Square Ⓣ.
Great coffee and lunch fare in a stylish space adorned with the

work of local artists. A focal point of the offbeat JP scene.

CAMBRIDGE

Algiers

Map 7, D5. 40 Brattle St ©492-1557. Harvard Ⓣ.

A fashionably cramped North African café popular with the artsy set; while the food is so-so and the service slow, there are few more atmospheric spots in which to sip first-rate coffee.

Bookcellar Café

Map 7, A1. 1971 Massachusetts Ave ©864-9625. Porter Ⓣ.

Relaxed basement coffeehouse with furnishings consisting primarily of a few old sofas and some folding chairs on the concrete floor, but the coffee is good – and cheap – and you can peruse the wide range of magazines and used books while you imbibe.

Café Gato Rojo

Map 7, D5. Basement of Lehman Hall (Dudley House), Harvard Yard ©496-4658. Harvard Ⓣ.

One of the least-known of the Harvard Square coffeehouses, this place is hip without being overbearing, run by and for grad students, though the general public is welcome too.

Café Pamplona

Map 7, E5. 12 Bow St. No phone. Harvard Ⓣ.

Eurochic hits its pretentious peak in this tiny basement café. The coffee is surprisingly average, the waitstaff a bit snooty. On balmy evenings, the patio seating provides refuge from thick blue clouds of clove cigarette smoke.

Caffé Paradiso

Map 7, D5. 1 Eliot St ©868-3240. Harvard Ⓣ.

This glossy Italian café strikes a bright, comfortable contrast to the atmospheric dimness of most Harvard Square coffeehouses.

The coffee is good (and reasonably priced); the service is swift, and the setting free of pretension.

Tealuxe

Map 7, D5. 0 Brattle St ©441-0077. Harvard Ⓣ.

In a twist on the standard coffeehouse, what was once a curiosity shop called Loulou's Lost and Found has reincarnated itself as the only teahouse in Harvard Square. They manage to stock over 100 varieties of the stuff – loose and by the cup – though the place is smaller than a teacup. Art Deco trimmings help you "skip the java in flavor of tea" in style.

1369 Coffeehouse

Map 7, G2. 757 Massachusetts Ave ©576-4600. Central Ⓣ; 1369 Cambridge St ©576-1369. #69 bus.

The *1369* mixes earnest thirty-something leftists with youthful hipsters in a relaxed environment; your best bets are the standard array of caffeinated beverages and particularly exquisite desserts.

Nightlife

In recent years Boston's nightlife has received something of a wake-up call, although for a major American city, its scene feels small and is geared primarily to a buttoned-down college crowd; you'll find that even at the wildest venues, locals tend to sport the reserved preppy look characteristic of Boston's universities. A few stylish new clubs have sprung up in places, such as Downtown Crossing, that were previously mere ghost towns by night. Though the city is by no means a 24-hour one, these new hotspots have breathed a bit of fresh air into a scene that once lived in the shadow of the city's so-called highbrow culture. Elsewhere, the same old clubs reinvent themselves every few years in the hopes of catching up with current trends.

For listings of classical music venues, see p.237.

Live music plays a huge role in the city's nightlife arena, with bars and clubs catering to a young crowd, especially around Kenmore Square and Harvard Square, where you're as likely to hear a garage band as a DJ. Boston has spawned its share of enormous **rock** acts, from the ever-enduring Aerosmith to pop ska-sters Mighty Mighty Bosstones, hip-hop heartthrobs Marky Mark and the New Kids on the

Block, and a smattering of post-punk and indie groups such as the Pixies, Sebadoh, Lemonheads, Push Stars and Morphine. There is a bit less in the way of **jazz** and **blues**, but you can usually find something cheap and to your liking almost any day of the week.

For **club and music listings**, check Thursday's *Boston Globe* "Calendar," the *Boston Phoenix*, the *Improper Bostonian* and *Stuff@night*. You'll also find a number of Web sites helpful for up-to-date listings; for details on these, see p.8.

LIVE MUSIC

The strength of Boston's **live music** is in the intimacy of its smaller venues, though superstar performers make the city a regular stop on their world tours as well. Two of the biggest concert halls are a ways out of town: the *Tweeter Center*, south of the city in Mansfield (✆508/339-2333; *www.tweetercenter.com*), and the *Worcester Centrum*, an hour or so west in Worcester (✆508/755-6800; *www.centrumcentre.com*). On a more human scale, plenty of alternative venues serve up everything from name bands to obscure new acts; if all else fails, there's always street music at "The Pit" in Harvard Square (p.121), where you're bound to hear some free amateur acts, whether you like it or not.

ROCK

BankBoston Pavilion

Map 2, J4. Fan Pier, Northern Ave ✆374-9000; *www.harborlights.com*. South Station Ⓣ.

Formerly the Harborlights Pavilion; during the summer, concerts by well-known performers from Mel Tormé to the Gipsy Kings are held here under a huge white tent at Boston Harbor's edge.

FleetCenter

50 Causeway St ✆624-1750; *www.fleetcenter.com*. North Station Ⓣ.

This arena, up in the West End, attracts many of the big-name acts that pass through New England, usually at a hefty price.

Lizard Lounge

Map 7, C4. 1667 Massachusetts Ave ✆547-0759. Harvard or Porter Ⓣ.

The downstairs portion of the *Cambridge Common* restaurant (p.208), a favorite among local students, featuring rock and jazz acts almost nightly for a fairly nominal cover charge.

Middle East

Map 7, H5. 472 Massachusetts Ave ✆864-3278; *www.mideastclub.com*. Central Ⓣ.

Local and regional acts of every sort – salsa to ska and mambo to hardcore – stop in regularly at this Cambridge institution. Bigger acts are hosted downstairs; smaller ones ply their stuff in a tiny upstairs space. A third venue, the "Corner" has free acts every night, with belly dancing every Wednesday. The attached restaurant has decent - you guessed it - Middle Eastern food.

Orpheum Theater

Map 3, F5. Hamilton Place ✆679-0810. Park or Downtown Crossing Ⓣ.

Once an old-school movie house, this is now a venue for big-name music acts. The small space means you're closer to the action, but it sells out quickly and the cramped seating discourages dancing.

Paradise Rock Club

Map 6, C3. 967 Commonwealth Ave ✆562-8800. Kenmore Ⓣ.

Usually a dance club (see *M-LXXX*, p.234), but occasionally hosts mid-level music shows. Crazy decor and pricey drinks, but it rarely sells out and the acoustics are quite good.

T.T. the Bear's

Map 7, I5. 10 Brookline St ©492-2327. Central Ⓣ.

A downmarket version of the *Middle East*, with less popular acts in a space with a gritty intimacy its neighbor lacks. All kinds of bands appear, mostly punk, rock, and electronica.

JAZZ, BLUES, AND FOLK

Club Passim

Map 7, D5. 47 Palmer St, Harvard Square ©492-7679; *www.clubpassim.com*. Harvard Ⓣ.

Folkie hangout where Joan Baez and Suzanne Vega got their starts. World music and spoken word performances in windowed basement setting.

House of Blues

Map 7, D5. 96 Winthrop St, Cambridge ©491-2583; *www.hob.com*. Harvard Ⓣ.

The first in the corporate monolith spawned by the same evil geniuses that started the Hard Rock Cafe conglomerate. The faux-roadhouse decor and stiff, middle-class patrons are painfully inauthentic, but the *House* still features top blues acts.

Johnny D's

17 Holland St, Somerville ©776-2004; *www.johnnyds.com*. Davis Ⓣ.

A mixed bag with talent ranging from the sublime to the ordinary. Acts include garage bands, progressive jazz sextets, traditional blues artists, and some uncategorizables.

Regattabar

Map 7, D5. 1 Bennett St ©661-5000. Harvard Ⓣ.

This place draws top jazz acts, though, as its location in the swish *Charles Hotel* suggests, the atmosphere - and clientele - is decidedly sedate. Dress nicely and prepare to pay at least $10 cover; it's sometimes necessary to purchase tickets ahead of time.

Ryles

Map 7, G2. 212 Hampshire St, Cambridge ©876-9330; *www.rylesjazz.com*. Central Ⓣ.

Two levels of live music – swing and salsa upstairs, and smooth jazz and blues downstairs.

Scullers

Map 7, F7. 400 Soldiers Field Rd, Cambridge ©783-0090; *www.scullersjazz.com*.

Upscale jazz club in the *DoubleTree Guest Suites* draws five-star acts, including some of the stars of the contemporary jazz scene. Hop in a taxi to get here, as the walk along the river at night can be dodgy.

Wally's Cafe

Map 3, G8. 427 Massachusetts Ave, Roxbury ©424-1408; *www.wallyscafe.com*. Massachusetts Ⓣ.

This refreshingly unhewn bar hosts lively jazz and blues shows that draw a vibrant crowd. It gets pretty packed on weekends, but that's part of the experience. No cover.

Western Front

Map 7, G6. 343 Western Ave, Cambridge ©492-7772. Central Ⓣ.

The *Front* puts on rollicking jazz, blues, and reggae shows for a dance-crazy audience. Drinks are cheap, and the Jamaican food served on weekends is delectably authentic.

NIGHTCLUBS

Boston's **nightclubs** are mostly clustered in downtown's Theater District and around Kenmore Square, with a few prominent ones in Back Bay and the South End. Many of the venues in the latter neighborhoods are **gay clubs**, often the most happening places in town; for a complete listing see "Gay Boston," p.245. The music at clubs changes almost nightly; to keep apprised of what's on, check the "Calendar" section in Thursday's *Boston Globe* or the listings in the weekly *Boston Phoenix*. **Cover charges** are generally in the $5–10 range, though sometimes there's no cover at all. Boston's venues tend to be easily entered – no New York style selection at the door – though there is a tendency for bouncers to frown upon sneakers and jeans. Weekends, clubs can be overrun with suburban yuppies.

DOWNTOWN, BACK BAY, AND THE SOUTH END

The Big Easy

Map 3, E8. One Boylston Place ©351-7000. Boylston Ⓣ.
New bar and jazz club with a New Orleans theme; for the best people-watching go on a weeknight.

Club Europa/Buzz

Map 3, E9. 67 Stuart St ©267-8969; *www.buzzboston.com*. Boylston Ⓣ.
On the edge of the Theater District, this is one of Boston's better dance clubs. Most of the action is on the third floor; the second tends to be louder and more crowded. On Saturday night the club becomes "Buzz," long the most plugged-in gay disco in Boston.

Envy

Map 3, E8. 25 Boylston Place ©542-3689. Boylston Ⓣ.
The musical menu at this small, casual (but no baseball caps or sneakers, please) club ranges from classic alternative to Top 40 and high energy house, depending on which DJ happens to be on duty.

Pravda 116

Map 3, E8. 116 Boylston St ©482-7799. Boylston Ⓣ.

You'll hear everything from Eurohouse and classic dance hits to traditional Greek music at the small dance club tucked into the rear of this popular restaurant/bar (p.192).

The Roxy

Map 3, F7. 279 Tremont St ©338-7699. Boylston Ⓣ.

Located in the former grand ballroom of the *Tremont House* hotel, this Theater District club is a magnet for Eurotrash, who brave the most byzantine admission process – long queues, even in winter, and lots of doors – to gyrate to loud house, techno, and salsa music.

Sugar Shack

Map 3, E8. One Boylston Place ©351-2510. Boylston Ⓣ.

This perennial favorite with the collegiate set features a decor of fake broken windows. Dance to the sounds of the 1970s, 1980s and 1990s at this cheezy top-40 club, and discover what college guys look like without their baseball caps on the sweaty dance floor.

Yesterdays

Map 3, G6. 533 Washington St ©338-6999. Downtown Crossing Ⓣ.

Located on the fringe of Downtown Crossing near a cluster of abandoned grand old theaters, this bi-level club packs in the international poseur crowd for its mix of techno music.

KENMORE SQUARE AND THE FENWAY

Avalon

Map 6, C3. 15 Lansdowne St ©262-2424. Kenmore Ⓣ.

Avalon's 1500-person capacity makes it the biggest dance club in Boston, and any weekend night the place is positively jamming. The cavernous central floor is flanked on either side by bars. Sunday is gay night.

Gay nightclubs can be found starting on p.246.

Axis

Map 6, C3. 13 Lansdowne St ©262-2437; *www.axisboston.com*. Kenmore Ⓣ.

Adjacent to *Avalon* but with more techno and trance leanings. On certain nights, the two clubs open their doors to each other, forming one megaclub, check current listings.

Karma Club

Map 6, C3. 9 Lansdowne St ©421-9595. Kenmore Ⓣ.

This multi-roomed, faux-hip dance club aspires with limited success to a futuristic Hindu temple decor. Wednesday is gay night.

Lava Bar

Map 6, C2. 575 Commonwealth Ave ©267-7707; *www.lavabar.com*. Kenmore Ⓣ.

Glass-walled club in the unlikely location of the Kenmore Square *Howard Johnson's*. The music is primarily house – from high-energy Latin to ambient deep house and old school hip-hop – and the dancing covers a broad range, including breakdancing. Saturday is "Tabu," which caters to a lesbian crowd.

M-LXXX (M-80)

Map 6, A1. 967 Commonwealth Ave ©562-8800; *www.m80.com*. Boston University Ⓣ.

Boston's substantial pack of international students dances here to redubbed mainstream hits and foreign disco beats. Everyone's dressed to the nines and able to afford the exorbitant prices for drinks; there's also a $10 cover. Open Wed, Fri and Sat.

The Modern

Map 6, C3. 36 Lansdowne St ©351-2581. Kenmore Ⓣ.

Although *Mama Kin* once resided here, the *Modern* bears little resemblance to the legendary rock palace co-owned by Aerosmith; the plush forest-green velvet chairs, relaxed lounge atmosphere and variety of DJ nights make it hard to believe grungy bands once cut their teeth here.

Sophia's

Map 6, D3. 1270 Boylston St ©354-7001. Kenmore Ⓣ.

Lively dance club with a Latin beat. There's a roof to cool off on, plus a stylish downstairs restaurant serving Spanish tapas and full meals. No cover, but a strictly enforced dress code (no blue jeans or sneakers) keeps the crowd looking posh.

Performing arts and film

Boston's cultural scene is famously vibrant, and many of the city's artistic institutions are second to none in the US. Foremost among these is the Boston Symphony Orchestra, which gave its first concert on October 22, 1881; indeed Boston is arguably at its best in the classical music department, and there are many smaller but internationally known chamber and choral music groups – from the Boston Symphony Chamber Players to the Handel & Hayden Society – to shore up its reputation. The Boston Ballet is also considered world-class, though it's probably best known in Boston itself for its annual holiday production of *The Nutcracker.*

The **theater** here is quite active too, even if it is a shadow of its 1920s heyday, when more than forty playhouses were crammed into the **Theater District**, south of Boston Common. Boston remains a try-out city for Broadway productions, however, and smaller companies have an increasingly high visibility; it's a real treat to see a play or musical at one of the opulent old theaters such as the Colonial or Emerson Majestic. For current productions, check the listings in the *Boston Globe*'s Thursday "Calendar" section, *Boston Phoenix*, or the *Improper Bostonian*, or consult the Web sites listed on p.8.

The Theater District is described in detail on p.41.

The **film** scene is dominated by the Sony conglomerate, which runs several cinema multiplexes featuring major first-run movies. For foreign, independent, classic or cult cinema, you'll have to look mainly to other municipalities – Cambridge is best in this respect, though Brookline and Somerville have their own art-movie and rerun houses.

CLASSICAL MUSIC

Boston prides itself on being a sophisticated city of high culture, and nowhere does that show up more than in its proliferation of **orchestras** and **choral groups** and the venues that house them. This is helped in no small part by the presence of four of the foremost music academies in the nation: the Peabody Conservatory, the New England Conservatory, the Berklee College of Music, and the Longy School of Music across the river in Cambridge.

Berklee Performance Center

Map 6, F6. 135 Massachusetts Ave ©747-2261. Symphony Ⓣ.
Berklee College of Music's main performance center, known for its contemporary repertoire. Call ©747-8820 for information on free faculty and student concerts.

Isabella Stewart Gardner Museum

Map 6, A7. 280 The Fenway ©734-1359. Museum Ⓣ.
Chamber and classical concerts, including many debuts, are held regularly at 1.30pm on weekends in the museum's Tapestry Room. The $16 ticket price includes admission to the museum.

Chamber Music Ensembles

Boston has a formidable range of **chamber music** groups, many affiliated with the local universities. Except where otherwise noted, the companies perform at various venues; check the usual listings sources for concert information, or call the groups directly.

Alea III (©353-3340) and **Boston Musica Viva** (©354-6910). Two regulars at BU's Tsai Performance Center.

Boston Baroque (©484-9200). One of the country's oldest Baroque orchestras.

Boston Camerata (©262-2092). Regular performances of choral and chamber concerts, from medieval to early American, at various locations.

Boston Chamber Music Society (©422-0086). This society has soloists of international renown; they perform in Jordan Hall and the Sanders Theater at Harvard.

Boston Symphony Chamber Players (©266-1492). The only permanent chamber group sponsored by a major symphony orchestra and made up of its members; they perform at Jordan Hall.

The Cantata Singers & Ensemble (©267-6502). Boston's premier choral group, which also performs at Jordan Hall.

Handel & Hayden Society (©262-1815). Performing chamber and choral music since 1815, these distinguished artists can be heard at Symphony Hall.

Pro Arte Chamber Orchestra (©661-7067). Cooperatively run chamber orchestra in which musicians have full control. Sunday afternoon concerts in Harvard's Sanders Theater.

Jordan Hall

Map 6, E6. 30 Gainsborough St ©536-2412. Symphony Ⓣ.

The impressive concert hall of the New England Conservatory, just one block west from Symphony Hall, is the venue for many chamber music performances as well as those by the Boston Philharmonic (©868-6696).

Museum of Fine Arts

Map 6, B7–C7. 465 Huntington Ave ©369-3300. Museum Ⓣ.

During the summer, the MFA's "Concerts in the Courtyard" take place each Wednesday at 7.30pm; a variety of indoor performances are also scheduled for the rest of the year.

Symphony Hall

Map 6, F6. 301 Massachusetts Ave ©266-2378 for concert information or 1-800/274-8499 for tickets. Symphony Ⓣ.

This is the regal, acoustically perfect venue for the Boston Symphony Orchestra; the famous Boston Pops concerts happen in May and June; in July and August, the BSO retreats to Tanglewood, in the Berkshires.

Tsai Performance Center

Map 6, A1. 685 Commonwealth Ave ©353-8724. Boston University Ⓣ.

Improbably tucked into Boston University's School of Management, this mid-sized hall is a frequent venue for chamber music performances, prominent lecturers, and plays; events are often affiliated with BU and either free or very inexpensive.

DANCE

The longest-running **dance** company in the city is the **Boston Ballet** (©695-6950), with an unparalleled reputation in America and beyond. The troupe performs at the Wang Center (p.241). For a more modern take, **Dance Umbrella** (©482-7570) represents and promotes a number of contemporary acts, and most often performs at the Emerson Majestic (see opposite).

THEATER

It's quite possible to pay dearly for a night at the **theater**. Tickets to the bigger shows range from $25 to $75 depending on the seat, and there is, of course, the potential of a pre- or post-theater meal (see p.184 for restaurants in the Theater District). Your best option is to pay a visit to **Bostix** (©482-BTIX) – a half-price, day-of-show ticket outlet as well as a Ticketmaster center at three locations: Faneuil Hall (Tues–Sat 10am–6pm, Sun 11am–4pm), Copley Square (Mon–Sat 10am–6pm, Sun 11am–4pm), and the Holyoke Center in Harvard Square (same hours as Copley Square). The half-price tickets here go on sale at 11am, and only cash is accepted. For full price tickets, you may also phone **Ticketmaster** (©931-2000) or contact the individual theater directly in advance of the performance. The **smaller venues** tend to showcase more offbeat and affordable productions; shows can be under $10 – though you shouldn't bank on that.

MAJOR VENUES

American Repertory Theater at the Loeb Drama Center

Map 7, C5. 64 Brattle St ©547-8300. Harvard Ⓣ.

Excellent theater near Harvard Square known for staging plays by big names like Shaw and Wilde as well as postmodern heavyweights like Ionesco and Stoppard.

Charles Playhouse

Map 3, D8. 74 Warrenton St ©426-6912. Boylston Ⓣ.

The Charles has two stages, one of which is more or less the permanent home of *Shear Madness*, a participatory, comic murder mystery that's now the longest-running non-musical in American theater. The other stage hosts somewhat edgier material.

Colonial Theatre

Map 3, E8. 106 Boylston St ©931-2787. Boylston Ⓣ.
Built in 1900 and since refurbished, this is the glittering grande dame of Boston theaters, known primarily for its Broadway-scale productions.

Emerson Majestic Theatre

Map 3, E8. 221 Tremont St ©824-8727. Boylston Ⓣ.
Emerson College, a communications and arts school, took stewardship of this 1903 Beaux Arts beauty in 1983. A lavish venue, with its soaring Rococo ceiling and Neoclassical friezes, it hosts productions of the Emerson Stage company, the Boston Lyric Opera and Dance Umbrella.

Huntington Theatre Company

Map 6, F6. 264 Huntington Ave ©266-0800. Symphony Ⓣ.
Productions here range from the classic to the contemporary, but they are consistently well-staged at this small playhouse, the official theater of Boston University.

Shubert Theatre

Map 3, E9. 265 Tremont St ©482-9393. Boylston Ⓣ.
Stars from Sir Laurence Olivier to Kathleen Turner have played the Shubert at some point in their careers; today the 1680-seat theater accommodates mostly big Broadway-style productions.

Wang Center for the Performing Arts

Map 3, E9. 270 Tremont St ©482-9393. Boylston Ⓣ.
The biggest performance center in Boston opened in 1925 as the Metropolitan Theater, a movie house of palatial

proportions – its original Italian marble, gold leaf ornamentation, crystal chandeliers, and 3800 seats all remain. The Boston Ballet (✆695-6950) is headquartered here; when their season ends, Broadway musicals often take center stage.

Wilbur Theatre

Map 3, E8. 246 Tremont St ✆423-4008. Boylston Ⓣ.

A Streetcar Named Desire, starring Marlon Brando and Jessica Tandy, debuted in this small Colonial Revival theater before going to Broadway, and the Wilbur has been working on trying to live up to that production ever since. In winter, avoid the seats toward the back, where the loud, old heating system may leave you straining to hear.

SMALL VENUES

Boston Center for the Arts

Map 6, K7. 539 Tremont St ✆426-5000. Back Bay Ⓣ.

Several theater troupes, many experimental, stage productions at the BCA, which incorporates a series of small venues on a single South End property. One of these is the Cyclorama Building, originally built to house a monumental painting called *The Battle of Gettysburg* (see p.91).

Hasty Pudding Theatre

Map 7, D5. 12 Holyoke St ✆495-5205. Harvard Ⓣ.

Harvard University's Hasty Pudding Theatricals troupe, one of the country's oldest, mounts one show per year (usually a musical comedy; Feb & March) at this theater, then hits the road, after which the Cambridge Theatre Company takes over.

Institute of Contemporary Art Theatre

Map 6, G4. 955 Boylston St ✆927-6620. Hynes Ⓣ.

Count on the unconventional at the theater of the ICA, Boston's leading venue for all things postmodern and cutting-edge.

Lyric Stage

Map 6, K4. 140 Clarendon St ©437-7172. Copley Ⓣ.

Both premieres and modern adaptations of classic and lesser-known American plays take place at this small theater within the big YWCA building.

Terrace Room

Map 3, C9. *Park Plaza Hotel*, 64 Arlington St ©423-8632. Arlington Ⓣ.

An intimate space for small but worthwhile productions of musical comedies and other crowd pleasers like *Café Teatro*, a flamenco dance show.

FILM

In Boston, as in any other large American city, it's easy enough to catch general release **films** – the usual listings sources carry all the details you need. If you're looking for out-of-the-ordinary film fare, however, you'll have to venture out a bit from the center. Whatever you're going to see, admission will cost you about $8, though matinees before 6pm can be considerably cheaper. You can call ©333-FILM for automated film listings.

Brattle Theater

Map 7, D5. 40 Brattle St ©876-6837. Harvard Ⓣ.

A historic cinema that pleasantly looks its age. They have thematic film series plus occasional author appearances and readings.

Coolidge Corner Moviehouse

Map 2, D5. 290 Harvard St, Brookline ©734-2500. Coolidge Corner Ⓣ.

Film buffs flock to this classic theater for foreign and independent movies. The interior has balconies and is adorned with Art Deco murals.

Harvard Film Archive

Map 7, D5. Carpenter Center, 24 Quincy St ©495-4700. Harvard Ⓣ.
A mixed bag of artsy, foreign, and experimental films.

Kendall Square Cinema

Map 7, J3. One Kendall Square, Cambridge ©494-9800. Kendall Ⓣ.
All the neon decoration, cramped seating, and small screens of your average multiplex, but this one has the area's widest selection of first-rate foreign and independent films.

Museum of Fine Arts Theater

Map 6, B7–C7. 465 Huntington Ave ©267-9300. Museum Ⓣ.
Offbeat art films and documentaries, mostly by locals, and often accompanied by lectures from the filmmaker.

Somerville Theatre

55 Davis Square, Somerville ©625-5700. Davis Ⓣ.
Wacky home for camp, classic, cult, independent and foreign and first-run pictures. Also doubles as a venue for live music. It's way out there – in more ways than one – past Cambridge, but well worth the trip.

Sony Nickelodeon

Map 6, A1. 606 Commonwealth Ave ©424-1500. Kenmore Ⓣ.
Originally an art-flick place, now taken over by the Sony group, but it features the better of the first-run features.

Gay Boston

For a town with a Puritan heritage and long-entrenched Blue Laws, it may come as some surprise that Boston happens to be one of the more gay-friendly cities on the East Coast. Much of the action centers around the South End, a largely residential neighborhood whose gay businesses (primarily restaurants and cafés) are concentrated on a short stretch of Tremont Street above Union Park. There's a sense of community here not found elsewhere in Boston – the occasional gay pride flag flies openly, and same sex couples sit together on their stoops to enjoy summer nights along with the rest of the diverse neighborhood.

Adjacent to the South End, on the other side of Arlington Street, is tiny **Bay Village**, home to most of the gay bars and clubs in the city. Largely leftist Cambridge, at least around Harvard Square, meanwhile, is known for being gay-friendly, though with few established gay venues.

Although the city's gay nightlife does range from leathermen at the *Ramrod* to cocktail-swilling guppies at *Club Cafe*, it remains small and fairly concentrated; the **lesbian club scene**, meanwhile, is almost non-existent.

In the summer, the Charles River Esplanade between Dartmouth and Fairfield streets, at the northern perimeter of Back Bay, is a popular spot for cruising. Footbridges lead from the end of both streets over Storrow Drive to a narrow urban beach alongside the river. You can't swim in the Charles, but it's more than acceptable to **sun yourself** in a bathing suit here. The area can get a bit dodgy at night, as can the rest of the Esplanade.

INFORMATION AND RESOURCES

Boston's two free **gay newspapers** are *in newsweekly* (*www.innewsweekly.com*) and *Bay Windows* (*www.baywindows.com*). The latter is one of two good sources of **club information**, the other being the gay-friendly alternative paper, *The Boston Phoenix* (see p.7). All can be found in various venues and bookstores, notably Glad Day Bookstore, 673 Boylston St, and We Think the World of You, 540 Tremont St. In Glad Day's vestibule is a gay community bulletin board, with postings for apartment rentals, club happenings, and so forth. Other **resources** for the gay community include the Gay and Lesbian Helpline (©267-9001), a general information source; the AIDS Action Hotline (©1-800/235-2331 or 536-7733); and Fenway Community Health Center, 7 Haviland St (©267-0159), which offers HIV testing during weekdays. If you're looking for a **travel agent** to book your trip to or from Boston, the Travel Alternatives Group (©1-800/464-2987) will route your call to your nearest gay-friendly agent.

BARS, CLUBS, AND CAFÉS

Many of Boston's more popular clubs designate one or two nights a week as gay nights. Significant gay nights at clubs around Boston include *Karma Club* (Weds), *Campus/Manray* (Thurs), *Buzz* (Sat), and *Avalon* (Sun); see "Nightlife," p.227, for further details on these venues. Saturday night's Tabu at the *Lava Bar* is the hottest lesbian spot in town. For those night owls who haven't gotten their fill of dancing after the clubs close, ask around for an invite to Boston's hush-hush after-hours private party – currently known as "Ryse" – a stomping ground for gays and straights alike.

Campus/ManRay

Map 7, I5. 21 Brookline St ©864-0400; *www.manrayclub.com*. Central Ⓣ.

One massive space with five bars, two dance floors and two very different theme nights. *Campus* (Thurs & Sat) is relatively wholesome, with many J. Crew types and plenty of straights. The rest of the week, the club is *ManRay*, a fetish-and-bondage fest, replete with leather and dominatrixes galore.

Chaps

Map 6, L4. 100 Warrenton St ©422-0862; *www.chapsofboston.com*. Arlington Ⓣ.

The biggest and flashiest gay disco in town features a bar and lounge area (open from 1pm daily) as well as a cavernous dance room with two additional bars. Sounds range from house and techno to oldies and Latin; call ahead to see what's on the menu. Dancing starts at 10pm nightly; the cover varies.

Club Café/Moonshine

Map 6, J6. 209 Columbus Ave ©536-0966. Back Bay Ⓣ.

A combination restaurant, video bar (*Moonshine*) and club, the latter of which attracts jazz acts; home to a variety of South End guppies.

Eagle

Map 6, L7. 520 Tremont St ©542-4494. Back Bay Ⓣ.

Neighborhood bar whose eagle-bedecked interior has the looks of a biker hangout; the crowd is especially outgoing. A live DJ spins house and top 40 on the weekends; his recorded sessions are played back on weeknights.

Francesca's Espresso Bar

Map 6, K7. 565 Tremont St ©482-9026. Back Bay Ⓣ.

A great place to check out the Tremont Street crowd passing by the plate-glass windows, this coffee shop gets packed in the evenings before clubs open, with a largely gay clientele caffeinating itself for a night out.

Fritz

Map 6, L6. 26 Chandler St ©482-4428. Back Bay Ⓣ.

South End bar below *Chandler Inn*; the trophy-filled decor doesn't stop it from attracting a nice mix of casually attired locals and visitors.

Jacque's

Map 3, E8. 79 Broadway ©338-7472. Boylston Ⓣ.

Priscilla, Queen of the Desert invades New England at this drag dream where the action gets so intense they have to close at 2am. The scene: past-it divas lip-synch *I Love the Nightlife*, while youngsters explore gender issues and transvestive/ transexual prostitutes peddle their wares. Bring the family!

Luxor

Map 6, L4. 69 Church St ©423-6969. Arlington Ⓣ.

Downstairs is a plain gay sports bar; upstairs, a popular gay video bar with a modern finish. A good place to drink and cruise, with a small lounge area to the right of the main barroom offering a place to relax with friends.

Machine

Map 6, E4. 1254 Boylston St ©266-2986. Kenmore Ⓣ.

A favorite with the gay crowd, especially on Fridays when the club's large dance floor and top-notch music has the place pumping. The pool tables and bar near the dance floor let you take a breather and soak up the scene.

Mildred's

Map 6, K7. 552 Tremont St ©426-0008. Back Bay Ⓣ.

Another café in the heart of the South End popular with those preparing to hit the club scene as well as with those for whom this is the scene.

Ramrod

Map 6, E4. 1254 Boylston St ©266-2986; *www.ramrodboston.com*. Kenmore Ⓣ.

This Fenway meat market attracts a pretty hungry crowd with its strictly enforced Levi/leather dress code (Fri & Sat) – no shirts nor cologne allowed. Not quite as hardcore as it sounds, as it's directly upstairs from the harmless *Machine*.

Shopping

Though Boston has its share of chain stores and typical mall fare, there are plenty of unusual and funky places to shop here. The city is perhaps best loved for its bookstores, having established somewhat of a reputation as a literary haven and academic center, but on a more modern – and fashionable – note it has also become known for its small, exclusive boutiques that feature the work of local designers.

To read about Boston's literary past, see p.310.

No matter what you're looking for, Boston is an extremely pleasant place to shop for it, with unique, high-quality stores clustered on atmospheric streets like **Charles**, in Beacon Hill, and **Newbury**, in Back Bay. The former has a dense concentration of antique shops, while the latter is an eight-block stretch that starts off quite trendy and upmarket, then begins to cater to more of a student population as it moves west past Exeter Street where record stores and novelty shops take over, a theme continued out to **Kenmore Square**. This span also has its fair share of big bookstores, but the best are clustered in and around **Harvard Square**, across the Charles River in Cambridge.

Otherwise, most of the action takes place in various downtown quarters, first and foremost at the **Faneuil Hall**

Marketplace. This area has become more commercialized over the years, but there's still enough homespun boutiques, plus the many food stalls of **Quincy Market**, to make a trip here worthwhile. To the south, **Downtown Crossing**, at Washington and Summer streets, is centered on **Filene's Basement**, a bargain-hunter's delight for marked-down brand-name clothing.

Stores are generally open 9.30am or 10am to 6pm or 7pm Mon through Sat (sometimes later on Tues & Wed) and Sun noon to 6pm.

Shopping by category

ANTIQUES

Cunha, St John and Vining

Map 3, B3. 131 Charles St ©720-7808. Charles Ⓣ.

Tucked away on the first floor of a recessed building, it's easy to miss, but inside is a varied array of Continental antiques – eighteenth- and nineteenth-century English, Italian and French – and nineteenth-century Chinese formal pieces.

Judith Dowling Asian Art

Map 3, B3. 133 Charles St ✆523-5211. Charles Ⓣ.

A first-rate selection of Asian pieces from all periods, at prices that encourage browsing rather than buying.

Marcoz Antiques

Map 6, I3. 177 Newbury St ✆262-0780. Arlington Ⓣ.

An atmospheric antiques boutique with French, English, and American furniture and accessories.

Twentieth Century Limited

Map 3, B4. 73 Charles St ✆742-1031. Charles Ⓣ.

Antique pieces from the early twentieth century, with a focus on American Art Deco and works from the Roaring Twenties.

BOOKSTORES

Boston has a history as a literary city, enhanced by its numerous universities as well as the many traces of authors and publishing houses that once called it home. This legacy is well-reflected in the quality and diversity of **bookstores** found both in Boston and neighboring Cambridge.

For reviews of books written about or set in Boston, see p.313.

NEW

Barnes & Noble

Map 3, H4. Downtown Crossing ✆426-5502. Downtown Crossing Ⓣ.

Map 6, C2. 660 Beacon St ✆267-8484. Kenmore Ⓣ.

Two large outposts of the national bookstore chain, with a decent newsstand and a good selection of bargain books and calendars. The one on Beacon Street is topped off by the neon Citgo sign (p.94).

Brookline Booksmith

Map 2, D5. 279 Harvard St ©566-6660. Coolidge Corner Ⓣ.

With its hardwood floors and friendly staff, this cozy shop doesn't seem to have a particular specialty, but it's friendly staff makes it perfect for browsing; holds a good author-reading series, too.

Harvard Book Store

Map 7, E5. 1256 Massachusetts Ave ©661-1515. Harvard Ⓣ.

Three huge rooms of new books upstairs, a basement for used volumes and remainders downstairs. Academic and critical work in the humanities and social sciences dominate, with a healthy dose of fiction thrown in.

Trident Booksellers & Café

Map 6, G4. 338 Newbury St ©267-8688. Copley Ⓣ.

A preferred lair of Back Bay's New-Agers. If the aroma of one too many essential oils doesn't deter you, buy an obscure magazine and pretend to read it over coffee in the café (see p.224).

USED

Avenue Victor Hugo Bookshop

Map 6, G4. 339 Newbury St ©266-7746. Hynes Ⓣ.

One of Boston's best used bookstores, this upper Newbury fixture is the place to find recent editions at unbeatable prices. Vintage postcards and back issues of *Life* and other American magazines, dating from 1854 to the present, also fill the stacks.

Brattle Book Shop

Map 3, H4. 9 West St ©542-0210. Downtown Crossing Ⓣ.

In these fairly dingy digs is one of the oldest antiquarian bookstores in the country. Three levels, with a good selection of yellowing travel guides on the second.

Bryn Mawr Books

Map 7, A3. 373 Huron Ave ✆661-1770. Porter Ⓣ.

This neighborhood bookstore vends used titles in a friendly, relaxed Cambridge setting. Weather permitting, there are sidewalk displays for pedestrian browsers.

House of Sarah

Map 7, G2. 1309 Cambridge St ✆547-3447. Central Ⓣ.

A wacky Inman Square spot in which to peruse used fiction and scholarly work – sit in an overstuffed red couch and look up at various stuffed creatures hanging from the ceiling. You may find a 25¢ copy of a Danielle Steele novel or some remaindered Foucault, and there are often coffee and snacks, compliments of the proprietors.

Starr Bookshop

Map 7, E5. 29 Plympton St ✆547-6864. Harvard Ⓣ.

A bit like a library hit by a tornado, with books lying about or spilling over desks and tables, but if you're patient – or ask for help – you can find great discounts on literature and art criticism.

TRAVEL

Boston Globe Store

Map 3, H4. 1 School St ✆367-4000. Park Ⓣ.

Small shop in the historic Old Corner Bookstore (see p.22) building with New England travel guidebooks, Internet access, and lots of stuff emblazoned with the *Boston Globe* logo.

Globe Corner Bookstore

Map 6, K4. 500 Boylston St ✆859-8008. Copley Ⓣ.

Map 7, D5. 28 Church St ✆497-6277. Harvard Ⓣ.

These travel specialists are well stocked with maps, travel literature and guidebooks, with an especially strong New England section.

Willowbee & Kent

Map 6, K4. 519 Boylston St ©437-6700. Copley Ⓣ.
The first floor of this roomy store has a good range of travel guidebooks and gear; the second is given over to a travel agency.

GAY AND LESBIAN

Glad Day Bookshop

Map 6, J4. 673 Boylston St ©267-3010. Copley Ⓣ.
This second-floor gay bookstore is easily recognized from the sidewalk by the big rainbow flag in the window. A good selection of reasonably priced books, cards, and pornography, and a vast community bulletin board at the entrance.

We Think the World of You

Map 6, K7. 540 Tremont St ©423-1965. Back Bay Ⓣ.
With its cool music and good selection of international magazines, this bright, upscale South End gay bookstore invites lingering.

SPECIALTY

Grolier Poetry Bookstore

Map 7, E5. 6 Plympton St ©547-4648. Harvard Ⓣ.
Diminutive store specializing in in-print poetry. With 14,000 volumes of verse, it has gained an international following among poets and their fans, and it hosts frequent readings.

Lucy Parsons Center

Map 6, G8. 549 Columbus Ave ©267-6272. Mass Ave Ⓣ.
The radical left lives on in this shrine to socialism, with a

particular bent toward women's issues, labor issues and radical economics. They also have plenty of free pamphlets on local demonstrations, and occasional readings and lectures.

New Words

Map 7, H5. 186 Hampshire St ✆876-5310. Central Ⓣ.
Well-organized feminist bookstore with tons of books on history criticism, lesbian studies, and the like. It also serves as a community center for women's issues and feminist events.

Nini's Corner/Out of Town News

Map 7, D5. Harvard Square. Harvard Ⓣ.
These two good, old-fashioned newsstands lie directly across from each other in the heart of Harvard Square. Few published magazines cannot be found at one of these two spots.

CLOTHES

DESIGNER STORES

Alan Bilzerian

Map 6, K3. 34 Newbury St ✆536-1001. Arlington Ⓣ.
International haute couture from Jean-Paul Gaultier and Comme des Garçons alongside the owner's own label. Menswear and accessories occupy the first floor and womenswear the second; clubwear roosts in a small basement section.

Allston Beat

Map 6, F4. 348 Newbury St ✆421-9555. Hynes Ⓣ.
This small but dense fashion den may exceed the vinyl per square foot limit – cutting-edge designer wear, ogled by teenagers too young to afford it and others too old to wear it.

Gypsy Moon

Map 7, B2. 1780 Massachusetts Ave ©876-7095. Porter Ⓣ.

For the well-dressed Wiccan, eccentric women's wear sold by a staff that can help you look your best at the next coven meeting.

House of Culture

Map 6, G4. 286 Newbury St ©236-1090. Copley Ⓣ.

Even if you're not in the market for local designer Patrick Petty's trendy creations, nip into his suave shop to browse around and pick up flyers on club happenings.

Jet Screamer

Map 7, B2. 1735 Massachusetts Ave ©661-8826. Porter Ⓣ.

Aggressively hip shoe boutique aimed mostly at women, with everything from formal leather shoes to glittery silver platforms.

J. Press

Map 7, D5. 82 Mt Auburn St ©547-9886. Harvard Ⓣ.

Old Harvard lives on in J. Press' sober collection of high quality men's suits; rates are mid-level ($400–1000 per suit) for the store's genteel clientele.

Louis, Boston

Map 6, H4. 234 Berkeley St ©262-6100. Arlington Ⓣ.

Occupying a stately, freestanding building from 1863 that once housed Boston's Museum of Natural History (which became the Museum of Science), this is Boston's classiest and most expensive clothes emporium. Though mostly geared toward men, the top floor is reserved for designer womenswear.

Riccardi

Map 6, I3. 116 Newbury St ©266-3158. Arlington Ⓣ.

The hippest designer schmatta shop in Boston could hold its

own in Paris or New York. A few of the labels on parade are Dolce & Gabbana, Romeo Gigli, and Jean-Paul Gaultier.

Suzanne

Map 6, J3. 81 Newbury St ©266-4146. Arlington Ⓣ.

Women's special occasion apparel by leading international designers such as Montana and Thierry Mugler.

CHAIN STORES

Burberrys

Map 6, L3. 2 Newbury St ©236-1000. Arlington Ⓣ.

The famously conservative British clothier seems right at home in its four-story Newbury Street digs, across from the *Ritz-Carlton*.

Patagonia

Map 6, G4. 346 Newbury St ©424-1776. Hynes Ⓣ.

Patagonia invented the soft, synthetic fleece called "Synchilla," and there's still no better way to fend off a Boston winter than in a jacket or vest lined with the colorful stuff.

USED AND THRIFT

The Closet Upstairs

Map 6, H3. 223 Newbury St ©267-5757. Copley Ⓣ.

The most atmospheric of Newbury Street's numerous retro clothes stores, this oversized second-floor closet is stuffed with everything from silly hats to designer shoes.

Dollar-a-Pound

Map 7, J3. 200 Broadway ©876-1122. Kendall Ⓣ.

Warehouse full of bins crammed with used togs. If you have the time to sift through the leftovers of twentieth-century fashion, you'll happen upon some great bargains – all at the rate of $1.50 per pound of clothing. On Fridays that's reduced to 50¢.

Mass Army & Navy Store

Map 6, G4. 895 Boylston St ©267-1559. Hynes Ⓣ.
You can stock up on camouflage duds and combat boots at this military surplus store, and there's also a good and inexpensive range of (mostly men's) pants, shirts, and shoes worth inspecting.

Oona's

Map 7, E5. 1210 Massachusetts Ave ©491-2654. Harvard Ⓣ.
Since 1972, Oona has been the place to find vintage "experienced clothing" – in this case kimonos, flapper dresses, leather jackets, and various accessories.

CRAFTS

Beadworks

Map 6, G4. 349 Newbury St ©247-7227. Hynes Ⓣ.
With so many kinds of beads, it's a good thing sales staff can assist you in creating a "distinctly personal adornment." Buttons too.

The Cambridge Artists' Cooperative

Map 7, D5. 59A Church St ©868-4434. Harvard Ⓣ.
Three floors fill this Harvard Square shop with all kinds of crafts, from woodcarvings and glass sculptures to wearable art and beaded bags.

Rugg Road Paper Co

Map 3, B3. 105 Charles St ©742-0002. Charles Ⓣ.
They've got fancy paper products of all kinds, including lovely cards, stationery, and wrapping paper.

Simon Pearce

Map 6, J3. 115 Newbury St ✆450-8388. Arlington Ⓣ.
Hand-blown glassware from Irish-born, Vermont-based craftsman.

FOOD AND DRINK

BAKERIES

Bova's Bakery

Map 4, D4. 76 Prince St ✆523-5601. Haymarket Ⓣ.
The North End's all-night bakery, vending delights like plain and chocolate cannolis, oven-fresh cakes and whoopie pies, is famously cheap, with most items around $5.

LMNOP Bakery

Map 3, C9. 79 Park Plaza ✆338-4220. Arlington Ⓣ.
Purveyor of bread to neighboring restaurants, this hideaway is the best gourmet bakery in Boston. Besides those breads, pastries and cookies, they also have great sandwiches and pasta specials at lunchtime.

Mike's Pastry

Map 4, E5. 300 Hanover St ✆742-3050. Haymarket Ⓣ.
The famed North End bakery is one part Italian and two parts American, meaning in addition to cannoli and tiramisu, you'll find countersfull of brownies and cookies. The homemade ice cream is not to be missed.

Panini

Map 7, E2. 406 Washington St ✆666-2770. #86 bus.
Baguettes and bruschetta, desserts and Danishes – *Panini* offers a diverse array of baked goods, all created on the premises. It's hard to find a place to sit on weekends.

Rosie's Bakery

Map 7, G2. 243 Hampshire St ©491-9488. #69 bus.
This bakery features the richest, most decadent desserts in Cambridge. Their specialty is a fudge brownie called the "chocolate orgasm," though the less provocatively named lemon squares are just as good.

GOURMET FOOD AND WINE SHOPS

Barsamian's

Map 7, F5. 1030 Massachusetts Ave ©661-9300. Harvard or Central Ⓣ.
Gourmet meats, cheeses, coffee and bread plus a great range of desserts, including the best tart in Cambridge.

Formaggio Kitchen

Map 7, A4. 244 Huron Ave ©354-4750. Harvard Square Ⓣ.
Although regarded as one of the best cheese shops in Boston, the gourmet meats, salads, sandwiches, and baked goods here are also worth sampling.

Monica's Salumeria

Map 4, C5. 130 Salem St ©742-4101. Haymarket Ⓣ.
Lots of imported Italian cheeses, cooked meats, cookies, and pastas.

Polcari's Coffee

Map 4, B6. 105 Salem St ©227-0786. Haymarket Ⓣ.
Old and fusty, but brimming with coffees as well as every spice you could think of. Worth going inside for the aroma alone.

Savenor's

Map 3, B3. 160 Charles St ©723-6328. Charles Ⓣ.
Known for its meats, this small gourmet food shop in Beacon

Hill also has a better-than-average produce selection, in addition to prepared foods – ideal for taking to the nearby Charles River Esplanade for an impromptu picnic.

See Sun Co

Map 3, G7. 19 Harrison St ©426-0954. Chinatown Ⓣ.

The most accessible of Chinatown's markets, has all the basics – like huge bags of rice and a dizzying range of See Sun soy sauces – as well as more exotic delicacies like duck's feet.

V. Cirace & Sons

Map 4, D6. 173 North St ©227-3193. North Station Ⓣ.

A great liquor store, with the expected range of Italian wines – it's in the North End, after all – and much more.

HEALTH FOOD

Bread & Circus

Map 6, F6. 15 Westland Ave ©375-1010. Symphony Ⓣ.

The Boston branch of this New England wholefoods chain, near Symphony Hall, has all the alternative foodstuffs you'd expect, plus one of the best salad bars in town.

Nature Food Centers GNC

Map 6, I4. 545 Boylston St ©536-1226. Copley Ⓣ.

If you're looking for vitamin-enriched fruit juices, organic produce, and other healthful items, this small store in Copley Square is bound to have it.

GALLERIES

Dozens of Boston's major **art galleries** can be found on Newbury Street; most are generally browser-friendly. South Street, in downtown's so-called Leather District, tends to feature the most contemporary work.

For information on the Arts Festival of Boston and the Boston Open Studios Coalition, see "Festivals," p.287.

Alianza

Map 6, K3. 154 Newbury St ©262-2385. Arlington Ⓣ.

An artsy American crafts gallery where the strong suits are creative ceramics, glass work, and jewelry, with funky sculptural clocks and picture frames as well.

Arden Gallery

Map 6, K3. 129 Newbury St ©247-0610. Arlington Ⓣ.

Arden's focus is on abstractionist contemporary paintings, vivid examples of which are displayed in the oversized second-story bowfront window.

Galerie Europeenne

Map 6, K3. 123 Newbury St ©859-7062. Arlington Ⓣ.

Always something interesting on display – contemporary, figurative and abstract painting – all by living European artists.

Gallery NAGA

Map 6, L3. 67 Newbury St ©267-9060. Arlington Ⓣ.

Contemporary painting, sculpture, studio furniture, and photography from Boston and New England artists, located in the Gothic Revival Church of the Covenant (see p.80).

International Poster Gallery

Map 6, J3. 205 Newbury St ©375-0076. Copley Ⓣ.

More than 6000 posters on display from 1895 through World War II.

Mario Diacono Gallery

Map 3, I8. 207 South St ©350-3054. South Station Ⓣ.
Artist-specific shows, of a contemporary nature, on a rotating basis. Call ahead; the gallery has unpredictable hours.

The Society of Arts and Crafts

Map 6, K3. 175 Newbury St ©266-1810. Arlington Ⓣ.
The oldest non-profit crafts group in America has two floors here. The first is its commercial outpost, with a wide range of ceramics, glass and jewelry. The second floor is reserved for themed (and free) special exhibitions.

MALLS AND DEPARTMENT STORES

MALLS

CambridgeSide Galleria

Map 7, L1. 100 Cambridgeside Place ©621-8666. Kendall Ⓣ.
Not too different from any other large American shopping mall. The haze of neon and packs of hairsprayed teens can be exhausting, but there's no similarly dense and convenient conglomeration of shops in Cambridge.

Copley Place

Map 6, I5. 100 Huntington Ave ©375-4400. Copley Ⓣ.
This ambitious, upscale office-retail-residential complex features more than 100 stores and an 11-screen multiplex. The best of the shops are a Rizzoli bookshop, a Neiman Marcus department store, the gift shop for the Museum of Fine Arts, and the Artful Hand Gallery, representing solely American artists; the rest is pretty generic.

Faneuil Hall Marketplace

Map 3, I2. Faneuil Hall ©338-2323. Government Center Ⓣ.

The city's most famous market, with a hundred or so shops, plus next door's Quincy Market. It's a bit tourist-oriented, but still worth a trip (see p.32).

The Heritage on the Garden

Map 3, C8. Cnr of Arlington and Boylston sts ©423-0002. Arlington Ⓣ.

Not so much a mall as a very upscale mixed-use complex across from the Public Garden that consists of condos, restaurants, and boutiques. The latter include Arche Shoes, Escada, Sonia Rykiel, and St John boutiques, Villeroy Boch and Hermés.

The Shops at Prudential Center

Map 6, H5. 800 Boylston St ©267-1002. Prudential Ⓣ.

This is a fairly new conglomeration of a hundred or so mid-market shops, heavily patronized by local residents and conventioneers from the adjacent Hynes Convention Center who seem to genuinely enjoy buying commemorative T-shirts and ties from the center-atrium pushcarts.

DEPARTMENT STORES

Filene's

Map 3, G5. 426 Washington St ©357-2100. Downtown Crossing Ⓣ.

The merchandise inside downtown Boston's oldest department store is standard issue; the stunning 1912 Beaux Arts facade is not. You'll have better luck downstairs, in Filene's Basement.

Filene's Basement

Map 3, G5. 426 Washington St ©542-2011. Downtown Crossing Ⓣ.

Established in 1908, Filene's Basement is now a separate business from Filene's, though operating under debtor-in-possession status since the company filed for bankruptcy in

August of 1999. Still, nothing seems to diminish the flagship location's status as a Boston fixture. The discounted merchandise comes here not only from Filene's upstairs, but from other big-name department stores and a few Boston boutiques. The markdown system works like this: after 14 days, merchandise is discounted 25 percent, after 21 days, 50 percent and after 28 days, 75 percent. Anything that lasts more than 35 days goes to charity. Be warned: dressing rooms are communal.

The Harvard Coop

Map 7, D5. 1400 Massachusetts Ave ✆499-2000. Harvard Ⓣ.
Harvard's local department store, with a wide selection of fairly expensive insignia clothing and the like.

Lord & Taylor

Map 6, I4. 760 Boylston St ✆262-6000. Copley Ⓣ.
This human-scale department store is an excellent place to stock up on high-end basics, from sweaters and suits to jewelry and cosmetics.

Macy's East

Map 3, G5. 450 Washington St ✆357-3000. Downtown Crossing Ⓣ.
Much the generic urban department store, with all the basics covered, including a better-than-average cosmetics section and a men's department that outshines that of Filene's next door.

Neiman Marcus

Map 6, I5. 5 Copley Place ✆536-3660. Copley Ⓣ.
Part of a Texan chain, Neiman's is the most luxurious of Boston's department stores, with prices to match. Three levels, with an impressive menswear collection on the first.

NEW

Boston Beat

Map 6, G3. 279 Newbury St ✆247-2428. Hynes Ⓣ.

A first-floor store stocking lots of independent dance and techno labels.

Newbury Comics

Map 6, F4. 332 Newbury St ✆236-4930. Hynes Ⓣ.

Boston's biggest alternative record store carries lots of independent labels you won't find at the national chains along with a substantial array of vinyl, posters, 'zines, and kitschy T-shirts. It's also a good place to pick up flyers on local club happenings.

Nuggets

Map 6, B2. 486 Commonwealth Ave ✆536-0679. Kenmore Ⓣ.

American jazz, rock, and R&B are the strong suits at this venerable new and used record store.

Satellite

Map 6, F5. 49 Massachusetts Ave ✆536-5482. Hynes Ⓣ.

This storefront hideaway has a great selection of imported techno and trance, in both CD and vinyl format.

Tower Records

Map 6, F4. 360 Newbury St ✆247-5900. Hynes Ⓣ.

Typically vast representative of this music superstore chain, with a standard selection of popular music, as well as jazz, classical, world beat, and the like. The building itself started out as an early 1900s warehouse, but was given a postmodern eclectic overhaul by architect Frank Gehry in 1989. Word has it that a Virgin Megastore will take over ownership by 2001.

USED/VINTAGE

Cheapo

Map 7, H5. 645 Massachusetts Ave ✆354-4455. Central Ⓣ.

Narrow, two-story Cambridge shop stuffed with bargains on just about every genre of used music. Slogging through the dense collection will produce considerable discoveries.

Disc Diggers

401 Highland Ave, Somerville ✆776-7560. Davis Ⓣ.

The largest selection of used CDs in New England, though higher in quantity than quality. Forgotten albums by one-hit wonders abound.

Pipeline

Map 7, F2. 257 Washington St ✆591-0590. Bus #63.

This alluringly bizarre store defies categorization. Mainly used CDs and vinyl, particularly deep on indie and imports. Also new music, kitsch Americana, and videos of the Russ Meyer film ilk.

Planet Records

Map 7, D5. 54B JFK St ✆492-0693. Harvard Ⓣ.

Map 6, B2. 536 Commonwealth Ave ✆353-0693. Kenmore Ⓣ.

To buy that old Duran Duran or Styx LP missing from your collection – or to sell one you've listened to a tad too much – head to this basement, secondhand music shop in Harvard Square. Buys and sells CDs, too.

Skippy White's

Map 7, H5. 538 Massachusetts Ave ✆491-3345. Central Ⓣ.

Excellent collection of jazz, blues, R&B, gospel, funk, P-funk, funkadelic, and hip-hop. Hum a few bars and the salesfolk will guide you to the right section.

Stereo Jack's

Map 7, B2. 1686 Massachusetts Ave ©497-9447. Porter Ⓣ.
Jazz and blues specialists, mostly used, but with some new stuff too. CDs, tapes, and vinyl.

Twisted Village

Map 7, D5. 12 Eliot St ©354-6898. Harvard Ⓣ.
A really weird mix of fringe styles, among them avant-garde, beat, spoken word, and psychedelic rock.

SPECIALTY SHOPS

Black Ink

Map 3, B3. 101 Charles St ©723-3883. Charles Ⓣ.
Eclectic assortment of things you don't really need but are cool anyway: rubber stamps, a smattering of clothes, campy refrigerator magnets, and a panoply of Tintin paraphernalia.

Fresh 21st Century

Map 6, K3. 121 Newbury St ©421-1212. Arlington Ⓣ.
Pear Chocolate and Fig Apricot are only two varieties of the several sweet-sounding soaps you will find in this chic bath and body store. They carry over three hundred varieties of French milled soaps, lotions, oils, and makeup, packaged so exquisitely you won't want to open them.

Justin Tyme Emporium

Map 7, G6. 91 River St ©491-1088. Central Ⓣ.
Justin's is all about pop culture artifacts, featuring boffo American detritus like lava lamps, Donny and Marie Osmond pin-ups, and campy T-shirts with iron-ons.

Kakadu

Map 6, J3. 291 Newbury St ©437-6666. Arlington Ⓣ.

This uplifting shop offers brightly painted wooden houseware items from Israel and animal-themed ceramics from South Africa.

Koo de Kir

Map 3, B4. 34 Charles St ©723-8111. Charles Ⓣ.

Their motto, "Ars longa, vita brevis," reflects their sales philosophy – to make even the most everyday objects artistic and beautiful. For a pretty penny, you can buy such beautified *objets* here.

Leavitt and Pierce

Map 7, D5. 1316 Massachusetts Ave ©547-0576. Harvard Ⓣ.

Old-school tobacconists that have been around almost as long as Harvard. An outstanding selection of cigars, imported cigarettes, and smoking paraphernalia (lighters, rolling papers, ashtrays), plus an upstairs smoking loft right out of the carefree past.

The London Harness Company

Map 3, H5. 60 Franklin St ©542-9234. Downtown Crossing Ⓣ.

Chiefly known for its high quality luggage goods, this atmospheric shop reeks of traditional Boston – indeed, Ben Franklin used to shop here. They also vend a wide array of items like chess sets, clocks, candlesticks, and inlaid decorative boxes.

Loulou's Lost & Found

Map 6, I3. 121 Newbury St ©859-8593. Arlington Ⓣ.

They say Loulou scours the globe in search of such essentials as tableware embossed with French cruise ship logos and silverware from long-gone five-star restaurants. A fine place to indulge your inner Martha Stewart.

Marquis de Sade Emporium

Map 6, L5. 73 Berkeley St ©426-2120. Back Bay Ⓣ.

Proffering a wide range of leather items and hardcore sexual paraphernalia, this South End shop leaves little to the imagination.

Matsu

Map 6, H3. 259 Newbury St ©266-9707. Copley Ⓣ.

A hip little shop featuring a medium-sized range of sleek Japanese clothing, knickknacks (desk clocks, stationery, funky pens) and contemporary home decor items.

Million-Year Picnic

Map 7, D5. 99 Mt Auburn St ©492-6763. Harvard Ⓣ.

For the comic obsessive. Japanese anime and Superman, Tank Girl and Dilbert. Stronger on current stuff than old material. The staff has encyclopedic knowledge, and is tolerant of browsers.

Sherman's

Map 3, G5. 26 Province St ©482-9610. Downtown Crossing Ⓣ.

Forget those overpriced travel boutiques in the malls; this cavernous Downtown Crossing emporium stocks not only an impressive range of luggage but just about every travel gadget imaginable.

Union Shop

Map 3, D8. 356 Boylston St ©536-5651. Arlington Ⓣ.

The retail outpost of this long-established private social services organization features quality handmade household knickknacks, toys, wrapping paper, stationery, and a range of antiques.

Sports, fitness, and outdoor activities

Bostonians have an acute love–hate relationship with their professional sports teams, obsessing over the four major franchises – baseball's Red Sox, football's Patriots, basketball's Celtics, and hockey's Bruins – with evangelical fervor. After years of watching their teams narrowly miss championship bids, hope is extended cautiously here, even if the Celtics are one of the more storied franchises in their sport. Boston's sports fans have an admirable tenacity, following their teams closely through good seasons and bad; indeed, supporters seem to love bemoaning their teams' woes nearly as much as they do celebrating their victories. This lively, vocal fan base makes attending a game a great way to get a feel for the city. While the Patriots' Foxboro Stadium is located out of town and has little to recommend it, the new FleetCenter, where the Celtics and Bruins play, is at least conveniently situated if lacking the history of the classic old Boston Garden – demolished a few years back. For fans of baseball, there is no more essential pilgrimage than the one to the Red Sox' idiosyncratic Fenway Park.

If you're a fan of an opposing team going to a game to root against Boston, be warned: you're in store for censure – and perhaps even violence – from the local faithful.

Boston isn't a city where **participatory sports** thrive particularly well, due mostly to the area's often dreary weather. There are, however, more than a number of good areas for jogging, biking, rollerblading, and the like. The **Metropolitan District Commisson (MDC)**, 20 Somerset St (©727-9650), oversees most facilities.

BASEBALL

The Boston **Red Sox** have tormented fans with an uncanny ability to choke late in the season: they haven't won a World Series since 1918, although they've come extremely close on several occasions (see p.96). In more recent years, they lost some of their faithful by not re-signing longtime players Roger Clemens and Mo Vaughn; however, new superstars like Pedro Martinez and Nomar Garciaparra have more than compensated, and have attracted a more diverse fan base, especially Dominicans, who revel in Martinez' pitching mastery. The pair have helped the Red Sox not just stay competitive, but make the playoffs as recently as 1999.

Even when the the Red Sox aren't performing so well, it's worth going to a game just to see **Fenway Park**, at 24 Yawkey Way (Map 6, 3B–3C), one of America's sports treasures. It's the oldest baseball stadium in the country, and one of bizarre dimensions – best represented by the abnormally tall (37ft) left-field wall, dubbed the "Green Monster." Though grandstand tickets can cost $28 or so, a bleacher seat is around $14–20 and puts you amid the raucous fans; there are few better ways to spend a Sunday summer afternoon in Boston. The stadium is near the Kenmore Ⓣ stop; for ticket information, call ©267-1700.

BASKETBALL

While Boston's other sports franchises may have a reputation for falling just short of victory, basketball's **Celtics** have won sixteen NBA championships – more than any other professional sports team except the New York Yankees. But while they enjoyed dynastic success in the 1960s and 1980s when they played on the buckling parquet floors of the beloved Boston Garden, the Celts have recently fallen on hard times, despite the importation of star coach Rick Pitino. Today, they play in the **FleetCenter**, 150 Causeway St (©624-1000), located near the North Station Ⓣ stop in the West End. Most tickets are pricey – good seats run between $50 and $90 – but you can sometimes snag some for as little as $10; for those, show up in front of the stadium and hope for the best.

FOOTBALL

For years, football's New England **Patriots** were saddled with the nickname "Patsies" and generally considered to be a laughing stock. But a change in ownership, and the addition of coach Bill Parcells brought respectability and a Super Bowl appearance in the mid 1990s. Unfortunately, Parcells is now long-gone, and the team is again struggling with mediocrity – despite some entertaining players, like quarterback Drew Bledsoe. In any case, going to a game isn't a very reasonable goal unless you have connections or are willing to pay a scalper upwards of $100; tickets are sold out far in advance, and the stadium is located in distant Foxboro, just north of the Massachusetts–Rhode

Island border (for information, call ©508/543-1776). Better to drop by a sports bar on a Sunday afternoon during the fall season; the best ones are located in the West End (see p.216).

HOCKEY

Until a few years ago, ice hockey's **Boston Bruins** were a consistently successful franchise, at one point running up a streak of 26 straight winning seasons – the longest in professional sports, including appearances in the Stanley Cup finals on two occasions, 1988 and 1990, both of which they barely lost. A series of retirements, injuries, and bad luck turned things around fast, and in the 1996-97 year they posted the worst record in the National Hockey League. The team has bounced back, though, and is again exciting to watch. You can catch the Bruins at the **FleetCenter**, 150 Causeway St (North Station Ⓣ; ©624-1000), where tickets are expensive ($20–77), especially if a good opponent is in town.

A cheap and exciting alternative to the Bruins is **college hockey**. The biggest event is the "Beanpot," an annual competition that takes place on the first two Mondays in February, in which the four big local teams – **Boston University**, who play at Walter Brown Arena, 285 Babcock St (©353-3838); **Harvard**, at Bright Hockey Center, N Harvard St, Allston (©495-2211); **Boston College**, at the Conte Forum, Chestnut Hill (©552-3000); and **Northeastern**, at Matthews Arena, St Botolph St (©373-4700) – compete for city bragging rights. BU tends to dominate the Beanpot and are consistently at the top of the national rankings, though BC and Harvard are generally competitive as well. Beanpot tickets are hard to come by, but regular-season seats go for around $5 and the games are quite fun.

FITNESS CENTERS

If you're staying at a hotel without a gym and are in need of a workout, a number of **health clubs** and **fitness centers** offer one-time daily memberships for out-of-towners. The **Beacon Hill Athletic Club**, with locations at 261 Friend St (©720-2422) and 3 Hancock St (©367-2422), vends such a pass for $10, as does the **City Gym and Aerobic Center**, at 542 Commonwealth Ave (©536-4008). **Fiticorp**, 133 Federal St (©542-1010), has a $12 daily rate, and **Boston Athletic Club**, 653 Summer St (©269-4300), charges $20.

RUNNING, ROLLERBLADING, AND CYCLING

On the rare days that Boston is visited by pleasant weather, residents take full advantage of it, turning up in droves to engage in **outdoor activities**. The most popular of these are **running**, **rollerblading**, and **cycling**, and they all pretty much take place along the banks of the Charles River, where the **Esplanade** provides eighteen miles of well-kept, picturesque trails stretching from the Museum of Science all the way down to Watertown and Newton. On the Cambridge side of the Charles is **Memorial Drive**, closed off to traffic between Western Avenue and Eliot Bridge (May–Oct daily 11am–7pm) – a prime place for blading and tanning. Blades are available for rent at Beacon Hill Skate Shop, 135 S Charles St (©482-7400), or Blades, Boards and Skates, 349 Newbury St (©437-6300), for about $15 per day.

Call the Metropolitan District Commission (©727-9650) for local hiking and cycling trail information.

Paintball

Among all the miscellaneous forms of sportslike entertainment in the city, perhaps the oddest (and most fun, if you're into this type of thing) is **paintball** – a kind of simulated warfare, where you shoot paintballs rather than bullets (and they do sting), while scampering around an area full of bunkers and obstacles. The proceedings take place in an old North End warehouse at **Boston Paintball**, 131 Beverly St, sixth floor (North Station Ⓣ; reservations ©742-6612; $39).

Two of the most popular **bike trails** in the area are the Dr Paul Dudley White Bike Path (really just another name for the Esplanade loop) and the Minuteman Bikeway, which runs 10.5 miles from Alewife station on the Red Line in Cambridge through Lexington to Bedford. The MDC has information about these trails, as does the Massachusetts Bicycle Coalition, 44 Bromfield St, Room 207 (©542-2453), and 214A Broadway, Cambridge (©491-7433), which also sells a Boston bike map ($5). The Charles River Wheelmen (©332-8546 or 325-BIKE for a recorded listing of rides) organize frequent, usually free, bike tours. You can rent bikes (around $20 per day) at Community Bicycle Supply, 496 Tremont St (Boylston Arlington Ⓣ; ©542-8623); Back Bay Bikes, 336 Newbury St (Hynes Ⓣ; ©247-2336); Earth Bikes, 35 Huntington Ave (Copley Ⓣ; ©267-4733); or at the Bicycle Workshop, 259 Massachusetts Ave, Cambridge (Harvard Ⓣ; ©876-6555), which also does repairs.

ICE SKATING

The MDC operates several **ice skating rinks** in the Boston area, of which the best-kept and most convenient to downtown is the **Steriti Memorial Rink**, at 550

Commercial St (©523-9327) in the North End, though it's closed for renovations until winter of 2000-2001. When it's cold enough, Frog Pond on Boston Common and the lagoon in the Public Garden offer free skating; skate rentals are available (adults $5, children $3). To find out dates and times and keep tabs on skating availability throughout the city, call the MDC skating hotline (©727-5283).

BOWLING

Boston's variation on tenpin bowling is **candlepin bowling**, in which the ball is smaller, the pins narrower and lighter, and you have three rather than two chances to knock the pins down. It's somewhat of a local institution, and popular with all types of recreational bowlers to boot, as it's difficult to be very bad or very good at candlepins – Boston's serious bowlers stick to the tenpin variety. The best candlepin spot is the Ryan Family Amusement Center, 82 Lansdowne St (Kenmore Ⓣ; Sun, Mon, Wed & Thurs noon–11pm, Tues 9am–11pm, Fri & Sat noon–midnight; ©267-8495), while Lanes and Games, 195 Concord Turnpike out in Somerville (Alewife Ⓣ; daily 9am–midnight; ©876-5533), is a good spot for both tenpin and candlepin bowling.

POOL

There are plenty of places to shoot **pool** in the Boston area, and not just of the divey variety you'll invariably find in some of the city's more down-and-out bars. One of the best is *Boston Billiard Club*, 126 Brookline Ave (Kenmore Ⓣ; ©536-7665), a classy and serious pool hall that also has a nice bar. *Flat Top Johnny's*, at One Kendall Square in Cambridge (Kendall Ⓣ; ©494-9565), draws a diverse young clientele to its smoky environment; and there's also *The Rack* at 24 Clinton St across from Faneuil Hall (Government Center Ⓣ; ✆725-1051), a slick joint that draws as many well-heeled yuppies as it does ardent pool players.

Kids' Boston

One of the best aspects of traveling with kids in Boston is the feeling that you're conducting an ongoing history lesson; while that may grow a bit tiresome for teens, younger children tend to eat up the Colonial-period costumes, cannons and the like. Various points on the Freedom Trail are, of course, best for this, though getting out of the city to Lexington and Concord will point you along a similar path. The city's parks, notably Boston Common, Franklin Park, and the Public Garden – where you can ride the Swan Boats in the lagoon – make nice settings for an afternoon with the children too. The best outdoor option, however, may be Fenway Park, as the country's oldest baseball stadium is easily reached and games here are affordable (see p.273). Harbor cruises are also a fairly popular and unique way to see Boston – as is ascending to the tops of various city skyscrapers. There are also a number of museums aimed at kids, most of them located along one waterfront or another.

MUSEUMS AND SIGHTS

Though kids might not have historical attractions at the top of their list of favorite places, most of Boston's major museums manage to make the city's history palatable to youngsters, especially at the **Boston Tea Party Ship & Museum**, a celebration of that revolutionary action (see p.36). More history is on display at the **USS Constitution**, the old warship moored in the Charlestown Navy Yard (see p.55). The **Children's Museum** (see p.38) and the **Museum of Science** (see p.72) are two obvious places to let the little ones loose for a while; both provide a lot of hands-on interactive fun that's easy to get lost in yourself. For animal sightings, the **Franklin Park Zoo** (see p.114) and the **New England Aquarium** (see p.36) can't be beat, and views from the dizzying heights of the **John Hancock Observatory** (see p.86) are always sure to thrill.

SHOPS

If and when the history starts to wear thin, there's always the failsafe of Boston's **malls** to divert the kids attention (see p.264). To combine history with your shopping, you could head to Faneuil Hall and Quincy Market; indeed, the latter holds a store sure to please, the Chocolate Dipper, 200 State St (Map 3, I2; ©439-0190), where strawberries, pineapple slices, cookies, brownies, and more all get a quick bath in chocolate, either milk or dark.

For descriptions of Faneuil Hall and Quincy Market, see p.30.

Few kids can resist FAO Schwarz, 440 Boylston St (Map 6, H4; Arlington Ⓣ; ©262-5900), and whether or not you're turned off by toys, the huge bronze teddy bear plunked on the sidewalk in front of this colorful emporium is worth a glance. Inside is a two-level childrens' paradise of huge stuffed animals, a Barbie boutique, the latest home video games, and many other useless but fun pieces of molded plastic.

Kids' tours

Boston is a great place for kids to see on a tour, in part due to the typical means of public transportation: mostly trolleys and ships. Of the latter, the best options are Boston Harbor Cruises (©227-4321) and Boston Duck Tours (©723-3825; see p.10). You can also take a ride on the schooner *Liberty* (summers noon, 3pm & 6pm, adults $30, children $18; ©742-0333), which departs from Long Wharf and sails for two hours around Boston's Harbor Islands. The New England Aquarium offers whale-watching excursions into the harbor (summers only; ©973-5277), as does Boston Harbor Cruises (see p.35). One tour designed specifically for kids is Boston By Little Feet (summer Sat & Mon 10am, Sun 2pm; $6; ©367-2345), which is a one-hour Freedom Trail walk for ages six to twelve. Tours begin in front of the statue of Samuel Adams at Faneuil Hall and include a free map and kids' *Explorer's Guide*.

THEATER AND PUPPET SHOWS

If you want to take the tots to the theater, you can try the **Boston Children's Theater**, at 55 Temple St (©424-6634), where productions of kids' classics are performed at the C. Walsh Theater, on the Beacon Hill campus of Suffolk University. Otherwise, head out to Brookline for the **Puppet Showplace Theater**, 32 Station St (©731-6400); tickets are $6 a head – big or small.

Festivals

It's always good to know ahead of time what festivals or annual events are scheduled to coincide with your trip to Boston, though even if you don't plan it, there's likely to be some sort of parade, public celebration or seasonal shindig going on. For detailed information, call the Boston Convention and Visitors Bureau (©1-888/SEE-BOSTON; *www.bostonusa.com*), although the schedule below should give you a good starting point.

JANUARY

Chinese New Year

Dragon parades and firecrackers punctuate these festivities throughout Chinatown. It can fall in February, too, depending on the Chinese lunar calendar (©1-888/SEE-BOSTON).

FEBRUARY

The Beanpot

First two Mondays. Popular college hockey tournament (©624-1000; see p.275 for more details).

MARCH

St Patrick's Day Parade and Festival

March 17. Boston's substantial Irish-American community, along with much of the rest of the city, turns out for this parade through South Boston, which culminates in Irish folk music, dance, and food at Faneuil Hall. This also happens to be "Evacuation Day," or the anniversary of the day that George Washington drove the British out of Boston during the Revolutionary War, which gives Bostonians another historical excuse to party (©536-4100).

New England Spring Flower Show

Winter-weary Bostonians turn out in droves to gawk at hothouse greenery in this week-long horticulture fest, which takes place down in Dorchester's Bayside Expo Center either the second or third week in March (©536-9280).

APRIL

Patriot's Day

Third Monday. A celebration and re-creation of Paul Revere's (and William Dawes') famous ride, from the North End to Lexington, that alerted locals that the British army had been deployed against the rebel threat (©536-4100).

Boston Marathon

Third Monday. Runners from all over the world gather for this 26.2-mile affair, one of America's premier athletic events. It crosses all over Boston, ending in Back Bay's Copley Square (©236-1652).

MAY

Blacksmith House Dulcimer Festival

Early May in Cambridge, workshops and performance by experts of both mountain and hammer dulcimers (©547-6789).

Greater Boston Kite Festival

In mid-May, Franklin Park gets taken over by kite-lovers during this celebration, which features kite-making, flying clinics, and music (©635-4505).

Lilac Sunday

Third Sunday of May. You can view more than three hundred lilac varieties in full bloom at the Arnold Arboretum (©524-1718).

JUNE

Boston Dairy Festival

First week of June. Cows and other animals are brought back to Boston Common to graze. There's also an event here known as the "Scooper Bowl," which, for a modest donation, allows you unlimited samples of Boston's best ice creams.

Bunker Hill Weekend

Sunday nearest June 17. In Charlestown, a parade celebrates the Battle of Bunker Hill, even though the bout was actually lost by the Americans (©242-5641).

Boston Early Music Festival

Taking place every odd-numbered year, this huge Renaissance fair with a strong music theme puts on concerts, costumes shows and exhibitions throughout town (✆661-1812; *www.bemf.org*).

Boston Globe Jazz Festival

The city's leading newspaper sponsors a weeklong series of jazz events at various venues, usually in mid- to late June. Some are free, though shows by big names can be pricey (✆929-2000 or 1-800/SEE-BOSTON).

Harborfest

From late June, culminating in the weekend nearest July 4, Harborfest hosts a series of concerts on the waterfront, mostly jazz, blues, and rock. On the July 4 weekend there's the annual turnaround cruise of the *USS Constitution*, the highly competitive "Chowderfest," and tons of fireworks (✆227-1528).

Boston Pops Concert and Fireworks

July 4. The Boston Pops' wildly popular annual evening concert in the Hatch Shell; people sometimes line up at dawn in order to get good seats (✆266-1492).

AUGUST

August Moon Festival

Near the end of the month, Chinatown's merchants and restaurateurs hawk their wares on the street amid dragon parades and firecrackers (✆536-4100).

Italian Festas

The last two weekends in August feature music, dancing, and games throughout the North End. In weekend parades, statues of the Virgin Mary are borne through the streets as locals pin dollar bills to the floats.

SEPTEMBER

Cambridge River Festival

In mid-September, Memorial Drive is closed off from JFK Street to Western Avenue for music shows, dancing, and eclectic food offerings, all along the Charles River (©349-4380).

Boston Film Festival

Boston theaters screen independent films, with frequent discussions by directors and screenwriters, for approximately two weeks in early to mid-September (©1-888/SEE-BOSTON).

Arts Festival of Boston

Around Labor Day weekend, the city is transformed into a giant gallery – five days of exhibits, arts and crafts pavilions, fashion shows, evening galas, receptions and outdoor musical performances at various locations. Phone 451-ARTS for specific locations, times and, when applicable, entrance fees.

Open Studios

Each fall the **Boston Open Studios Coalition** arranges for local artists to showcase their paintings, pottery, photographs, and other works of art to the public, on a neighborhood by neighborhood basis. Exhibitors include: United South End Artists (©267-8862), Jamaica Plain Artists (©524-3816), ACT Roxbury (©445-1061 ext 222), Mission Hill Art Association ©427-7399) and Fort Point Channel Arts Community (©423-4299). Check newspapers for listings.

OCTOBER

Columbus Day Parade

Second Monday of October. Kicked off by a ceremony at City Hall at 1pm, the raucous, Italian-flavored parade continues into the heart of the North End.

Head of the Charles Regatta

Hordes of college students descend on the banks of the Charles River between Central and Harvard Squares, ostensibly to watch the crew races that take place on the second to last weekend in October, but really more to pal around with their cronies and get loaded (©441-2884).

Salem Haunted Happenings/Halloween

The two weeks of witch-related kitsch – seances and the like – end fittingly with the Halloween celebrations (©1-800/777-6848).

NOVEMBER

Thanksgiving

In Plymouth, they commemorate the first thanksgiving ever held with tours of old houses and traditional feasts (information ©1-800/USA-1620, reservations ©508/746-1622).

DECEMBER

Boston Tea Party Reenactment

Sunday nearest Dec 16. A lusty reenactment of the march from Old South Meeting House to the harbor, and the subsequent tea-dumping that helped spark the American

Revolution, hosted by the Boston Tea Party Museum (✆338-1773).

First Night

December 31–January 2. A family-friendly festival to ring in the New Year, featuring parades, ice sculptures, art shows, plays, and music throughout downtown and the Back Bay, culminating in a spectacular fireworks display over Boston Harbor. A button, granting admission to all events, tends to run around $20 (✆542-1399).

City directory

AIRLINES American Airlines ©1-800/433-7300; British Airways ©1-800/247-9297; United Airlines ©1-800/241-6522; US Airways ©1-800/428-4322; Virgin Atlantic ©1-800/862-8621. American and United have offices in the *Park Plaza Hotel* (in addition to one at Logan Airport); the British Airways office is across from the Government Center Ⓣ station.

BANKS AND ATMS Fleet Financial Group and its newly acquired Bank of Boston together make up the biggest bank – Fleet Boston – with branches and ATMs throughout the city.

BICYCLES Back Bay Bikes & Boards, 336 Newbury St (©247-2336) and Community Bicycle Supply, 496 Tremont St (©542-8623). A copy of *Boston's Bike Map* ($4) will help you find all the trails and bike-friendly roads in the area.

CONSULATES Australia, 20 Park Plaza ©542-8655; Canada, 3 Copley Place ©262-3760; France, 31 St James Ave ©542-7374; Ireland, 525 Boylston St ©267-9330; UK, 600 Atlantic Ave ©248-9555.

DISABILITY For people with mobility impairments, getting around Boston is possible for the simple reason that the city is relatively flat and curb cuts abound. Many MBTA buses and Ⓣ

stops are wheelchair accessible (information: ©222-5976 or 1-800/543-8287) and most major taxi companies have some vehicles with wheelchair lifts, though getting one can be difficult. Very Special Arts (©350-7713; *www.accessexpressed.net*) has superior information on the accessibility of museums, sights, movie theaters, and other cultural venues in the Boston area. Anything else, call the Massachusetts Office on Disability (©727-7440).

EMERGENCIES Dial ©911 for emergency assistance.

EXCHANGE There are bureaux de change at Logan Airport Terminal E (International); Thomas Cook, 399 Boylston St, and American Express, 1 State St.

FILM AND PHOTOGRAPHY Almost any kind of film can be found at pharmacies and camera specialty shops around town. For one-hour developing service, try Moto Photo, with locations in the Financial District, 101 Summer St (©423-6848); Back Bay, 657 Boylston St (©266-6560); and Harvard Square, 35 JFK St (©497-0731).

HEALTH Massachusetts General Physician Referral Service ©726-5800.

HOSPITALS Massachusetts General Hospital, 55 Fruit St (©726-2000); Beth Israel Deaconess Medical Center, 330 Brookline Ave (©667-7000); Brigham and Women's Hospital, 75 Francis St (©732-5500); New England Medical Center, 750 Washington St (©636-5000); and Children's Hospital, 300 Longwood Ave (©355-6000).

INTERNET The best way to access the Internet is to pop in to a local university and access a Web-based email account from a public computer. Boston's main public library also has

Internet access, but cybercafés are few and far between; *Designs For Living*, 52 Queensberry St (©536-6150; Kenmore Ⓣ), is a rare exception, charging $8 per hour for Internet access.

LAUNDRY Back Bay Laundry Emporium, 409-A Marlborough St (daily 7.30am–11pm, last wash at 9pm), is a good, clean bet; drop-off service is 80¢ per pound.

MAIL The biggest post office downtown is J. W. McCormack Station in Post Office Square, 90 Devonshire St (Mon–Fri 7.30am–5pm; ©720-4754); another central branch is at 125 Mt Auburn St, in Harvard Square (Mon–Fri 7.30am–6pm, Sat 7.30am–3pm; ©876-6483). The General Post Office, 25 Dorchester Ave, by Fort Point Channel, is open 24 hours (©654-5326).

NEWSPAPERS The *Boston Globe* (50¢) is Boston's best general daily paper; its fat Sunday edition ($2) includes sections on art, culture, and lifestyle. The *Boston Herald* (50¢) is the *Globe*'s tabloid competitor. To know what's on, the weekly *Boston Phoenix* ($1.50) is essential, offering extensive entertainment listings as well as good feature articles. There are also the freebies *Improper Bostonian* and *Stuff@Night*, each of which have decent, though ad-driven, features. The free *Cambridge TAB* has news articles and listings exclusively about local Cambridge events.

PARKING This can be an absolute nightmare, definitely to be avoided if possible. Garages cost $15–20 per evening, more overnight. There are metered spots on main streets like Newbury, Boylston, and Charles, but the chances of finding an empty one on any given evening are slim at best. Heed, too, the ubiquitous "Permit Parking Only" signs along residential streets: without the requisite parking sticker, you will be ticketed $20 or towed (expect to pay well over $50 to get your car back).

The parking limit at nonmetered spots is two hours, whether posted or not.

PHARMACIES The CVS drugstore chain has locations all over the city, though not all have pharmacies. For those, try the branches at 155–157 Charles St, in Beacon Hill (open 24 hours; ✆227-0437, pharmacy ✆523-1028), and 35 White St, in Cambridge's Porter Square (open 24 hours, ✆876-4037, pharmacy ✆876-5519).

POLICE Dial ✆911 for emergencies; for non-emergency situations, contact the Boston Police, headquartered at 154 Berkeley St, in Back Bay (✆343-4200).

PUBLIC TOILETS There aren't too many of these around. The cleanest ones are in the visitors' center on the fourth floor of the City Hall building in Government Center, and in the National Park Service visitors' center across from the Old State House. If desperate, you can always try ducking into a restaurant, bar, or hotel.

RADIO The best stations are on FM, including WGBH (89.7), which carries National Public Radio shows, plus jazz, classical, and world music; WBUR (90.9), earnest leftist talk radio; WJMN (94.5), for good hip-hop beats; WFNX (101.7), mainstream alternative hits; and WODS (103.3), an oldies station.

TELEPHONES Local calls cost 35¢; just deposit your change and dial the number. To call Boston from long distance, dial 1+617 then the number. For a long-distance call from Boston, dial 1+area code+number and wait for the operator to prompt you for the required payment or the option to make collect, reverse-charge, or credit card calls. Operator assistance (✆0) and directory information (✆411) are toll-free.

TELEVISION You'll find CBS on channel 4, ABC on channel 5, NBC on channel 7, and Fox on channel 25. Local channel 68 is of interest for its frequent broadcasts of regional sports action.

TIME Boston follows Eastern Standard Time (five hours behind Greenwich Mean Time). Daylight Savings Time runs from April to October.

TRAVEL AGENTS Council Travel, 12 Eliot St, 2nd Floor, Harvard Square, Cambridge (©497-1497), specializes in student and youth travel; American Express Travel, 170 Federal St (©439-4400), provides general travel services.

CONTEXTS

A brief history of Boston

Early exploration and founding

The first indications of explorers "discovering" the Boston area are the journal entries of **Giovanni da Verrazano** and **Estevan Gomez**, who – in 1524 and 1525, respectively – passed by Massachusetts Bay while traveling the coast of North America. The first permanent European settlement in the Boston area was undertaken by a group of 102 British colonists, around half of them Separatists – better known now as **Pilgrims** – chased out of England for having disassociated themselves entirely from the Anglican Church.

They had tried to settle in Holland, but the Dutch didn't want them either, so they boarded the ship *Mayflower* to try the forbidding, rugged coast of North America, where they landed in 1620 near Plymouth Bay – after a short stopover at the tip of Cape Cod – and founded Plimoth Plantation. Within the first decade, one of them, a disillusioned scholarly loner by the name of **William Blackstone**, began searching for land on which to make a new start and found it on a peninsula at the mouth of the Charles River known as Shawmut by the local Indians. He became Boston's first white settler, living at the foot of modern-day Beacon Hill with a few hundred books and a Brahma bull.

In 1630, close to one thousand **Puritans** led by **John Winthrop**, settled just across the river to create **Charlestown**, named after the king of England. Unlike the Pilgrims, the Puritans didn't necessarily plan to disconnect themselves completely from the Anglican Church, but merely hoped to purify themselves by avoiding what they considered to be its showy excesses. Blackstone eventually lured them to his side of the river with the promise of a better water supply, then sold them the entire Shawmut Peninsula, keeping only six acres for himself. The Puritans renamed the area after the town in England from which many of their company hailed: **Boston**.

The Colonial period

Early Bostonians enjoyed almost total political autonomy from England and created a remarkably democratic system of government, whose primary body was the **town meeting**, in which white male church members debated over and voted on all kind of matters. This liberal approach was counterbalanced, however, by religious intolerance: four Quakers and Baptists were hanged for their non-Puritan beliefs from 1649 to 1651.

With the restoration of the British monarchy in 1660, the crown tried to exert more control over the increasingly prosperous Massachusetts Bay Colony, appointing a series of governors, notably the despotic Sir **Edmund Andros**, who was chased from the colony by locals in 1689, only to be reinstalled by the crown the following year. Britian's relentless mercantilist policies, designed to increase the nation's monopolistic hold on the new colonies, resulted in a decrease in trade that both plunged Boston into a depression and fanned the anti-British resentment which would eventually reach a boiling point. The **Molasses Act** of 1733, for example, taxed all sugar purchased outside the British Empire, dealing a stiff economic blow to the colonies, dependent upon foreign sources for their sugar supply.

The American Revolution

At the outset of the 1760s, governor Francis Bernard informed the colonists that their success was a result of "their subjugation to Great Britain," before green-lighting the **Writs of Assistance**, which gave British soldiers the right to enter colonists' shops and homes to search for evidence of their avoiding duties. The colonists reacted with outrage at this violation of their civil liberties, and a young Boston lawyer named **James Otis** persuaded a panel of judges headed by lieutenant governor Thomas Hutchinson to repeal the acts. After listening to his four-hour oration, many were convinced that revolution was justified, including future US president **John Adams**, who wrote of Otis' speech: "Then and there the child liberty was born."

Nevertheless, in 1765 the British introduced the **Stamp Act**, which required stamps to be placed on all published material (the revenue on the stamps would go to the Imperial coffers), and the **Quartering Act**, which stipulated that colonists had to house British soldiers on demand. These acts galvanized the opposition to the English government, a resistance based in Boston, where a group of revolutionary firebrands headed by **Samuel Adams** and known as the "Sons of Liberty" teamed up with more level-headed folks like **John Hancock** and John Adams to organize protest marches and petition the King to repeal the offending legislation. Though Parliament repealed the Stamp Act, in 1766 it issued the **Declaratory Acts**, which asserted the Crown's right to bind the colonists by any legislation it saw fit, and, in 1767, with the **Townshend Acts**, which prescribed more tariffs on imports to the North American colonies. This was followed by a troop increase in Boston; by 1768, there was one British soldier in the city for every four colonists.

The tension erupted on March 5, 1770, when a group of British soldiers fired into a crowd of taunting townspeople. The **Boston Massacre** was hardly a massacre – only five people were killed, and the accused soldiers were actually defended in court by John Adams and Josiah Quincy – but the occupying troops were forced to relocate to **Castle Island**, at the tip of South Boston. The crisis was postponed for a few years, until December 16, 1773, when Samuel

Adams led a mob from the Old South Meeting House to Boston Harbor as part of a protest against a British tax on imported tea. A segment of the crowd boarded the brig *Beaver* and two other ships and dumped their entire cargo overboard, the so-called **Boston Tea Party**; Parliament responded by closing the port of Boston and passing the **Coercive Acts**, which deprived Massachusetts of any self-government. They also sent in more troops and cut off the Dorchester Neck, the only land entrance to Boston. Soon after, the colonies convened the first **Continental Congress** in Philadelphia, with the idea of creating an independent government.

Two months after the province of Massachusetts was declared to be in a state of rebellion by the British government, a "shot heard 'round the world" was fired at Lexington on April 18, 1775, when a group of American militiamen skirmished with a company of British regulars; they lost that fight but defeated the Redcoats in a subsequent incident at Concord Bridge, and the **Revolutionary War** had begun. The British troops left in Boston were held under siege, and the city itself was largely evacuated by its citizens.

The first major engagement of the war was the **Battle of Bunker Hill**, in which the British stormed what was actually Breed's Hill, in Charlestown, on three separate occasions before finally dislodging American battlements. Despite the loss, the conflict, in which the outnumbered Americans suffered fewer casualties than the British, bolstered the patriots' spirits and confidence.

George Washington took over the Continental troops in a ceremony on Cambridge Common on July 2, 1775; however, his first major coup didn't even require bloodshed. On March 16, 1776, under cover of darkness, Washington ordered much of the troops' heavy artillery to be moved to the top of Dorchester Heights, in view of the Redcoats.

The British awoke to see battlements sufficient to destroy their entire fleet of warships; on March 17, they evacuated the city, never to return.

This was largely the end of Boston's involvement in the war; the focus soon turned inland and southward. After the Americans won the Battle of Saratoga in 1778, the French joined the war as their allies; on October 19, 1781, Cornwallis surrendered to Washington at Yorktown; and the **United States of America** became an independent nation with 1783's **Treaty of Paris**.

Economic swings and the Athens of America

Boston quickly emerged from the damage wrought by British occupation. By 1790, the economy was already booming, due primarily to the maritime industry. A merchant elite – popularly known as the "cod millionaires" – developed and settled on the sunny south slope of Beacon Hill. These were the Boston **Brahmins** – though that name would not be coined until seventy years later – infamous for their stuffed-shirt elitism and fiscal conservatism. Indeed, the **trust fund** was invented in Boston at this time as a way for families to protect their fortunes over the course of generations.

The outset of the nineteenth century was less auspicious. Severe restrictions on international trade, notably Jefferson's **Embargo Act** in 1807, plunged the port of Boston into recession. When the War of 1812 began, pro-British Bostonian Federalists derided the conflict as "Mr. Madison's War" and met in Hartford in 1814 with party members from around New England to consider seceding from the union – a measure that was wisely, though narrowly, rejected. America's victory in the war shamed Bostonians back into their patriotic ways, and they reacted to further trade restrictions by developing manufacturing industries, soon becoming prominent in textiles and shoe production.

This industrial revival and subsequent economic growth shook the region from its recession. By 1820, Boston's population had grown to 43,000 – more than double its total from the 1790 census. The city stood at the forefront of American intellectual and political life – earning Boston the moniker "Athens of America." The country's first college, **Harvard University**, was founded here in 1636. In the late eighteenth century, a controversial sect of Christianity known as **Unitarianism** – premised on the rational study of scripture, voluntary ethical behavior, and (in Boston only) a rejection of the Trinity – became the city's dominant religion (and one still practiced at King's Chapel), led by Reverend **Ellery Channing**. His teachings were the basis for **transcendentalism**, a philosophy propounded in the writings of Ralph Waldo Emerson and premised on the idea that there existed an entity known as the "over-soul," to which man and nature existed in identical relation. Emerson's theory, emphasizing intuitive (*a priori*) knowledge – particularly in contemplation of nature – was put into practice by his fellow Harvard alumnus, **Henry David Thoreau**, who, in 1845, took to the woods just northwest of the city at **Walden Pond** in an attempt to "live deliberately." Boston was also a center of literary activity at this time: historical novels by **Nathaniel Hawthorne**, such as *The Scarlet Letter*, tweaked the sensibilities and mores of New England society, and poet **Henry Wadsworth Longfellow** gained international renown during his tenure at Harvard.

This intellectual flowering was complemented by a variety of social movements. Foremost among them was **abolitionism**, spearheaded by the fiery **William Lloyd Garrison**, who, besides speechmaking, published the anti-slavery newspaper *The Liberator*. Beacon Hill resident **Harriet Beecher Stowe**'s 1852 novel, *Uncle Tom's Cabin*, turned the sentiments of the nation against slavery. Other

Bostonians who made key contributions to social issues were **Horace Mann**, who reformed public education; **Dorothea Dix**, an advocate of improved care for the mentally ill; **Margaret Fuller**, one of America's first feminists; and **William James**, a Harvard professor who pioneered new methods in psychology, coining the phrase "stream of consciousness."

Social transformation and decline

The success of Boston's maritime and manufacturing industries attracted a great deal of immigrants; the **Irish**, especially, poured in following the Potato Famine of the 1840s. By 1860, the city was marked by massive social divide, with overcrowded slums abutting beautiful mansions. The elite that had ruled for the first half of the century tried to ensure that the lower classes were kept in place: "**No Irish Need Apply**" notices accompanied job listings throughout Boston. Denied entry into "polite" society, the lower classes conspired to grab power in another way: the popular vote.

To the chagrin of Boston's WASP elite, **Hugh O'Brien** was elected mayor in 1885. His three-term stay in office was followed by that of John "Honey Fitz" Fitzgerald, and in the 1920s, the long reign of **James Michael Curley** began. Curley was to serve several terms as mayor, and one each as governor and congressional representative. These men enjoyed tremendous popularity among their supporters, despite the fact that their tenures were often characterized by rampant corruption: Curley was elected to his last term in office while serving time in a Federal prison for fraud. Still, while these mayors increased the visibility and political clout of otherwise disenfranchised ethnic groups, they did little to improve the lot of their constituents, which was steadily worsening – along with the city's economy. Competition with the railroads, following the Civil War, crippled the shipping industry, and with it, Boston's prosperous waterfront.

Soon after, the manufacturing industry felt the impact of bigger, more efficient factories in the rest of the nation. The shoe and textile industries had largely disappeared by the 1920s, and the **Great Depression** of the 1930s made a bad state of affairs even worse. World War II turned Boston's moribund shipbuilding industry around almost overnight, but this economic upturn wasn't enough to prevent a massive exodus from the urban center.

The 1950s to the 1980s

A turnaround began under the mayoral leadership of **John Collins**, who undertook a massive plan to reshape the face of Boston. Many of the city's oldest neighborhoods and landmarks were razed, though it's questionable whether these changes beautified the city. Still, the project created jobs and economic growth, while making the downtown area more attractive to businesses and residents. By the end of the 1960s, a steady economic resurgence had begun. Peripheral areas of Boston, however, did not share in this prosperity. Collins' program paid little attention to the poverty that afflicted outlying areas, particularly the city's southern districts, or to the city's growing **racial tensions**. The demographic redistribution that followed the "white flight" of the 1940s and 1950s made Boston one of the most racially segregated cities in America by the mid-1970s: Charlestown's population was almost entirely white, while Roxbury was almost entirely black.

Along with other cities nationwide, the city was ordered by the Supreme Court to implement **busing** – sending students from one neighborhood to another and vice-versa in an attempt to achieve racial balance. More than two hundred area schools were involved, and not all reacted kindly: Charlestown parents, for their part, staged hostile demonstrations and boycotted the public school system. This was especially embarrassing for Boston considering its history of racial tolerance. City officials finally scrapped their plan for desegregation after only a few years. The racial scars it left began to heal, thanks, in part, to the policies of **Ray Flynn**, Boston's mayor during the upbeat 1980s, helping to make the decade one of the city's healthiest in recent memory, both economically and socially.

The 1990s into the Twenty-first century

That resurgence spilled over into the 1990s, a decade that saw the job market explode and rents spiral upward in reaction to it. The increase in housing prices was aided as well by the 1996 state vote to abolish **rent control** in the city, a decision that has pushed much of the lesser-paid working class out. In any case, it seems everyone who can afford a posh apartment these days works for some biotech company or dot-com startup, not unlike the way it is in a number of major US cities.

Meanwhile, civic programs that aim to improve the city infrastructure continue, not least downtown's **Big Dig**, which is at over $1 billion per mile the most expensive highway construction project in US history. More successfully, the **cleanup of Boston Harbor** has had a great effect in reclaiming abandoned beaches and reinvigorating species of long disappeared fauna.

Architecture and urban planning

The land to which William Blackstone invited John Winthrop and his Puritans in 1630 bore almost no resemblance to the contemporary city of Boston. It was virtually an island, spanning a mere 785 acres, surrounded on all sides by murky swamps and connected to the mainland only by a narrow isthmus, "the Neck," that was almost entirely submerged at high tide. It was also very hilly: three peaks formed its geological backbone and gave it the name that Puritans used before they chose Boston – the **Trimountain** – echoed today in downtown's Tremont Street.

The first century and a half of Boston's existence saw this sleepy Puritan village slowly expand into one of the biggest shipping centers in the North American colonies. Narrow, crooked footpaths became busy commercial boulevards, though they retained their sinuous design. The pasture land of **Boston Common** became the place for public gatherings. By the end of the eighteenth century, Boston was faced with the dilemma of how to accommodate its growing population and thriving industry on a tiny geographical center. Part of the answer was to create more land. This had been accomplished in Boston's early years almost accidentally, by means of a process known as **wharving out**. Owners of shoreside properties with wharves found that rocks and debris collected around the pilings, until eventually the wharves were on dry land, necessitating the building of more wharves further out to sea. In this way, Boston's shoreline moved slowly but inexorably outward.

Post-Revolution development

Boston's first great building boom began in earnest following the American Revolution. Harrison Gray Otis' company, the **Mount Vernon Proprietors**, razed Boston's three peaks to create tracts for new townhouses. The land from their tops was placed where Boston Common and the Charles River met to form a swamp, extending the shoreline out even farther to create what is now known as "the flat of the hill." Leftover land was used to fill some of the city's other coves and ponds, most significantly Mill Pond, near present-day North End. The completion of the Mount Vernon Proprietors' plans made the resulting area, **Beacon Hill**, the uncontested site for Boston's wealthy and elite to build their ideal home – as such, it holds the best examples of American architecture of the late eighteenth and early nineteenth centuries, ranging in styles from Georgian to early Victorian.

This period also ushered in the first purely American architectural movement, the **Federal style**. Prime examples of its flat, dressed-down facades are prevalent in townhouses throughout downtown and in Beacon Hill. **Charles Bulfinch** was its leading practitioner; his most famous work was the 1797 gold-domed **Massachusetts State House** looming over Boston Common, a prototype for state capitols to come.

The expansion of the city

Boston continued to grow throughout the 1800s. Mayor **Josiah Quincy** oversaw the construction of a large marketplace, **Quincy Market**, behind the overcrowded Faneuil Hall building. These three oblong Greek Revival buildings pushed the Boston waterfront back several hundred yards, and the new surface area was used as the site for a symbol of Boston's maritime prosperity, the **US Custom House**. While Boston had codes prohibiting overly tall buildings, the Federal Government was not obligated to obey them, and the Custom House building, completed in 1847, rose a then-impressive sixteen stories.

Meanwhile, the city was trying to create enough land to match the demand for housing, in part by transforming its swampy backwaters into useable land. **Back Bay** was originally just that: a marsh along the banks of the Charles. In 1814, however, Boston began to dam the Charles and fill the resulting area with debris. When the project was completed in 1883, Back Bay was one of Boston's choicest addresses, drawing some prominent families from their dwellings on Beacon Hill. The layout followed a highly ordered French model of city planning: gridded streets, with those running perpendicular to the Charles arranged alphabetically. The district's main boulevard, **Commonwealth Avenue**, surrounded a strip of greenery that terminated in the **Public Garden**, a lush space completed by George Meachum in 1859, with ponds, statuary, weeping willows, and winding pathways that is the jewel of Back Bay, if not all Boston.

Back Bay's **Copley Square** was the site of numerous high-minded civic institutions built in the mid- and late-1800s, foremost among which were H. H. Richardson's Romanesque **Trinity Church** and the **Public Library**, a High Victorian creation of Charles McKim, of the noted firm McKim, Mead and White. But the most impressive accomplishment of the century was Frederick Law Olmsted's **Emerald Necklace**, a system of parks that connected Boston Common, the Public Garden, and Commonwealth Avenue Mall to his own creations a bit further afield, such as the **Back Bay Fens**, **Arnold Arboretum**, and **Franklin Park**.

While Boston's civic expansion made life easier for its upper classes, the middle and lower classes were crammed into the tiny downtown area. The city's solution was to annex the surrounding districts, beginning with **South Boston** in 1807 and ending with **Charlestown** in 1873 – with the exception of **Brookline**, which remained a separate entity. Toward the end of the century, Boston's growing middle class moved to these surrounding areas, particularly the southern districts, which soon became known as the "streetcar suburbs." These areas, once the site of summer estates for the wealthy, were built over with one of Boston's least attractive architectural motifs: the **three-decker**. Also known as the "triple-decker," these clapboard rowhouses held a family on each floor, models of efficiency.

Modernization and preservation

New construction waned with the economic decline of the early 1900s, reaching its lowest point during the **Great Depression**. The streetcar suburbs were hardest hit – the white middle class migrated to Boston's nearby towns in the 1940s and 1950s, and the southern districts became run-down low-rent areas. Urban renewal began in the late 1950s, with the idea of creating a visibly modern city, and while it provided Boston with an economic shot in the arm, the drastic changes erased some of the city's most distinctive architectural features. The porn halls and dive bars of **Scollay Square** were demolished to make way for the dull gray bureaucracy complexes of Government Center. The **West End**, once one of Boston's liveliest ethnic neighborhoods, was flattened and covered over with high-rise office buildings. Worst of all, the new elevated **John F. Fitzgerald expressway** tore through downtown, cutting off the North End and waterfront from the rest of the city.

Soon, the fury of displaced and disgruntled residents forced planners to create structures that either reused or integrated extant features of the city. The **John Hancock Tower**, designed by I. M. Pei and completed in 1975, originally outraged preservationists, as this Copley Square high-rise was being built right by some of the city's most treasured cultural landmarks; however, the tower managed a delicate balance – while it rises sixty stories smack in the middle of Back Bay, its narrow wedge shape renders it quite unobtrusive, and its mirrored walls literally reflect its stately surroundings. Quincy Market was also redeveloped, and, by 1978, what had been a decaying, nearly defunct series of fishmongering stalls was transformed into a thriving tourist attraction. Subsequent development has, for the most part, kept up this theme, preserving the city's four thousand acres – and most crucially its downtown – as a virtual library of American architecture.

Literary Boston in the 1800s

America's literary center has not always been New York; indeed, for much of the nineteenth century, **Boston** held that mantle, and since then – largely due to the lingering effects of those sixty or so years – it has managed to retain a somewhat bookish reputation despite no longer having the influence it once did on American publishing.

The origins for that period actually go back to colonial times and the establishment of Puritanism. **John Winthrop** and his fellow colonists who settled here had a vision of a theocratic and utopic "City on a Hill." The Puritans were erudite and fairly well-off intellectuals, but religion always came first, even when writing: in fact, Winthrop himself penned *A Model of Christian Charity* while crossing the Atlantic. Religious **sermons** were the real literature of the day – those and the now-forgotten explorations of Reverend **Cotton Mather** such as *The Wonders of the Invisible World*, a look at the supernatural that helped foment the Salem Witch Trials.

In the years leading up to the Revolutionary War, Bostonians began to pour their energy into a different kind of sermon – that of anti-British sentiment, such as rants in radical newspapers like the *Boston Gazette*. Post-Revolution, the stifling atmosphere of Puritanism remained to some extent – the city's first theater, for example, built in 1794, had to be billed as a "school of virtue" in order to remain open. But writers began to shake off Puritan restraints and explore their newfound freedom; in certain instances, they drew upon the repressiveness of the religion as a source of inspiration.

Ironically enough, Boston's deliverance from parochialism started in the countryside, specifically Concord, scene of the first battle of the Revolutionary War. The **transcendentalist movement** of the 1830s and 1840s, spearheaded by **Ralph Waldo Emerson**, was borne of a passion for rural life, intellectual freedom and belief in intuitive knowledge and experience as a way to enhance the relationship between man, nature, and the "over-soul." The free thinking it unleashed put local writers at the vanguard of American literary expression. Articles by Emerson, **Henry David Thoreau**, **Louisa May Alcott**, **Bronson Alcott** (Louisa's father), and other members of the Concord coterie filled the pages of *The Dial*, the transcendentalist literary review, founded by Emerson around 1840 and edited by **Margaret Fuller**. Fuller, an early feminist, also wrote essays prodigiously; while Alcott penned the classic *Little Women*, and Thoreau authored his famous study in solitude, *Walden*. Meanwhile, a writer by the name of **Nathaniel Hawthorne**, known mainly for short stories like "Young Goodman Brown," published *The Scarlet Letter*, in 1850, a true schism with the past that examined the effects of the repressive Puritan lifestyle and legacy.

The abolitionist movement also helped push Boston into the literary limelight. Slavery had been outlawed in Massachusetts since 1783, and Boston attracted the likes of activist **William Lloyd Garrison**, who published his firebrand newspaper, *The Liberator*, in a small office downtown beginning in 1831. Years later, in 1852, **Harriet Beecher Stowe**'s slave narrative *Uncle Tom's Cabin* hit the printing press in Boston and sold more than 300,000 copies in its first year of publication. It, perhaps more than anything else, turned the nation against slavery, despite that its writer was a New Englander with little firsthand knowledge of the South or the slave trade.

Another involved with the cause was **John Greenleaf Whittier**, who also happened to be among the founding members of Emerson's famed "**Saturday Club**," the name given to a series of informal literary gatherings that took place at the *Parker House Hotel* beginning in 1855. **Oliver Wendell Holmes** and poet **Henry Wadsworth Longfellow** were among the moneyed regulars at these **salons**, which metamorphosed two years later into *The Atlantic Monthly*, from its inception a respected, if staid, literary and political journal. One of its more accomplished editors, **William Dean Howells**, wrote *The Rise of Silas Lapham*, in 1878, a novel on the culture of commerce that set the stage for American Realism. Around the same time, more literary salons were being held at the **Old Corner Bookstore**, down the street from the Parker House, where leading publisher **Ticknor & Fields** had their headquarters. Regulars included not only the likes of Emerson and Longfellow, but visiting British authors like William Thackeray and Charles Dickens, who were not only published by the house as well but friends with its charismatic leader, Jamie T. Fields. Meanwhile, Longfellow was well on his way to becoming America's most popular poet, writing "The Midnight Ride of Paul Revere," among much other verse, while a professor at Harvard University.

In the last burst of Boston's literary high tide, sometimes resident **Henry James** recorded the sedate lives of the moneyed – and miserable – elite in his books *Watch and Ward* (1871) and *The Bostonians* (1886). His renunciation of hedonism was well-suited to the stifling atmosphere of Brahmin Boston, where well-appointed homes were heavily curtained so as to avoid exposure to sunlight; however, his look at the emerging battle of the sexes was in fact fueled by the liberty-loving principles of Emerson and colleagues in Concord thirty years before.

The fact that Boston's literary society was largely a members-only club contributed to its eventual undoing. **Edgar Allen Poe** slammed his hometown as "Frogpondium," in reference to the Saturday Club-style chumminess of its literati. Provincialism reared its head in the Watch & Ward Society, which as late as 1878 instigated boycotts of books and plays it deemed out of the bounds of common decency, spawning the phrase "**Banned in Boston**." To many observers, Howells' departure from *The Atlantic Monthly* in 1885 to write for *Harper's* in New York signaled the end of Boston's literary golden age.

Books

In the reviews, publishers are listed in the format US/UK, unless the title is only available in one country, in which case the country has been specified. Out of print titles are indicated by o/p.

History and biography

Cleveland Amory *The Proper Bostonians* (Parnassus Imprints US). First published in 1947, this surprisingly upbeat volume remains the definitive social history of Boston's old-moneyed aristocracy.

Jack Beatty *The Rascal King: The Life and Times of James Michael Curley, 1874–1958* (Addison Wesley o/p). A thick and thoroughly researched biography of the charismatic Boston mayor and Bay State governor, valuable too for its depiction of big city politics in America.

David Hackett Fischer *Paul Revere's Ride* (University of Massachusetts Press/Oxford University Press). An exhaustive account of the patriot's legendary ride to Lexington, related as a historical narrative.

Jonathan Harr *A Civil Action* (Vintage Books US). The story of eight families in the community of Woburn, just north of Boston, who took a major chemical company to court in 1981, after a rash of leukemia cases raised suspicion about the purity of the area's water supply.

Jonathan Kozol *Death at an Early Age: The Destruction of the Hearts and Minds of Negro Children in the Boston Public Schools* (Penguin US). Winner of the National Book Award, an intense portrait of prejudice and corruption in Boston's 1964 educational system.

J. Anthony Lukas *Common Ground: A Turbulent Decade in the Lives of Three American Families* (Vintage US). A Pulitzer Prize-winning account of three Boston families – one Irish-American, one black, one white middle class – against the backdrop of the 1974 race riots sparked by court-ordered busing to desegregate public schools.

Michael Patrick MacDonald *All Souls: A Family Story from Southie* (Beacon Press US). A moving memoir of growing up in South Boston in the 1970s among the sometimes life-threatening racial, ethnic, class, and political tensions of the time.

Douglass Shand-Tucci *The Art of Scandal: The Life and Times of Isabella Stewart Gardner* (HarperCollins US). Astute biography of this doyenne of Boston society, who served as the inspiration for Isabel Archer in Henry James' *Portrait of a Lady*. The book includes evocative photos of Fenway Courtyard in Gardner's Venetian-style palace – which is now the Gardner Museum.

Dan Shaughnessy *The Curse of the Bambino* (Penguin US). Shaughnessy, a Boston sportswriter, gives an entertaining look at the Red Sox' "curse" – no championships since 1918 – that began after they sold Babe Ruth to the Yankees. His *At Fenway: Dispatches from Red Sox Nation* (Crown Publishing US) is another memoir of a Red Sox fan.

Hiller B. Zobel *The Boston Massacre* (W. W. Norton). A painstaking account of the circumstances that precipitated one of the most highly propagandized pre-Revolution events – the slaying of five Bostonians outside the Old State House.

Travel and specific guides

Charles Bahne *The Complete Guide to Boston's Freedom Trail* (Newtowne Publishing US). Unlike most souvenir guides of the Freedom Trail, which have lots of pictures but little substance, this one is chock full of engaging historical tidbits on the stories behind the sights.

John Harris *Historic Walks in Old Boston* (Globe Pequot US). In most cases you'll be walking in the footsteps of long-gone luminaries, but Harris infuses his accounts with enough lively history to keep things going.

Walt Kelley *What They Never Told You About Boston (Or What They Did Were Lies)* (Down East Books). Who would have guessed that in 1632, Puritans passed the world's first law against smoking in public? This slim book is full of such Boston trivia.

Architecture, urban planning, and photography

Philip Bergen *Old Boston in Early Photographs 1850–1918* (Dover Publications). Fascinating stuff, including a photographic record of Back Bay's transition from swampland to swanky residential neighborhood.

Robert Campbell and Peter Vanderwarker *Cityscapes of Boston: An American City Through Time* (Houghton Mifflin US). An informative pictorial tome with some excellent photos of old and new Boston.

Mona Domosh *Invented Cities: The Creation of Landscape in Nineteenth Century New York and Boston* (Yale University Press US). Fascinating historical account of how these very different cities were shaped according to the values, beliefs, and fears of the people and society who built them.

Matthew W. Granade and Joshua H. Simon (eds) *50 Successful Harvard Application Essays* (St Martin's Press US). Just in case you want to know who they actually let into this hallowed university anyhow.

Jane Holtz Kay *Lost Boston* (Houghton Mifflin US). A photographic essay of long-gone architectural treasures.

Lawrence W. Kennedy *Planning the City Upon a Hill: Boston Since 1630* (University of Massachusetts Press US). This is the book to have if you want to delve deeper into how Boston's distinct neighborhoods took shape over the centuries.

Alex Krieger, David Cobb, Amy Turner, and Norman B. Leventhal (eds) *Mapping Boston* (MIT Press US). Irresistible to any map-lover, this thoughtfully compiled book combines essays with all manner of historical maps to help trace Boston's conception and development.

Barbara Moore and Gail Weesner *Back Bay: A Living Portrait* (Centry Hill Press US). If you're dying to know what Back Bay's brownstones look – and looked – like inside, this book of hard-to-find photos is for you. They do a similar book on Beacon Hill.

Susan and Michael Southworth *AIA Guide to Boston* (Globe Pequot US). The definitive guide to Boston architecture, organized by neighborhood. City landmarks and dozens of notable buildings are given exhaustive but readable coverage.

Walter Muir Whitehill *Boston: A Topographical History* (Harvard University Press US). How Boston went from a tiny seaport on the Shawmut Peninsula to the city it is today, with detailed descriptions of the city's many land reclaiming projects.

Fiction

James Carroll *The City Below* (Houghton Mifflin US). Gripping historical novel of later-twentieth-century Boston, centered on two Irish brothers from Charlestown.

Nathaniel Hawthorne *The Scarlet Letter* (Penguin). Puritan Boston comes to life, in all its mirthless repressiveness, starring the adulterous Hester Prynne.

William Dean Howells *The Rise of Silas Lapham* (Penguin). This 1878 novel was the forerunner to American Realism. Howells' less-than-enthralling tale of a well-off Vermont businessman's failed entry into Boston's old-moneyed Brahmin caste gives a good early portrait of a uniquely American hero: the self-made man.

Henry James *The Bostonians* (Penguin). James' soporific satire traces the relationship of Olive Chancellor and Verena Tarrant, two fictional feminists in the 1870s.

Dennis Lehane *Darkness Take My Hand* (Avon Books US). Perhaps the best in Lehane's Boston-set mystery series; two private investigators tackle a serial killer, the Boston mafia, and their Dorchester upbringing in this atmospheric thriller.

Michael Lowenthal *The Same Embrace* (Penguin US). A young man comes out to his Jewish, Bostonian parents after his twin brother disowns him for his homosexuality; courageous and complex.

John Marquand *The Late George Appley* (Buccaneer Books US o/p). Winner of the 1937 Pulitzer Prize, this novel satirizes a New England gentry on the wane.

Carole Maso *Defiance* (Penguin US). A Harvard professor sits on death row after having murdered a pair of her own star students, in this fragmentary, moving confessional.

Edwin O'Connor *The Last Hurrah* (Little, Brown & Co/Back Bay). Fictionalized account of Boston mayor James Michael Curley, starring a 1950s corrupt politician; the book was so popular that the bar at the *Omni Parker House Hotel* was named after it.

George Santayana *The Last Puritan* (The MIT Press). The philosopher's brilliant "memoir in the form of a novel," set around Boston, chronicles the short life and education of protagonist Oliver Alden coming to grips with Puritanism.

Jean Stafford *Boston Adventure* (Harcourt Brace US). Narrated by a poverty-stricken young girl who gets taken in by a wealthy elderly woman, this long but rewarding novel portrays upper-class Boston in all its magnificence and malevolence.

William F. Weld *Mackerel by Moonlight* (Pocket Books US). The former federal prosecutor and governor of Massachusetts turns his hand to writing, in this uneven – though not unworthy – political mystery.

Boston on film

Boston has served as the setting for surprisingly few major **films** despite its historic importance in shaping US culture. Here are a dozen titles to start with if you want to see how it's shown up thus far.

Two Sisters from Boston (Henry Koster 1946)
Walk East on Beacon (Alfred L. Werker 1952)
The Actress (George Cukor 1953)
The Boston Strangler (Richard Fleischer 1968)
Love Story (Arthur Hiller 1970)
Between the Lines (Joan Micklin Silver 1977)
Starting Over (Alan J. Pakula 1979)
The Bostonians (James Ivory 1984)
Tough Guys Don't Dance (Norman Mailer 1987)
Good Will Hunting (Gus Van Sant 1997)
A Civil Action (Steve Zaillian 1998)
Next Stop Wonderland (Ben Anderson 1998)

Boston terminology and language

Boston has a **language** all its own, plus a truly unmistakeable regional accent. A guide to local parlance appears in this section, along with some architectural terms used in the guide.

One of Boston's most recognizable cultural idiosyncrasies is its strain of American English, distinguished by a tendency to drop one's "r"s, as on the ubiquitous T-shirts that exhort you to "Pahk the cah in Havvid Yahd." Watch, too, for the greeting "How why ya?" or the genial assent, "shuah." The lost "r"s crop up elsewhere, usually when words that end in "a" are followed by words that begin in a vowel – as in "I've got no idear about that." When the nasal "a" (as in "cat") is not followed by an "r", it can take on a soft, almost British tenor: "after" = "ahfta." And the "aw" sound (as in "body") is inverted, like "wa": "god" = "gwad."

If in doubt, the surest way to fit in with the locals is to use the word "wicked" as an adverb at every opportunity: "Joo guys see the Celts game lahst night? Theah gonna be wicked wasome this yeah!"

BC Boston College

Beantown Nickname for Boston – a reference to the local specialty, Boston baked beans – that no one uses any longer.

The Big Dig The ongoing project to put the elevated highway I-93 underground (see p.4).

Brahmin An old-moneyed Beacon Hill aristocrat.

Brownstone Originally a nineteenth-century terraced house with a facade of brown stone; now any row- or townhouse.

BU Boston University

Bubbler Water fountain.

The Cape Shorthand for Cape Cod.

The Central Artery The stretch of I-93 that runs through downtown, separating the North End and the Waterfront from the rest of the city.

Colonial Style of Neoclassical architecture popular in the seventeenth and eighteenth centuries.

Combat Zone The once-busy strip of Washington Street just north of Chinatown designated for adult entertainment.

Comm Ave Commonwealth Avenue.

Dot Ave Dorchester Avenue.

Federal Hybrid of French and Roman architecture popular in the late eighteenth and early nineteenth centuries.

Frappe Milkshake (meaning milk, ice cream, and syrup) – the "e" is silent. Order a *milkshake* in Boston and you'll likely get milk flavored with syrup – distinctly devoid of ice cream.

Georgian Architectural style popular during the late Colonial period, highly ornamental and rigidly symmetrical.

Greek Revival Style of architecture that mimicked that of classical Greece. Popular for banks and larger houses in the early nineteenth century.

Grinder A sandwich made of deli meats, cheese, and condiments on a long roll or bun.

Hamburg Ground beef *sans* bun. Add an –er for the classic American sandwich.

Hub Like Beantown, a nickname for Boston not really used anymore.

JP Jamaica Plain.

Mass Ave Massachusetts Avenue.

MBTA (Massachusetts Bay Transportation Authority) The agency in charge of all public transit – buses, subways, commuter trains, and ferries.

MGH Massachusetts General Hospital, also "Mass General."

Packie Liquor store. Many signs say "Package Store."

The Pike The Massachusetts Turnpike (I-90).

P-town Provincetown.

Scrod Somewhat of a distasteful generic name for cod or haddock. Almost always served breaded and sold cheap.

Southie South Boston.

Spa An independently-owned convenience store.

The T Catch-all for Boston's subway system.

Three-decker Three-story house, with each floor a separate apartment. Also called a "triple-decker."

Townie Originally a term for residents of Charlestown, it now refers to hardcore residents of Boston and its outlying suburbs most readily identified by their heavy accents.

Victorian Style of architecture from the mid to late 1800s that is highly eclectic and ornamental.

Wicked The definitive word in the Bostonian patois, still used to intensify adjectives, as in "wicked good."

Boston people

ADAMS Samuel (1722–1803). A standard-bearer for the Revolution, Adams's patriotic pursuits included founding the "Sons of Liberty" in 1765, creating the Committee of Correspondence – basically a hype machine for the Revolutionary cause – in 1772, and leading the Boston Tea Party a year later. And yes, he brewed beer, too.

ALCOTT Bronson (1799–1888). Perpetually penniless father of author Louisa May, Alcott launched a series of progressive though short-lived elementary-type schools in Boston, most notably the Temple School. He also spearheaded the failed utopian community of Fruitlands, outside Boston, in 1843.

ALCOTT Louisa May (1832–1888). Writer of *Little Women* and other works that drew on her close-knit family, who lived in and around Boston. While a Civil War nurse, she was treated with mercury for a fever, beginning a painfully long demise that ended just a day after her father's funeral.

ATTUCKS Crispus (1723?–1770). Ex-slave who was killed in the Boston Massacre of 1770, the only one of the five slain to be remembered by history and the only one who was black.

BELL Alexander Graham (1847–1922). Scottish-born professor who moved to Boston in the 1870s and invented the telephone in a Boston University laboratory.

BLACKSTONE William (1595–1675). English reverend who was the first European settler on the Shawmut Peninsula, now Boston.

BOYLSTON Zabdiel (1679–1766). Boston doctor who invented a smallpox inoculation first used during the plague of 1721–1722. To allay fears about his cure, Boylston inoculated his son first.

BULFINCH Charles (1763–1844). Boston's leading architect of the Federalist style, he designed the State House and many townhouses on Beacon Hill that can still be seen today.

BULGER James "Whitey" (1935–). Reportedly on the lam in Ireland, the wayward brother of the president of the University of Massachusetts, is one of America's Most Wanted mobsters; though hard to locate, his name keeps coming up in the press in connection with long missing persons who've recently turned up as dead bodies in empty lots around town.

CHILD Julia (1912–). Cookbook author, famed for simplifying French cuisine for the middle American dinner table, who calls Cambridge her home.

COPLEY John Singleton (1738–1815). A painter best known for his portraits of prominent Colonial-era Bostonians, Copley relocated to London in 1775.

CURLEY James Michael (1874–1958). Four-time Democratic Mayor of Boston, this charismatic – and corrupt – Irish-American politician ruled for 35 years, also serving as a Massachusetts congressman and governor.

EDDY Mary Baker (1821–1910). The founder of Christian Science, a church with its world headquarters in Boston. Healed of an injury while reading a section of the New Testament in 1866, she was inspired to write *Science and Health*, the original Christian Science textbook.

EMERSON Ralph Waldo (1803–1882). Literary giant and renowned lecturer whose essay "Nature," penned in Concord, signaled the birth of transcendentalism.

FANEUIL Peter (1700–1743). Wealthy merchant of French Huguenot origin who donated the eponymous town hall to the town of Boston in 1742.

FIELDS James T (1817–1881). Partner in the local publishing firm Ticknor & Fields, he helped persuade Nathaniel Hawthorne to publish *The Scarlet Letter*.

FRANKLIN Benjamin (1706–1790). American statesman and inventor born and raised in Boston, he apprenticed to his brother, publisher of the independent-minded *New England Gazette* newspaper, before settling in Philadelphia.

FULLER Margaret (1810–1850). Literary critic who was the editor of *The Dial*, the transcendentalist journal of the 1840s.

GARDNER Isabella Stewart (1840–1919). This socialite and art collector, described once as a "millionaire Bohemienne," enjoyed shocking Boston's high society with antics such as having John Singer Sargent paint a low-neckline portrait of her and, reputedly, walking her pet lions down Tremont Street.

GARRISON William Lloyd (1805–1879). Abolitionist who at 23 made his first public address in favor of emancipation, in Boston's Park Street Church. Also the publisher of *The Liberator*, an anti-slavery newspaper.

HANCOCK John (1737–1793). Wealthy Colonial-era merchant and Declaration of Independence signer who helped finance the early Revolutionary campaign; after the war he served as the first governor of the Commonwealth of Massachusetts.

HOLMES Oliver Wendell (1809–1894). Doctor, author, and pundit, Holmes coined the phrase "Boston Brahmins," describing Beacon Hill aristocrats, in a series of *Atlantic Monthly* articles entitled "Autocrat of the Breakfast Table."

HOMER Winslow (1836–1910). Boston-born, self-taught naturalist painter best known for his watercolors of New England seascapes.

KENNEDY Edward M. (1932–). Brother of JFK and longtime liberal Massachusetts Democratic senator.

KENNEDY John F. (1917–1963) The youngest president to be elected, and the first Catholic one, Kennedy was born just outside Boston proper in Brookline. He served as Boston congressman and Massachusetts senator before gaining high office in 1960. He was assassinated on November 22, 1963.

LOWELL Robert (1917–1977). Pulitzer Prize-winning Boston-born poet whose most famous collection, *For the Union Dead*, was inspired by the Robert Gould Shaw and 54th Massachusetts Regiment statue on the Beacon Street promenade.

MATHER Cotton (1663–1728). Puritan minister who entered Harvard College at the age of 12, and proceeded to pen many esoteric books, including the 1300-page *Magnalia Christi Americana*, which traced the ecclesiastical history of America.

MATHER Increase (1639–1723). Father of Cotton Mather, this minister secured a new royal charter for the Massachusetts Bay Colony in 1692 and served some time as president of Harvard College.

MENINO Thomas (1942–). Boston's current Mayor and the first one of Italian descent.

QUINCY Josiah (1772–1864). Popular Mayor of Boston in the 1820s who cleaned up Beacon Hill of prostitution and stopped development of the land that would become the Public Garden.

REVERE Paul (1735–1818). Silversmith and principal rider for Boston's Committee of Public Safety, he made his midnight ride to Lexington and Concord to warn the rebels that the British were coming, an event immortalized in an 1863 Longfellow poem of questionable accuracy.

RICHARDSON Henry Hobson (1838–1886). Architect noted for his oversized Romanesque Revival works such as Trinity Church.

STUART Gilbert (1755–1828). Early American painter who made his mark with a series of portraits of George Washington – one of which is replicated on the US one-dollar bill.

INDEX

C

NOTES

NOTES

NOTES

ROUGH GUIDES: Travel

Amsterdam
Andalucia
Australia
Austria
Bali & Lombok
Barcelona
Belgium & Luxembourg
Belize
Berlin
Brazil
Britain
Brittany & Normandy
Bulgaria
California
Canada
Central America
Chile
China
Corfu & the Ionian Islands
Corsica
Costa Rica
Crete
Cyprus
Czech & Slovak Republics
Dodecanese
Dominican Republic
Egypt
England
Europe
Florida
France
French Hotels & Restaurants 1999
Germany
Goa
Greece
Greek Islands
Guatemala
Hawaii
Holland
Hong Kong & Macau
Hungary
India
Indonesia
Ireland
Israel & the Palestinian Territories
Italy
Jamaica
Japan
Jordan
Kenya
Laos
London
London Restaurants
Los Angeles
Malaysia, Singapore & Brunei
Mallorca & Menorca
Maya World
Mexico
Morocco
Moscow
Nepal
New England
New York
New Zealand
Norway
Pacific Northwest
Paris
Peru
Poland
Portugal
Prague
Provence & the Côte d'Azur
The Pyrenees
Romania
St Petersburg
San Francisco
Scandinavia
Scotland
Sicily
Singapore
South Africa
Southern India
Southwest USA
Spain
Sweden
Syria
Thailand
Trinidad & Tobago
Tunisia
Turkey
Tuscany & Umbria
USA
Venice
Vienna
Vietnam
Wales
Washington DC
West Africa
Zimbabwe & Botswana

Rough Guides on the Web

www.travel.roughguides.com

We keep getting bigger and better! The Rough Guide to Travel Online now covers more than 14,000 searchable locations. You're just a click away from access to the most in-depth travel content, weekly destination features, online reservation services, and an outspoken community of fellow travelers. Whether you're looking for ideas for your next holiday or you know exactly where you're going, join us online.

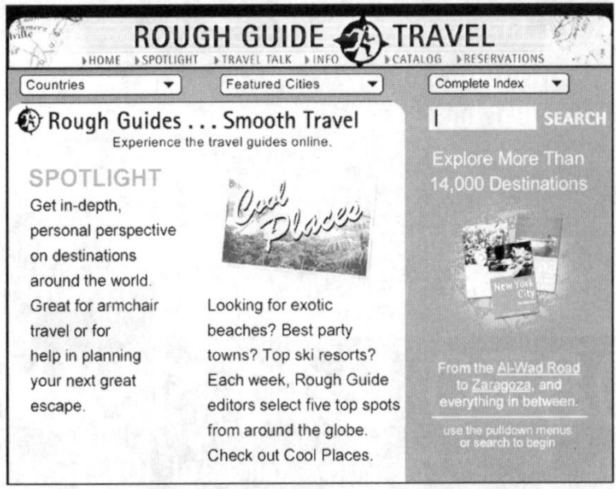

You can also find us on Yahoo!® Travel (http://travel.yahoo.com) and Microsoft Expedia® UK (http://www.expediauk.com).

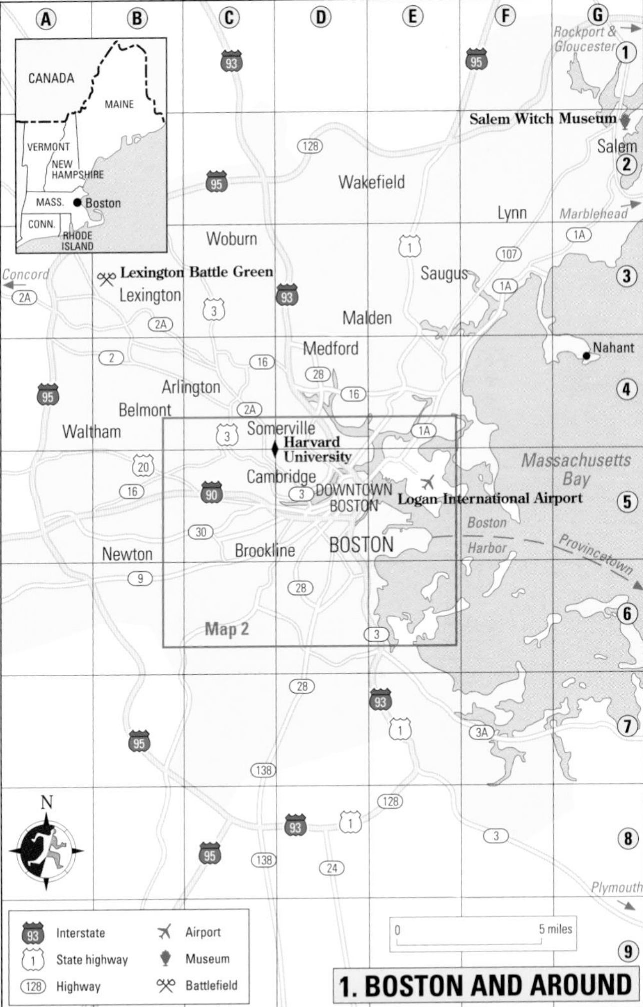

1. BOSTON AND AROUND
A
B
C
D
E
F
G
1
2
3
4
5
6
7
8
9
CANADA
MAINE
VERMONT
NEW HAMPSHIRE
MASS.
Boston
CONN.
RHODE ISLAND
Rockport & Gloucester
Salem Witch Museum
Salem
Wakefield
Lynn
Marblehead
Woburn
Saugus
Concord
Lexington Battle Green
Lexington
Malden
Medford
Nahant
Arlington
Belmont
Waltham
Somerville
Harvard University
Cambridge
DOWNTOWN BOSTON
Logan International Airport
Massachusetts Bay
Boston Harbor
Provincetown
Newton
Brookline
BOSTON
Map 2
Plymouth
N
0
5 miles
Interstate
State highway
Highway
Airport
Museum
Battlefield

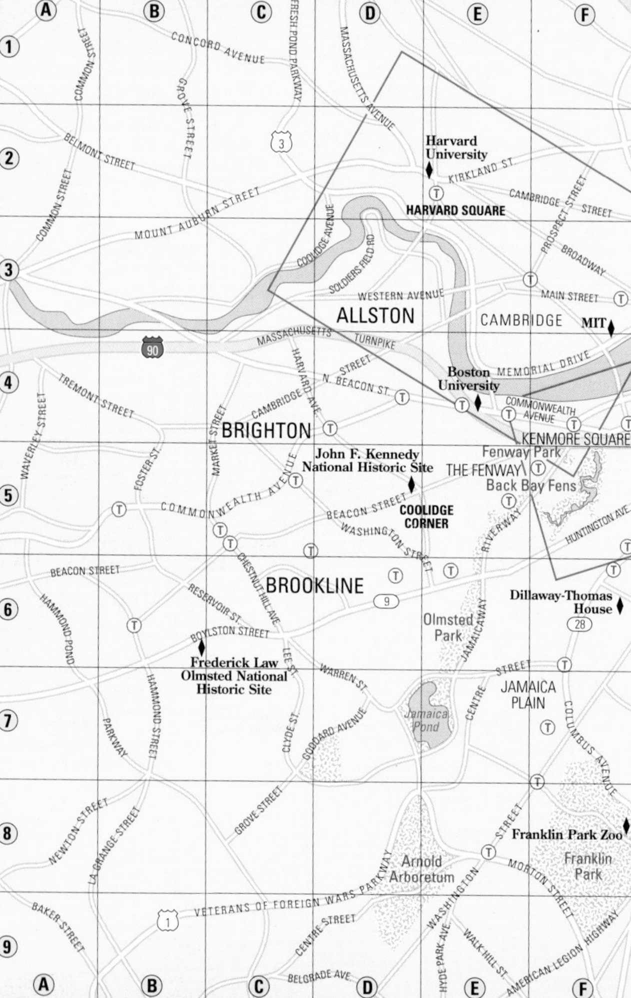

A
B
C
D
E
F
1
2
3
4
5
6
7
8
9
CONCORD AVENUE
COMMON STREET
GROVE STREET
FRESH POND PARKWAY
MASSACHUSETTS AVENUE
3
BELMONT STREET
Harvard University
KIRKLAND ST.
HARVARD SQUARE
CAMBRIDGE STREET
PROSPECT STREET
MOUNT AUBURN STREET
COOLIDGE AVENUE
SOLDIERS FIELD RD
BROADWAY
WESTERN AVENUE
MAIN STREET
ALLSTON
CAMBRIDGE
MIT
90
MASSACHUSETTS TURNPIKE
HARVARD AVE.
MEMORIAL DRIVE
Boston University
N. BEACON ST.
STREET
TREMONT STREET
CAMBRIDGE
COMMONWEALTH AVENUE
WAVERLEY STREET
MARKET STREET
BRIGHTON
KENMORE SQUARE
Fenway Park
John F. Kennedy National Historic Site
THE FENWAY
FOSTER ST.
COMMONWEALTH AVENUE
Back Bay Fens
BEACON STREET
COOLIDGE CORNER
RIVERWAY
HUNTINGTON AVE.
WASHINGTON STREET
BEACON STREET
CHESTNUT HILL AVE.
BROOKLINE
Dillaway-Thomas House
HAMMOND POND
RESERVOIR ST.
9
Olmsted Park
28
BOYLSTON STREET
JAMAICAWAY
Frederick Law Olmsted National Historic Site
LEE ST.
WARREN ST.
STREET
HAMMOND STREET
CENTRE
JAMAICA PLAIN
COLUMBUS AVENUE
PARKWAY
Jamaica Pond
CLYDE ST.
GODDARD AVENUE
GROVE STREET
NEWTON STREET
LA GRANGE STREET
STREET
Franklin Park Zoo
Arnold Arboretum
MORTON STREET
Franklin Park
WASHINGTON
VETERANS OF FOREIGN WARS PARKWAY
BAKER STREET
1
CENTRE STREET
HYDE PARK AVE.
WALK HILL ST.
AMERICAN LEGION HIGHWAY
BELGRADE AVE.

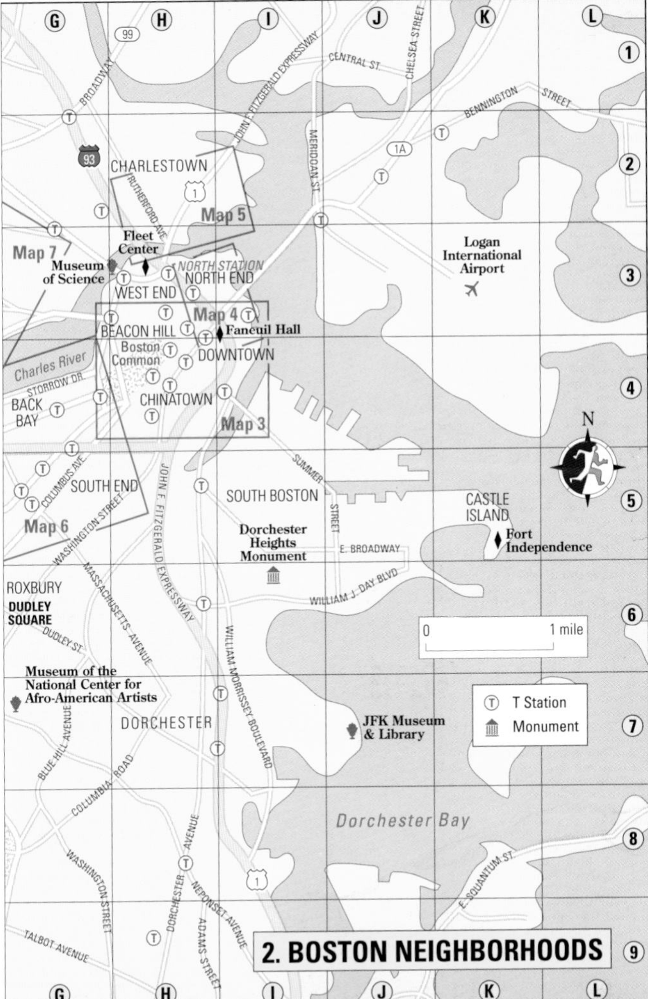

2. BOSTON NEIGHBORHOODS
CHARLESTOWN
Map 5
Fleet Center
Map 7
Museum of Science
NORTH STATION
NORTH END
WEST END
Map 4
BEACON HILL
Faneuil Hall
Boston Common
DOWNTOWN
Charles River
STORROW DR.
BACK BAY
CHINATOWN
Map 3
SOUTH END
Map 6
SOUTH BOSTON
Dorchester Heights Monument
E. BROADWAY
WILLIAM J. DAY BLVD
CASTLE ISLAND
Fort Independence
Logan International Airport
ROXBURY
DUDLEY SQUARE
DUDLEY ST.
Museum of the National Center for Afro-American Artists
DORCHESTER
JFK Museum & Library
Dorchester Bay
E. SQUANTUM ST.
BROADWAY
RUTHERFORD AVE
JOHN F. FITZGERALD EXPRESSWAY
CENTRAL ST.
CHELSEA STREET
BENNINGTON STREET
MERIDIAN ST.
SUMMER STREET
COLUMBUS AVE.
WASHINGTON STREET
MASSACHUSETTS AVENUE
WILLIAM MORRISSEY BOULEVARD
BLUE HILL AVENUE
COLUMBIA ROAD
DORCHESTER AVENUE
NEPONSET AVENUE
ADAMS STREET
TALBOT AVENUE
0
1 mile
T Station
Monument
N

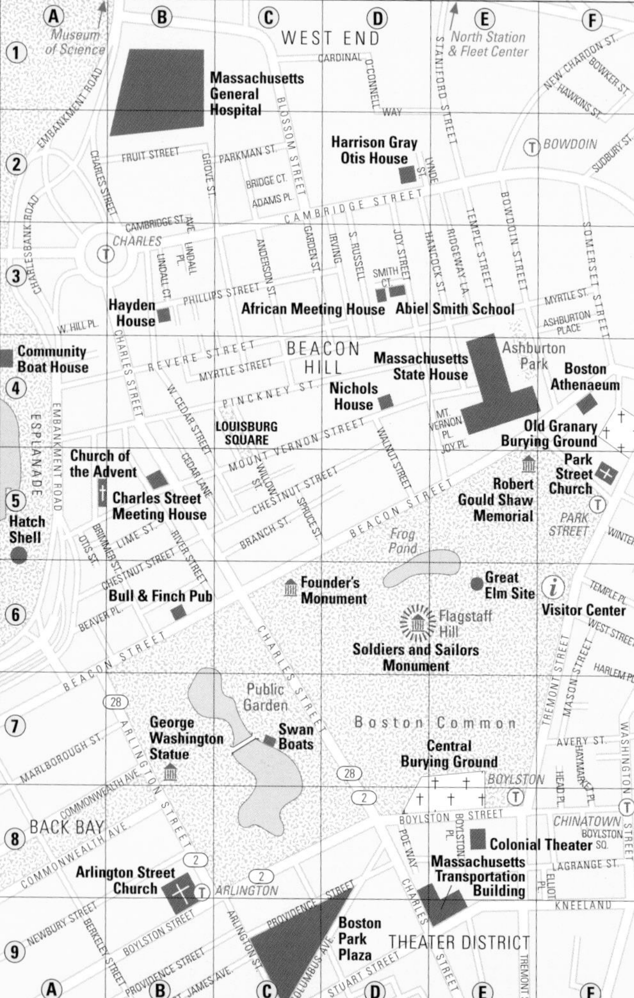

WEST END
Museum of Science
North Station & Fleet Center
Massachusetts General Hospital
Harrison Gray Otis House
BOWDOIN
CHARLES
Hayden House
African Meeting House
Abiel Smith School
Community Boat House
BEACON HILL
Ashburton Park
Massachusetts State House
Boston Athenaeum
Nichols House
LOUISBURG SQUARE
Old Granary Burying Ground
Park Street Church
Church of the Advent
Charles Street Meeting House
Hatch Shell
ESPLANADE
Robert Gould Shaw Memorial
PARK STREET
Frog Pond
Founder's Monument
Great Elm Site
Visitor Center
Bull & Finch Pub
Flagstaff Hill
Soldiers and Sailors Monument
Public Garden
Boston Common
George Washington Statue
Swan Boats
Central Burying Ground
BOYLSTON
BACK BAY
CHINATOWN
Colonial Theater
Massachusetts Transportation Building
Arlington Street Church
ARLINGTON
Boston Park Plaza
THEATER DISTRICT
CAMBRIDGE STREET
BEACON STREET
CHARLES STREET
ARLINGTON STREET
TREMONT STREET
BOYLSTON STREET

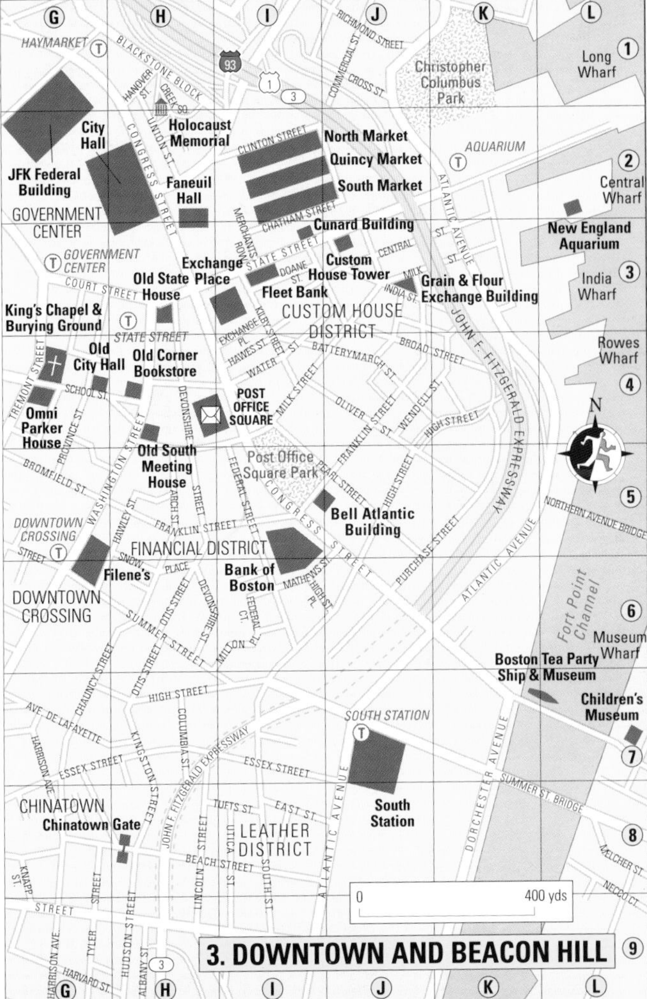

3. DOWNTOWN AND BEACON HILL
HAYMARKET
City Hall
JFK Federal Building
GOVERNMENT CENTER
Holocaust Memorial
Faneuil Hall
North Market
Quincy Market
South Market
Christopher Columbus Park
Long Wharf
AQUARIUM
Central Wharf
New England Aquarium
India Wharf
Rowes Wharf
Cunard Building
Custom House Tower
Grain & Flour Exchange Building
Exchange Place
Old State House
Fleet Bank
CUSTOM HOUSE DISTRICT
King's Chapel & Burying Ground
Old City Hall
Old Corner Bookstore
POST OFFICE SQUARE
Omni Parker House
Old South Meeting House
Post Office Square Park
Bell Atlantic Building
FINANCIAL DISTRICT
DOWNTOWN CROSSING
Filene's
Bank of Boston
Fort Point Channel
Museum Wharf
Boston Tea Party Ship & Museum
Children's Museum
SOUTH STATION
South Station
CHINATOWN
Chinatown Gate
LEATHER DISTRICT
JOHN F. FITZGERALD EXPRESSWAY
0
400 yds

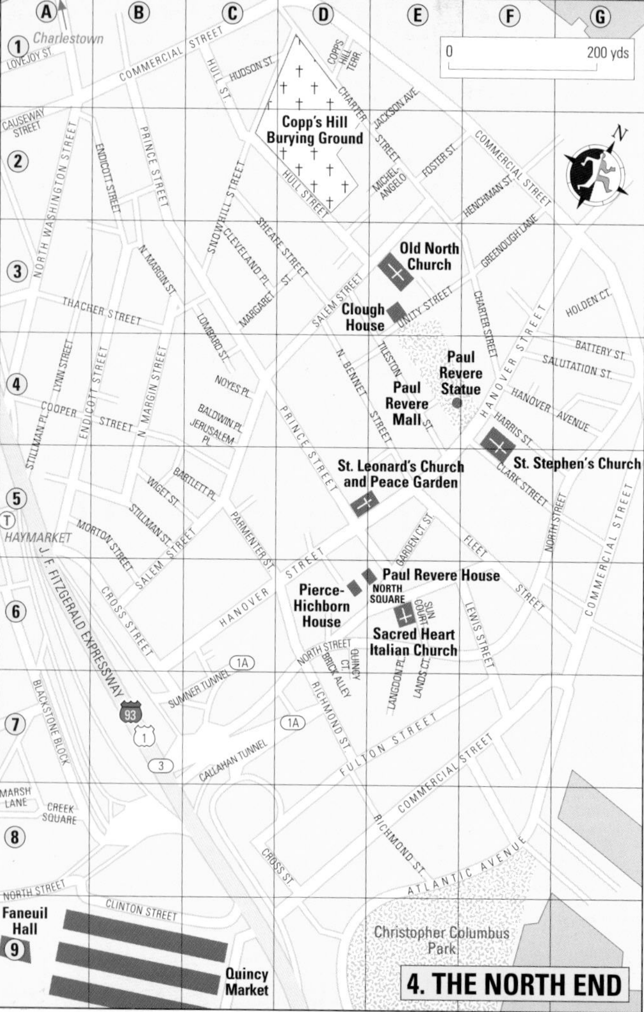
Charlestown
0
200 yds
N
Copp's Hill Burying Ground
Old North Church
Clough House
Paul Revere Statue
Paul Revere Mall
St. Leonard's Church and Peace Garden
St. Stephen's Church
Paul Revere House
Pierce-Hichborn House
NORTH SQUARE
Sacred Heart Italian Church
HAYMARKET
J. F. FITZGERALD EXPRESSWAY
SUMNER TUNNEL
CALLAHAN TUNNEL
MARSH LANE
CREEK SQUARE
Faneuil Hall
Quincy Market
Christopher Columbus Park
COMMERCIAL STREET
HANOVER STREET
SALEM STREET
PRINCE STREET
NORTH STREET
CLINTON STREET
ATLANTIC AVENUE
FULTON STREET
FLEET STREET
CROSS STREET
NORTH WASHINGTON STREET
4. THE NORTH END

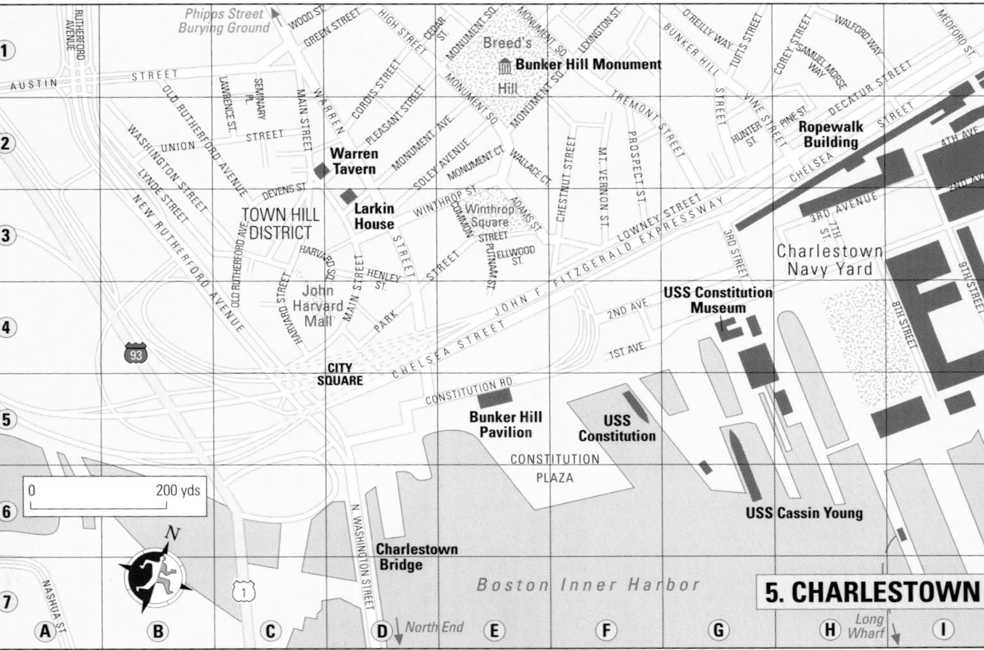
5. CHARLESTOWN
Phipps Street Burying Ground
Breed's Hill
Bunker Hill Monument
Warren Tavern
Larkin House
TOWN HILL DISTRICT
John Harvard Mall
Winthrop Square
CITY SQUARE
Ropewalk Building
Charlestown Navy Yard
USS Constitution Museum
USS Constitution
USS Cassin Young
Bunker Hill Pavilion
CONSTITUTION PLAZA
Charlestown Bridge
Boston Inner Harbor
North End
Long Wharf
RUTHERFORD AVENUE
AUSTIN STREET
WOOD ST.
GREEN STREET
HIGH STREET
CEDAR ST.
MONUMENT SQ.
LEXINGTON ST.
O'REILLY WAY
TUFTS STREET
BUNKER HILL STREET
COREY STREET
SAMUEL MORSE WAY
WALFORD WAY
MEDFORD ST.
DECATUR STREET
PINE ST.
HUNTER ST.
VINE STREET
TREMONT STREET
PROSPECT ST.
MT. VERNON ST.
CHESTNUT STREET
WALLACE CT.
ADAMS ST.
MONUMENT CT.
SOLEY AVENUE
MONUMENT AVE.
PLEASANT STREET
CORDIS STREET
WARREN STREET
MAIN STREET
SEMINARY PL.
LAWRENCE ST.
UNION STREET
OLD RUTHERFORD AVENUE
WASHINGTON STREET
LYNDE STREET
NEW RUTHERFORD AVENUE
DEVENS ST
OLD RUTHERFORD AVE
HARVARD SQ.
HARVARD STREET
HENLEY ST.
PARK STREET
WINTHROP ST.
COMMON STREET
PUTNAM ST.
ELLWOOD ST.
LOWNEY STREET
JOHN F. FITZGERALD EXPRESSWAY
CHELSEA STREET
CONSTITUTION RD.
2ND AVE.
1ST AVE.
3RD STREET
3RD AVENUE
7TH ST.
4TH AVE
2ND AVE
8TH STREET
9TH STREET
N. WASHINGTON STREET
NASHUA ST.
93
1
N
0
200 yds
1
2
3
4
5
6
7
A
B
C
D
E
F
G
H
I

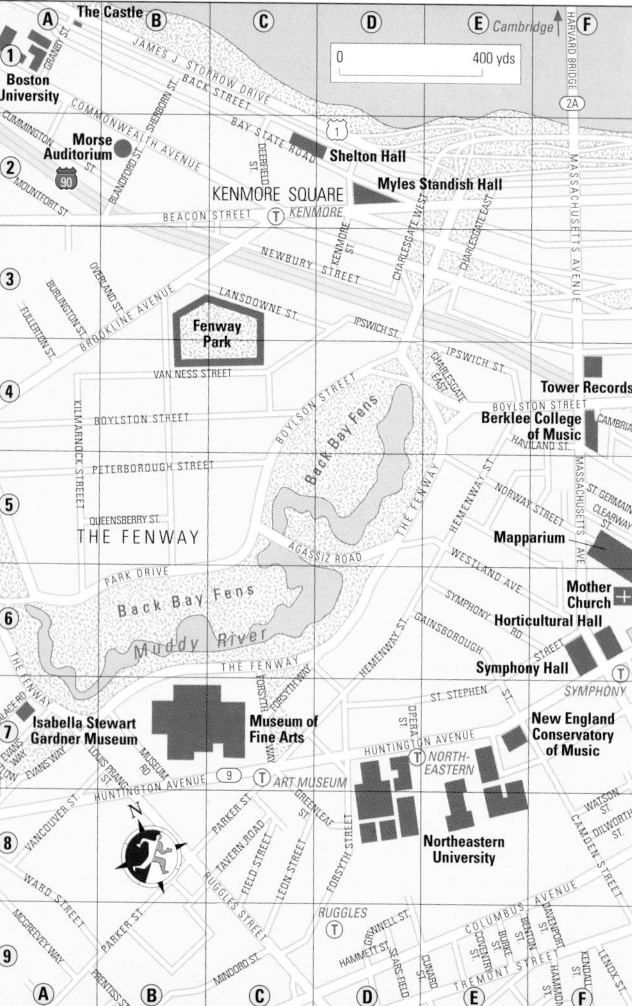

The Castle
Boston University
Morse Auditorium
Shelton Hall
Myles Standish Hall
KENMORE SQUARE
KENMORE
Cambridge
0
400 yds
JAMES J. STORROW DRIVE
BACK STREET
COMMONWEALTH AVENUE
BAY STATE ROAD
BEACON STREET
NEWBURY STREET
LANSDOWNE ST.
IPSWICH ST.
BROOKLINE AVENUE
Fenway Park
VAN NESS STREET
BOYLSTON STREET
PETERBOROUGH STREET
QUEENSBERRY ST.
THE FENWAY
Back Bay Fens
AGASSIZ ROAD
PARK DRIVE
Muddy River
HARVARD BRIDGE
MASSACHUSETTS AVENUE
Tower Records
Berklee College of Music
Mapparium
Mother Church
Horticultural Hall
Symphony Hall
SYMPHONY
Isabella Stewart Gardner Museum
Museum of Fine Arts
HUNTINGTON AVENUE
ART MUSEUM
NORTH-EASTERN
New England Conservatory of Music
Northeastern University
RUGGLES
COLUMBUS AVENUE
TREMONT STREET
RUGGLES STREET
WARD STREET
PARKER ST.
FORSYTH STREET
CAMDEN STREET

6. BACK BAY TO THE FENWAY
Charles River
Charles River Esplanade
BACK BAY
Gibson House
First Baptist Church
Church of the Covenant
Ritz Carlton
Arlington St. Church
Institute of Contemporary Art
New Old South Church
HYNES/ICA
COPLEY
ARLINGTON
Trinity Church
Prudential Center & Skywalk
Boston Public Library
COPLEY SQUARE
John Hancock Building & Observatory
Hynes Convention Center
Copley Place
Christian Science Center
PRUDENTIAL
BACK BAY
Reflecting Pool
Southwest Corridor Park
Cyclorama Building
SOUTH END
MASS. AVE.
Union Park Square
Blackstone Square
Franklin Square

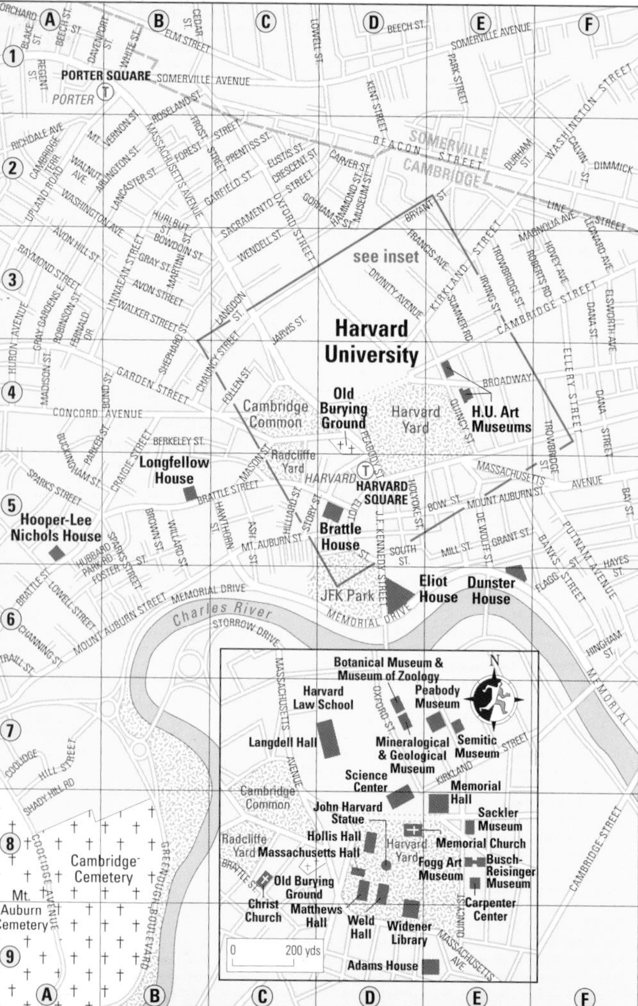

A
B
C
D
E
F
1
2
3
4
5
6
7
8
9
PORTER SQUARE
PORTER
SOMERVILLE AVENUE
ELM STREET
BEECH ST.
SOMERVILLE AVENUE
PARK STREET
KENT STREET
LOWELL ST.
CEDAR ST.
WHITE ST.
DAVENPORT ST.
BEECH ST.
BLAKE ST.
ORCHARD
REGENT ST.
WASHINGTON STREET
CALVIN ST.
DIMMICK
SOMERVILLE
CAMBRIDGE
BEACON STREET
DURHAM ST.
RICHDALE AVE.
CAMBRIDGE TERR.
UPLAND ROAD
WALNUT AVE.
MT. VERNON ST.
ARLINGTON ST.
LANCASTER ST.
ROSELAND ST.
MASSACHUSETTS AVENUE
FROST STREET
FOREST STREET
PRENTISS ST.
GARFIELD ST.
EUSTIS ST.
CRESCENT ST.
CARVER ST.
HAMMOND ST.
MUSEUM ST.
GORHAM ST.
OXFORD STREET
SACRAMENTO STREET
WENDELL ST.
WASHINGTON AVE.
HURLBUT ST.
BOWDOIN ST.
MARTIN ST.
GRAY ST.
AVON HILL ST.
RAYMOND STREET
AVON STREET
WALKER STREET
LINNAEAN STREET
GRAY GARDENS E.
ROBINSON ST.
FERNALD DR.
HURON AVENUE
MADISON ST.
BOND ST.
SHEPHARD ST.
GARDEN STREET
LANGDON ST.
CHAUNCY STREET
FOLLEN ST.
JARVIS ST.
BRYANT ST.
FRANCIS AVE.
DIVINITY AVENUE
see inset
KIRKLAND STREET
IRVING ST.
SUMMER RD.
TROWBRIDGE ST.
ROBERTS RD.
HOVEY AVE.
MAGNOLIA AVE.
LINE STREET
LEONARD AVE.
CAMBRIDGE STREET
DANA ST.
ELSWORTH AVE.
ELLERY STREET
Harvard University
BROADWAY
CONCORD AVENUE
Cambridge Common
Old Burying Ground
Harvard Yard
QUINCY ST.
H.U. Art Museums
TROWBRIDGE ST.
DANA STREET
BERKELEY ST.
BUCKINGHAM ST.
PARKER ST.
CRAIGIE STREET
Longfellow House
MASON ST.
Radcliffe Yard
HARVARD
PEABODY ST.
HARVARD SQUARE
MASSACHUSETTS AVENUE
SPARKS STREET
BRATTLE STREET
HAWTHORN ST.
ASH ST.
HILLIARD ST.
STORY ST.
ELIOT ST.
J.F. KENNEDY STREET
HOLYOKE ST.
BOW ST.
MOUNT AUBURN ST.
DE WOLFE ST.
BAY ST.
Hooper-Lee Nichols House
HUBBARD PARK RD.
SPARKS STREET
BROWN ST.
WILLARD ST.
MT. AUBURN ST.
Brattle House
SOUTH ST.
MILL ST.
GRANT ST.
BANKS ST.
PUTNAM AVENUE
HAYES ST.
FLAGG STREET
FOSTER ST.
BRATTLE ST.
LOWELL STREET
MEMORIAL DRIVE
JFK Park
Eliot House
Dunster House
MOUNT AUBURN STREET
Charles River
STORROW DRIVE
MEMORIAL DRIVE
CHANNING ST.
TRAILL ST.
HINGHAM ST.
MEMORIAL
COOLIDGE
HILL STREET
SHADY HILL RD
COOLIDGE AVENUE
Cambridge Cemetery
Mt. Auburn Cemetery
GREENOUGH BOULEVARD
CAMBRIDGE STREET
N
Botanical Museum & Museum of Zoology
Harvard Law School
OXFORD ST.
Peabody Museum
MASSACHUSETTS AVENUE
Langdell Hall
Mineralogical & Geological Museum
Semitic Museum
KIRKLAND STREET
Science Center
Memorial Hall
Cambridge Common
John Harvard Statue
Sackler Museum
Hollis Hall
Harvard Yard
Memorial Church
Radcliffe Yard
Massachusetts Hall
BRATTLE ST.
Fogg Art Museum
Busch-Reisinger Museum
Old Burying Ground
Christ Church
Matthews Hall
Weld Hall
Widener Library
QUINCY ST.
Carpenter Center
MASSACHUSETTS AVE.
0
200 yds
Adams House

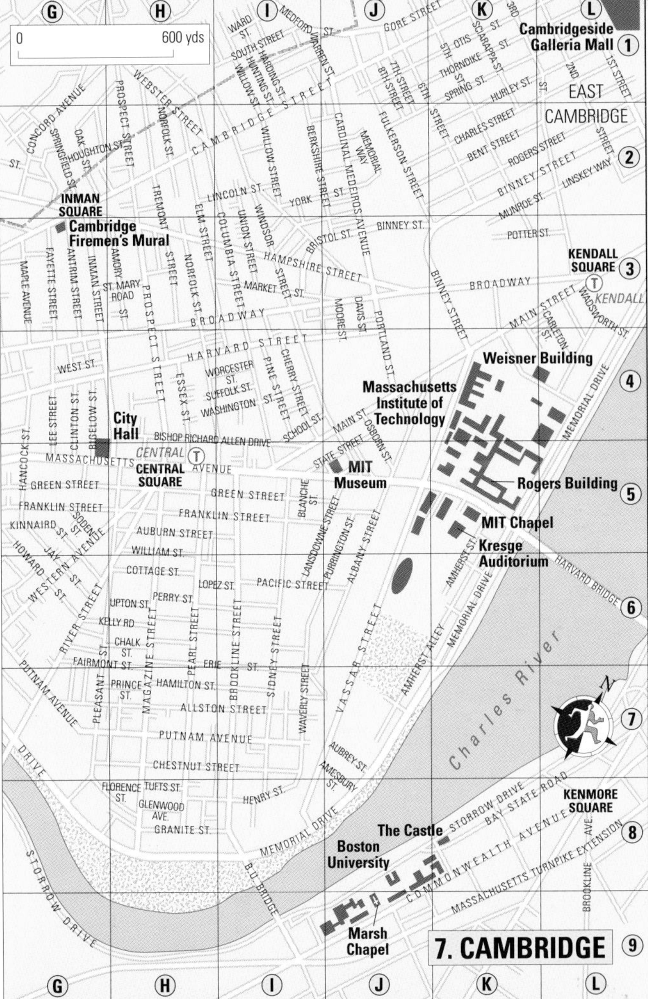

7. CAMBRIDGE
0
600 yds
Cambridgeside Galleria Mall
EAST CAMBRIDGE
INMAN SQUARE
Cambridge Firemen's Mural
KENDALL SQUARE
Weisner Building
Massachusetts Institute of Technology
City Hall
CENTRAL SQUARE
MIT Museum
Rogers Building
MIT Chapel
Kresge Auditorium
Charles River
KENMORE SQUARE
The Castle
Boston University
Marsh Chapel
CAMBRIDGE STREET
HAMPSHIRE STREET
BROADWAY
HARVARD STREET
MASSACHUSETTS AVENUE
MAIN STREET
MEMORIAL DRIVE
HARVARD BRIDGE
VASSAR STREET
STORROW DRIVE
COMMONWEALTH AVENUE
BAY STATE ROAD
MASSACHUSETTS TURNPIKE EXTENSION
B.U. BRIDGE

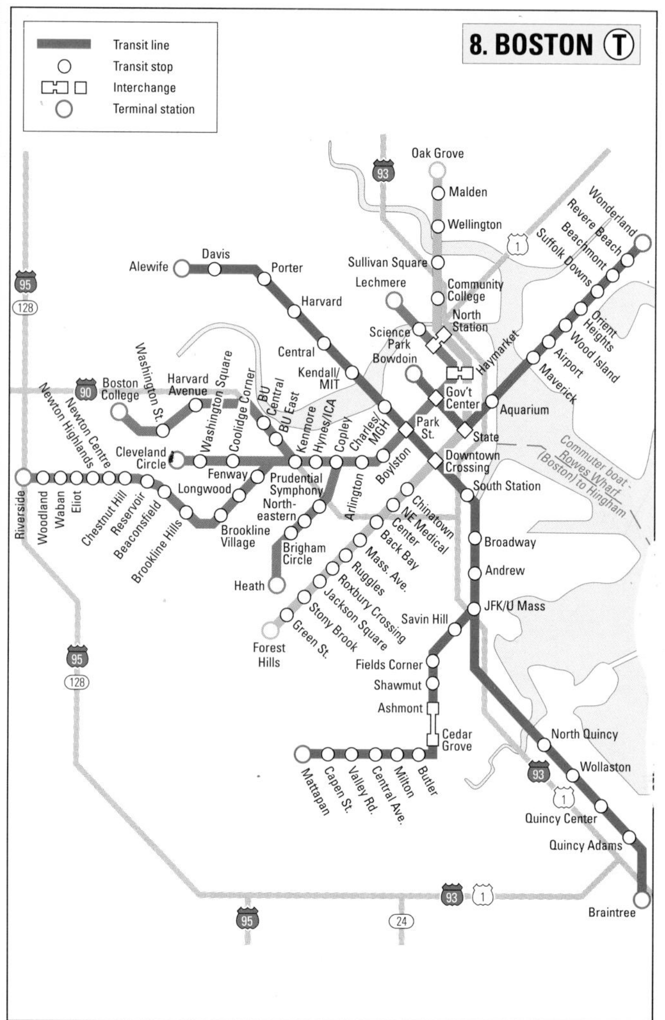
8. BOSTON T
Transit line
Transit stop
Interchange
Terminal station
Oak Grove
Malden
Wellington
Sullivan Square
Community College
North Station
Lechmere
Science Park
Bowdoin
Haymarket
Gov't Center
State
Aquarium
Wonderland
Revere Beach
Beachmont
Suffolk Downs
Orient Heights
Wood Island
Airport
Maverick
Alewife
Davis
Porter
Harvard
Central
Kendall/ MIT
Charles/ MGH
Park St.
Downtown Crossing
South Station
Broadway
Andrew
JFK/U Mass
Savin Hill
Fields Corner
Shawmut
Ashmont
Cedar Grove
Butler
Milton
Central Ave.
Valley Rd.
Capen St.
Mattapan
North Quincy
Wollaston
Quincy Center
Quincy Adams
Braintree
Commuter boat - Rowes Wharf (Boston) to Hingham
Boston College
Washington St.
Harvard Avenue
Washington Square
Coolidge Corner
BU Central
BU East
Kenmore
Hynes/ICA
Copley
Arlington
Boylston
Cleveland Circle
Fenway
Longwood
Brookline Village
Prudential
Symphony
North-eastern
Brigham Circle
Heath
Riverside
Woodland
Waban
Eliot
Newton Highlands
Newton Centre
Chestnut Hill
Reservoir
Beaconsfield
Brookline Hills
Chinatown
NE Medical Center
Back Bay
Mass. Ave.
Ruggles
Roxbury Crossing
Jackson Square
Stony Brook
Green St.
Forest Hills
93
95
128
90
1
24